The Author

Resistance on a Bicycle

—⁓—

Dirk van Leenen

A Note from the Author

—ɯ—

O ut of respect for the people described in this book, I have changed some of their names into fictitious names. In addition I have changed the names of some of the places the characters used to live and work in.

All characters in this book were real, live people. Their actions and activities truly happened during the period of war which started on May 10, 1940 until May 5, 1945.

Acknowledgements

—w—

Information to write this book has been gathered from the following sources:
Newspaper articles from "Trouw"
L.E. Winkel:De Ondergrondse Pers
Anne De Vries: De levensroman van Johannes Post
Dick Hendrikse: De Dag waarop mijn Vader Huilde.
E.H.Brongers: De oorlog in Mei 40.
"Ben's Story: Holocaust Letters," edited by Kees W. Bolle
Stedelijk Museum De Lakenhal Leiden: Joden in Leiden.
Articles from unknown authors: Gathered by Rijks Institute voor Oorlogs Documentatie.
Cover design by Larry Walker
Editing by Jordan Currier
Email the author: resistonabicycle@hotmail.com

Thanks to numerous survivors of the Holocaust who were willing to tell their stories.
Thanks to the many Resistance workers who finally were able to release their emotions.

Chapters

—m—

1. The Boy 13

2. The Workers in the Underground 23

3. The Occupation Leadership....................................29

4. The Singing Box..31

5. The Razzia..33

6. The Message..37

7. Resistance as an Artist..41

8. A Narrow Escape..43

9. The Ambulance Builders 49

10. The Haystack...55

11. The Secret Meeting...59

12. The Way to Freedom 61

13. The Illegal Press 65

14. The Most Secret Meeting 69

15. Life Under the Floor...75

16. Attack on the Generals 79

17. Trouble on the Way Back 83

18. The Evacuation of City Children..............................91

19. Many Roads which Led to Freedom 95

20. At Home in The Hague..99

21. The City Children...105

22. The Suffering of the Jews......................................109

23. Operation Isolation 113

24. The Little Spy 117

25. Moving the Driven and the Dislodged 119

26. The Factories of the War Machine.............................125
27. Distribution of Food Stamps 133
28. A Trip to Freedom 145
29. A Second Truck 149
30. From Farm to Farm 155
31. The Source of Resistance...................................163
32. The Hunger Winter 167
33. The Dutch and the Dutch Jews...............................171
34. The Jewish Council 185
35. A Dangerous Monk..189
36. How They Kept Going 201
37. Orphanages for Jewish Children 205
38. Saving Lives and Saving the Pig...........................209
39. Israel is Calling...219
40. The Israel Connection.....................................223
41. Always a Step Ahead of the Nazis 231
42. The NSB-er..245
43. Jumping from a Train 253
44. NSB-er Redeemed...263
45. Cornelius' Little Farm 271
46. Bicycles Seized...275
47. A Different Kind of Guest 279
48. Pigeon Eggs...293
49. Arriving in Palestine.....................................297
50. The Value of Food 301
51. Released from Camp Westerbork.............................305
52. Razzia Again and Again 311
53. Anything Which Can Burn...................................317
54. The Zionist Council.......................................321
55. The NSB-er Prison 323
56. The Old Spy...327
57. The Attack on the Jail....................................331
58. A Rabbi's Questions 335

Dedication

I dedicate this book to my Father and Mother, whom I respect more than ever before writing this book and to my Wife Cindy who stood by me and encouraged me to keep on writing. Above all, I thank God for the vivid memories he has brought back to my mind without which I would have never been able to put this book together.

Dirk van Leenen

Chapter One

THE BOY

—✳︎—

W When you lick the ice on a frozen window, your tongue may stick to it, but he made a little peephole by just breathing at the window. The frost flowers were fascinating. He would watch them for hours. This time, however, he had a different reason to be at the frosted window. He was standing on a chair. The heavy velvet curtain behind him prevented his shadow from being seen outside so he could freely violate the orders from his dad to stay away from the windows.

It was pitch dark outside in the Deiman Straat, because there was a city-wide blackout in the heavily bombed city of The Hague in Holland. His dad was gone to church, he had told him, but he hardly believed him. He knew he was doing something the Germans would not approve of and he was told never to tell anyone where they went during the day time.

It was exciting to look through the peephole he had made. Most of the time he saw German soldiers coming by, or he saw how one of his neighbors, would sneak and hide from the German soldiers. Sometimes he saw someone being arrested and taken away by a German truck and if he could see who it was, he would tell dad.

Dad was in the Underground. Whatever that meant he wanted to discover. Meanwhile, he helped dad and went on great trips with him. Tomorrow, he was told, they were going on a four day trip far,

far away. He knew the routine and could already feel the crushing packs of counterfeit food stamps on his body. He would get packed all over his body with thousands of them. It was not comfortable but he knew they were helping hundreds of people who could otherwise not get any food.

The Second World War was in its third year. Everywhere in the city there were bombed buildings. When it had begun, the Germans had tricked the Dutch army by using Dutch Army uniforms one early morning in May of 1940.

Two things happened which broke his quiet reflections in front of the frost-flowered window. All of a sudden the humming, scaring sound of the "flying bombs" broke the curfew that had put the city into such false peace and quiet.

Werner von Braun's world-changing invention was flying over The Hague. In the dark sky you could see the red dots humming onwards to their destructive destination, to the unsuspecting citizens of the city of London. Death and destruction would be imminent.

The humming sound was like the noise of an oncoming train far above the city. The red dots drew many people out to their backyards. Even though they had to be very quiet and whisper to each other, the fear was seen in their eyes because many of the "flying bombs" would drop out of the sky that night. The people knew that some of them would fail, the rocket motor could quit and it would come down straight where they were. That is why they were outside looking at the threat and listening intently to see if the humming would become less in one of the rockets.

Cornelius felt a hand on his leg and heard the voice of his mother, "Cornelius, go tell the friends under the floor that the rockets are coming over." He knew the routine he had done so many times before. Go to the bathroom, slide the wall panel to the left and squeeze through the opening. Then he would climb down the narrow ladder that brought him to the secret room beneath the floor of the house.

They were all awake and huddled together. Their scared faces looked at him and waited for the familiar message. It meant a sudden change in their slumbering times, they had to move from their places and go to the self-made bunker underneath the staircase. It could mean the difference between life and death for them.

Jacob Ivanowski, an orthodox Jew, was the leader tonight. Every day one of them was appointed as leader. From the youngest to the oldest, each had his or her turn as the group leader. Some had been in hiding at the Deiman Straat for as long as two weeks. Others had only arrived the day before and many had already left. The leader would brief them each day on what they could and could not do and what they could expect at the van Rijn residence.

Jacob pushed the heavy concrete block which had been part of the foundation of the solid concrete stairs, leading to the upstairs houses. The Deiman Straat was half a mile long, divided into four three-story blocks of houses on both sides of the cobbled stoned street. Each block had eight groups of six houses. In the center was a concrete staircase which went to a portico with four doors. Two were for the second floor houses and two others had a steep narrow staircase going up to the third floor.

Cornelius' dad had found out that the staircase was poured out of concrete and when he researched the bombed buildings further down the street, it was the only part of the block of houses that remained intact. He decided then and there that that was the best and safest place to hide the Jews during the bomb threats which hounded the city so many times. And so he had a group of friends come to help him create the shelter. No one in Holland had any idea what was coming until it started to happen. Suddenly, truck-loads of people were dragged out of their houses at gun-point.

First they were men – any man over 18 years of age. They were picked up for no reason other than the fact they were Dutch citizens. They were taken to local factories to be used as forced labor. Many men went into hiding to avoid being put to work for nothing. Most of the ones who went into hiding had other things to do. They were the underground army of the Netherlands, an army which could not be seen, an army which would become very detrimental to the German cause.

Jacob ushered all the visitors through the opening and closed the concrete wall. It was hardly noticeable that there had been an opening a few minutes before the wall was locked in place on the inside.

15

No one would ever think of trying to push the concrete wall to even find an opening.

When Cornelius was finished with his message and the Jews had all safely disappeared behind the concrete wall, he looked around the living area of the twenty people. He knew they were hiding from the Germans but he did not have a clue why.

According to his dad they were sought by the Germans because they were Jewish. Why was that? He wondered why his mother was not sought by the Germans. She was Jewish too, she had told him one day.

They were all such nice people, though they were loud sometimes. His dad often had to go down to urge them to be quiet.

One time they were singing. It was almost Christmas and all the people everywhere were singing Christmas songs. Not the Jews, they were singing in a different language and they were singing songs he had never heard before. It sounded really nice, though.

When his dad had come home they were still singing. His dad had gotten really mad and stormed to the closet to go down below. "Don't you understand that they can hear you right from the streets? All the neighbors can hear you too," he said. "Some of them are NSB-ers (collaborators with the Germans). Be quiet, sing in a whispering tone if you have to, better not at all."

Mrs. Silverstein had touched his arm gently and said, "But Kees, this is our Jewish Holiday Hanukkah. It is just as important to us as your Christmas is to you.

Hanukkah is the feast of Dedications, commemorating the purification of the Temple. We have no feast here with food. At least we can celebrate by singing."

Kees had listened and gently talked to all the friends down in the self-made, home-made shelter, deep below a simple portico home in the center of the city. It had become a home for the haunted, a home for those who were hunted like animals, a refuge in a spider hole, a living without a bath or a shower, a place filled with fear for every soul.

Every sound from above, every warning could mean arrest and deportation to a Concentration camp in Auswitz and a certain

16

death.

Kees had explained how neighbors would be willing to tell the Germans where they could be found, to betray their hiding place and spoil it for all the others to come. Several times one of the neighbors must have told the Germans about hearing unusual noises coming from the van Rijn residence. The Germans had followed up to the treason from fellow citizens. They had searched the home on many occasions.

Cornelius remembered it all too well. The first time there had been a "Razzia," the Germans came to the street with two trucks and many soldiers with guns. They had pounded on the door and yelled, "Aufmachen (open up!)" If you did not open very quickly they would kick in the door or shoot it from its hinges.

They would scream and yell at everyone and once they were inside the home they looked everywhere – under beds, in closets, even in the toilet.

Once, when Cornelius was only three years old, he had thought they were playing a game of hide and seek and he was ready to help the soldiers, to give them hints where to look. His mother, Johanna, had quickly pulled him away from the scene, putting her finger on her mouth as a gesture which he understood very well: keep it secret. That made the game even more exciting for him. That evening, after the soldiers had gone away and had found nothing, Johanna took Cornelius on her lap and explained, "The Germans are not always mean, Sweetie. They have a job to do. Their Commandant tells them what to do what he says, no matter if they like it or not.

Now, some of them are real mean and want to be even meaner then their Commandant. Those people would hit our Jewish friends and push them so they fall and kick them. We should never help them to find our friends lest they would harm them. Do you understand?" Cornelius nodded. He did understand, and from then on he was on the "inside" of the plan to save as many people as they could from the cruel intentions of the Germans.

Dad had come upstairs with tears in his eyes. He was a sensitive man.

His motto in life had always been, "do unto others as you would

17

do unto yourself." He lived this slogan and practiced it all the time.

"We have to help these people and see if we can give them some dignity.

They are God's chosen people but they can't even worship Jaweh," he said.

"I am going to talk to Frans Knecht right now and ask him if there is anything we can do about it."

He had left the house in the darkness of the curfew and the black-out. It was dangerous to be outdoors after curfew had started. The only people who were out on the streets legally were the Germans.

They would shoot anyone they saw, even before asking questions, or they would arrest anyone without asking questions and take them to the feared Gestapo.

So many Dutch citizens had disappeared daily and were never heard from again.

Kees moved stealthily through the dark streets, careful not to make any noise. He stopped and paused regularly in dark hallways or alleys. Everytime he would stand still he would hold his breath in order to listen for possible movement of other feet or breathing. He listened particularly for German voices and froze when he heard a gun-shot.

The hardest part was crossing a street because there was no cover for him then. He could be seen from the end of the street, even in the total darkness.

After more than an hour he reached the Goeverneur laan, the one mile-long lane which used to have beautiful trees in the middle but was now barren. Only the roots were still there where the trees had once been. They had all been chopped down by the people who risked their lives cutting them for some warmth in their houses.

When they had cut parts of the trees and hauled the limbs to their homes, many of them had been arrested. Some of them had been in jail for as long as a month.

Kees had moved slowly but safely toward his friend's house when he heard voices. He froze and slipped into a hallway with an open staircase under which he could hide. "Halt, Ausweiss!" he heard the German soldier yell harshly. The voice was close to him and he slipped a little lower into his hiding place. Was the command directed at him? He did not think so. He could see no one so how could they have seen him?

He heard a shuffle and more voices, and then a loud yell. The scream sounded like it was coming from a Dutch girl. Kees tried to look around the corner, but he saw nothing.

The screaming continued and he tried to listen to the words, "Ik ben Maartje." Then he heard some German words he could not distinguish. Then again, "Ik ben de weg kwijt (I got lost.)" He heard and quickly made a decision, a bold step. He took a dangerous risk.

He stepped out of his dark hiding place and before the soldiers even noticed him coming Kees yelled, "Maartje hier is Pappa, where were you?"

The German soldiers now turned to Kees and demanded his Ausweiss, (identification issued by the Germans), which he quickly produced.

Meanwhile, Maartje ran over to him and hugged him saying, "Pappa, Pappa, I was lost, it was so dark and I was so scared. Please, take me home!"

When the soldiers saw the display of affection they shrugged their shoulders and the Sergeant said, "Gehen see schnell, schnell. (Go quickly)." They did, and Maartje held both her arms around Kees as if she had found her father. The Sergeant could be heard saying, "Dumme Hollaender." Kees did not say a word, when they turned a street corner he pulled her into a dark hallway.

Now that he could talk, he gently pulled her arms from around him and he took hold of her by her two shoulders, asking, "What were you doing in the dark and so late into the curfew?" Maartje knew she could not answer and tell what she had really been doing even to the stranger who had rescued her. He could even be a Gestapo Man. She had learned during her two years of being a courier that she could not be careful enough.

At least she could say that she had to bring someone a message from her parents down the road. Then Kees broke the tension and said the one word the Germans could not pronounce, a word which was the common password in the Resistance. The word meant nothing to anyone not inside the Resistance. He said, "Graag." In the Underground it meant, "I am a messenger, I am one of us, and I am pleased to listen to what you have to say."

Maartje acknowledged and told him she was 14 years old and that her entire family, two brothers and three sisters as well as her parents, were a messenger family.

They would warn people or bring encouraging messages to other workers.

Their work was mostly done in the dark, sometimes they were part of a chain of people who passed messages on throughout the entire country.

Suddenly, the silence of the dark night and the forbidden presence of the citizens was broken by two different sounds. Just down the block where Kees was stealthily moving, loud German voices were heard, followed by crying sounds of several people. The German "Halt, ausweiss!" sounded cruelly between the sobs.

Kees carefully tried to look from his darkness. What he saw was heart-wrenching. An entire family was pushed and shoved toward the waiting truck with a loud German "Aufsteigen schnell (get on the truck fast)!" The crying people were pushed on the truck.

The older man, his wife and three children hardly carried anything, although one of them had a sack and the father carried a small suitcase. They were obviously Jews because the Star of David clearly showed on their clothes as the Germans had demanded just weeks ago.

Most Jews had seen that as an honor at first. They were proud to be Jews – God's chosen people – and why not? They all looked like Jews.

The way they wore dresses, their hair and their humble demeanor made them stand out among the Dutch.

The German Reich's Commissary, Seiss Inquart, had decreed that all Jews were to wear the Star of David. When the Germans had seized all the administrations in every city and town in Holland, they had access to all the personal information of the citizens.

They had quickly separated all the files of the Jews in the entire country. It had been the first step toward the "Final Solution," the complete annihilation of the Jewish race.

At the same time it was the most thorough way for the Nazis to weaken the Dutch population, because the Jews were the economic leaders of the country. They were the employers of many and they controlled the major part of the money.

As quickly as they had come, the Germans left the street. The truck followed two motorcycles, and a second vehicle carrying the soldiers disappeared in the darkness of the blackout.

The second they left and the stillness had almost returned, but a different sound rent the black curtain of quiet on the city.

All the sirens blared a loud, almost deafening sound, the warning of an impending arrival of planes. They could be German fighter planes or Allied bombers who would be on their way to the Ruhr area. Their target was the industrial part of Germany where the war machine was supplied from, to drop their destructive cargo.

Sometimes Allied, but more often German bombers would fly over the city and the darkness would hinder them from finding their targets. Even the German occupation feared the arrival of planes, and they would run and hide deep down in their bomb shelters as long as the sirens carried on with their deafening sound.

When the threat was over the sirens would change their sound into the "all-clear" monotonous blast and quit.

Chapter Two

THE WORKERS IN
THE UNDERGROUND

—— ɯɯ ——

K ees finally reached the house of Frans Knecht, the handyman
of the Underground. The inventor of many ways to deceive
the Germans was surprised to see Kees coming at this late hour, and
during a curfew. Before he could enter the house a simple ritual was
to be done before the door would open.

Kees waited in front of the door and looked intensely at the little
pond in the front yard.

He knew Frans was looking at him. A mirror on the bottom of
the pond was watched by anyone in the Knecht household, and they
had good reasons to. Underneath the front yard, Frans had dug a big
hole just before the war had started. He had seen the warning signs
of the pending war and he figured that if he could create a safe place
for his family and himself outside the home he might be able to use
it in many ways and circumstances.

He had been able to complete the hidden living quarters just
before the war on Holland had started in May of 1940, and he had
completed the final stage by building a small pond on top of the
shelter. With a one-sided mirror he was able to see anyone coming
or going without being seen. He had also made a hatch on the side
of the pond and if anyone would want to bring him something, a
book or an envelope with a message they would wrap it in plastic
and simply drop it in the pond. Frans would see it and collect it again

without being noticed.

He hardly knew how valuable his foresight would become two years after the war had begun. be done And it needed to be done quickly. The lives of so many would be at stake. A city without doctors would be in serious trouble.

Even though the war had started in May of 1940, and ten days later the Dutch Army surrendered, no Dutchman had ever really been subdued by the Germans. Every "Hollander," as they called each other, was ready to fight and fight they did.

As soon as the Germans thought they had gained some ground on the Hollanders, they had taken it back. Every right that was taken away by the enemy was taken back by the Underground's activities.

The right of communication was flourishing with the underground press.

The right to distribute food was taken back by clandestine purchases or by robbing the German occupied warehouses.

The only right that was taken away was the right of freedom and the right of freedom of speech, and that made the Dutch very angry, creating a determination to fight against the oppressors.

The overwhelming number of aggressors caused the Hollanders to ponder their options and it took almost two years for them to organize a full-scale resistance network all across the country and beyond.

The door finally opened quickly. Kees sliped inside and was welcomed enthusiastically. Franz exclaimed, "We have not seen you for more than two weeks Kees! What have you been up to?" He held his arms wide-open to embrace his friend and comrade in the underground army. "Oh, it's so nice to see you and so dangerous to come here, it must be something very important for you to risk violating the curfew?"

Neeltje, Frans' wife, came running to him from the tiny kitchen and gave him a big hug after wiping her wet hands on her flowery apron. "Kees tell me, how is Johanna? And how are your boys?"

Kees replied with a shrug and said, "It's the Jews that keep me worried, the boys are fine. They will soon be going to the farms in Friesland to stay for a while. My two boys and my one daughter are

24

scheduled to leave next week. They will be fine there, the German-sare not very active there and the farmers have collectively offered to take in about two thousand city children."

Kees had paused for a while and the silence created an atmosphere of expectation. "So what about the Jews?" Frans finally asked. Kees took a deep breath and began, "The Jews are getting restless at the Deiman Straat. All they can do is sit and wait. Johanna finally went to the library and got them some books. She made a big mistake, she told me. She had asked for the Jewish authors and within minutes the Gestapo was there interrogating her on why she was getting Jewish books. They let her go but I would not be surprised if they are going to watch our house more closely and more often."

"You can't keep them any longer?" Franz asked. "It was your idea to keep them under your home in the hiding place we made, to keep then ready for further transportation. Are you backing out now?"

Kees shook his head emphatically, "No, that is not the case at all. It is the lack of respect for them that is bothering me. We have to help them, at least enable them to practice their religion and even their personal communication without having to worry about being detected.

Whenever they talk, pray or sing they tend to make a lot of noise being so close together with twenty people. My house is surrounded by NSB-ers. If they hear something – anything – they will report it to the Germans, the shelter will be compromised and you'll know where I will get to go if that happens. Frans, what can you do to make my shelter under the floor sound proof?"

Frans made his usual gesture when he was thinking. He would place his arms cris-crossing his chest, his hands on his shoulders and his chin resting on his chest and arms.

Kees knew not to disturb him in that posture, because Frans'mind was working hard and fast. After a full six minutes he came out of his trance and nodded his head.

"I see what your problem is and I think I'll be able to solve it," Frans said. When Frans used the words "I think," he usually had found a solution as he always had in the past.

He moved towards the table and sat down reaching for a sheet of paper to doodle on. "This is what we can do," he said. He always used the word "we" even when he knew he was going to do the job himself. "We will make a 'singing box.' Insulating the entire shelter is virtually impossible and even if we could get the materials, it would never become fully sound proof and we still would have to be careful and be speaking in a whisper.

Here is what we will do. Fortunately, I have been saving newspapers for years, I don't know why. I have a huge stack of them in my shack.

The first thing is that tomorrow morning, we are going to move them to your place. You have any idea how we can do that without any suspicion, Kees?"

Kees took a few minutes to think it over and said, "My neighbor Groenendijk can help."

Next door to the van Rijn residence was a small warehouse; the three story block ended there and in between the van Rijn block and the next was a one story warehouse used by Willem Groenendijk as a box bicycle rental and repair shop.

The entrance was two double garage door sets, one of which remained mostly closed. Behind the set of door which was closed was a large work bench. It looked heavy but no one could see the rollers underneath the legs. The heavy bench could be moved in a split second. Below the bench was a trap hatch and when that was opened a staircase led down to the van Rijn house under the floor, through the seemingly solid concrete foundation which, when closed from the inside, could not move a centimeter.

All the bakers, the fish mongers, the greengrocers and any one wanting to move something would rent a box-cycle from Groenendijk. He had open boxes and typical closed ones for the bakers. He had ones with a canopy for the fish mongers and even ones with a water tank for the garbage can cleaners and the staircase washers.

Willem made a good living from his rentals, and now during the war he even made a profit off the Germans by letting them rent the tricycle box bikes as well.

Willem Groenendijk had played into their game by being a good fellow but always demanding to know where they were taking his rental he was often able to warn people in the neighborhood when the Germans were coming. He had thus saved the lives of many Jews. Most of them were unfortunate to lose their possessions, but at least not their lives.

When the German soldiers came to him it was mostly to rob and ransack some poor Jewish family's house when the soldiers only needed the box bicycles for their personal greed.

Even though Groenendijk had made friends with them his friendship was only for the good of the Resistance. The Germans wanted to be friends with him because they knew he would not tell their commanders. That fact gave Willem a power over the soldiers.

To fight right under the noses of the Germans and with soldiers almost always present in his ware house, Willem Groenendijk was a master double agent in the Resistance. He was also the master of transportation for the Underground, who used his services for free and more often than the Germans.

When Jews arrived at the van Rijn residence they would often arrive in one of his box tricycles. They would always arrive after closing time, just after the tradesmen had come in and after the Germans had left.

It was impossible for anyone other than the van Rijn family members to enter the house through the front door. So they arrived through Groenendijk's place and disappeared when the work bench was quickly rolled away. It would all take just seconds and no one had ever found out until the war ended.

Only because of Groenendijk's assistance and his warehouse was it possible to move almost a thousand Jews through the van Rijn residence and bring them to temporary safety at the farms in the country.

No one had ever seen them coming or going, even though some Jews would give the van Rijn's a hard time. "The Pillar of the Resistance," Willem Groenendijk, remained the Germans' "friend" until the end of the war and some citizens thought he was a collaborator.

As hunger in the war-torn country increased, so did the anxiety of the German soldiers who would do anything to take the scarce food supplies from the Hollanders.

"Here is what we will do tomorrow," Kees said. "I will ask Willem Groenendijk for the help of the Fish peddler to have him keep a load of fish guts and heads in his carrier and ask him to meet you here in the back alley. Make sure to have a lot of kids ready to help load up the newspaper. We will load them up underneath the smelly fish junk, the Germans would never even dream of looking underneath that.

Then we'll park the bike in Groenendijk's warehouse and unload the papers after he has closed the warehouse.

But what in heaven's name are you planning to do with all those newspapers, if I may ask?"

At last Frans explained what he was going to make. "Call it a 'sound box,' or a 'singing box.' I will make a square box of five feet wide, five feet deep and five feet high. All I have to do is make a light wooden frame of cheap slats, if I can find them, and cover it with lots of wet newspapers. If we keep doing that so many times then it becomes a four inch thick box.

Then I will cut two holes in the top and one lower in the middle- on each side of the box in such a way that twelve people can stick their heads in the holes at the same time. We will put some cloth around the hole for comfort and sound proofing.

Hence the sound box is created, and while twelve people sing or talk no one outside will hear a thing." The only thing Kees could say was, "Very clever Frans."

He thought this was the invention of the century and in his mind he could see Jacob and all the others singing their hearts out.

He smiled and said, "Isn't God good to have people like you who can invent things and create solutions in a time like this? I am sure our Jewish friends will be equally delighted."

With that he shook both of Frans's hands, gave Neeltje a hug and started to leave.

"Wait!" Frans called out urgently. "Don't you even touch the door until I give you an 'all clear!'" He leaped towards the wall which began to turn against his weight to reveal a narrow staircase which led to his secret dwelling and his observation pond outside

Chapter Three
THE OCCUPATIONAL LEADERSHIP

—ᚓᚓ—

A t the beautiful Binnenhof, the former Dutch Government had been chased away by the Germans.

The structure was like a medieval castle with a moat around it and gates at both sides for the entrance and exit.

Seiss Inquart, the Reich's Commissary for the Germans, was pacing the long dark conference room, watched by his secretary, members of staff, General Mussert, and several members of the feared Gestapo. Seiss Inquart and Mussert had just arrived from a visit to their worshipped Fuehrer in Berlin.

It had been a dangerous but secretive trip. Both men had been very nervous to travel even through their own country.

Opposition was everywhere and the Dutch resistance could strike at any corner they turned. That is why the trip was fast and the drivers raced through the streets of the country at full speed. Even if someone would aim at the convoy, he would have to be a very excellent marksman to hit his targets.

The visit turned out to be a total disgrace to them. The Fuehrer was not happy with the progress made in Holland. "Not enough Jews" had been deported and too many attacks on the Germans had taken place.

"We cannot defeat the Dutch by shooting them all," Mussert had replied to the angry Hitler.

"Kill them any other way, or starve them if you have to," the Fuehrer had told them. "And if you can't do it, I will replace you!" Hitler screamed with a rasping voice. The other Generals had shown their agreement with a loud applause and a "Heil Hitler!" The two top leaders of the German occupation in Holland had returned angry and determined. They would teach the Dutch a lesson they would never forget. Upon their return, they put all their trusted employees to work with a highly secret assignment.

"Operation Food Distribution" was a fair and honest way to feed the entire population of the Netherlands Protocol. Rauter, the General of the SS in Holland, had been charged with the details of the plan to literally starve the Dutch and thus break their resistance. From that moment on, all food transports had been seized, all distribution centers and wholesale companies had been occupied by German soldiers, and all shops were commanded not to sell food until the new distribution stamps had been issued. A different kind of war had begun.

Chapter Four

THE SINGING BOX

—⟐—

T here was a lot of excitement that day at the Van Rijn residence, and below the floor. After the fish peddler had arrived
and the doors of the warehouse were closed it was all hands on deck.
Every person was lined up through the house as an endless number
of newspaper stacks were passed on towards the secret shelter underneath the house.

Frans had come and Cornelius watched him make a frame for
the large "singing box" under the floor. Each of the Jews was in
anticipation of the changes which were ahead. To be able to talk,
sing and pray together was a treat they had forgotten existed. It was
a slow process to wet the newspapers and hang them over the frame,
but as the wall slowly grew thicker and thicker, the expectations
grew more.

To Cornelius, the entire busyness in the house was very exciting.
Finally, after three days of careful pasting and layering, the box was
almost completed. Only the carefully measured holes, into which
they would put their faces, were left.

It took the major part of a week before the first test could be
made. Frans showed them how it would have to be operated.

"No hole can remain open," he said, "and every one of you has
to keep your face pressed against the sides so that no sound can
come out."

31

It was a comical performance. By the time 12 people had been able to position themselves at the holes there was a lot of commotion. Everyone had forgotten that silence would be their means of survival, at least while they remained at the Van Rijn residence.

Until the board cracked and they all froze.

"The board" was a plank in the hallway upstairs. In fact, it was on the ground floor. The board, which had been positioned in such a way that no one would ever step on it by accident, was set on the side along the wall and served as an alarm device. Whenever the doorbell rang or knocks on the door sounded through the house, the Jews below would not be able to hear it and they remained unalarmed. So, before anyone opened the front door, someone would step on "the board."

It was a well rehearsed plan that went into operation. Without a word, the leader of the day would raise his hands, which meant: "Silence and move." He would then push the stone block in the foundation. This led to a space underneath the concrete staircase. Every time a newcomer joined them, the exercise had to be repeated. Their lives and the lives of Kees, Johanna and their children depended on it.

It would take thirty-five seconds for them to disappear behind the wall and move the concrete barrier into place. The Germans had never been down there. If they did discover the hiding place, all they would find would be some old mattresses and even that would need a lot of explaining by Kees.

Chapter Five

THE RAZZIA

—ɷ—

T he soldiers who had banged on the door demanding them to open it had only one mission. Their commander had told them that there were Jews in that house. Their command was to "go get them."

When they entered the hallway they screamed as if Johanna had committed a crime and pushed away the children as if they were cattle. They opened all the closets and pushed away the table in the center of the room and yelled "Who Sind sie (where are they?)" at Kees.

Kees kept his composure and simply said, "I don't know what you are talking about."

Then one of the soldiers pulled the rug away from where the table once had stood and barked, "Jawohl hier Sind Sie!" and pointed at the square lines which indicated a hatch in the floor.

The other soldiers pointed their guns at the wooden floor and began to shoot through the planks. They were waiting for screams of someone who would be hit by a bullet, but no sound could be heard from below.

Then one of the soldiers took his bayonet and pried open the hatch. They all thought they had found what they wanted and what they had been looking for.

You could see the disappointment on their faces when they shot

33

into the hatchway and the bullets bounced back on the thick concrete. They looked again; one of them dropped on his knees to look inside the opening and shook his head. "Nur beton," he said.

The sergeant turned to Kees and asked in his broken Dutch, "Where are they? We are sure they are here." Kees shook his head and said, "I work for Simowitz and I don't know what you are talking about."

These last words from Kees made an impression on the Sergeant whose final command followed, "Night hier, abfahren (not here, let's go!)" They all flocked to the door and left.

Amazingly, Kees had kept his composure for at least five minutes but then he dropped in his chair and broke out in a sweat. "That was a close call," he said to Johanna. "It shows that our precautions were very much needed."

Just a few months before Frans and Kees had decided to cut the hatch underneath the table, several other hiding places had been discovered at the same place. They knew that one day the soldiers would come and look for it.

In order to distract any searcher they had poured a concrete box underneath the hatch. Now it looked like a place to hide papers or some valuables.

It was way too small to hide people, not to speak of twenty live Jews who had exchanged their daily dwelling for the temporary one beneath the stairway. The concrete box was impenetrable for the German bullets and hidden from any keen eye.

His wife Johanna was crying. She could not stand the intrusion but in particular the treason that had been committed against them.

Who in the world would have betrayed them and had told the Germans that they were hiding people? "We have to be more careful, especially now that they have been here," she said.

Being practical, she went to the hallway and stepped on the alarm board twice, which was the sign of "all clear" for her Jewish guests.

During all the commotion of the scary event little Cornelius had watched the scene.

He was not yet aware of the severity of the event, he thought it was more a game of hide and seek. One of the soldiers had stroked his blond hair. Cornelius had reminded him of his own son far back in the south of Germany. He had felt compassion for the little boy.

Cornelius had felt his sympathy and was tempted to help the soldier find the people he was looking for. Johanna quickly pulled him away from the crowding group of men. She had pushed him gently towards the bedroom and held a finger in front of her lips.

After the soldiers left she took Cornelius on her lap. With tears in her eyes she began to tell him a story. "Corrie, these fine men were here to do bad things to us and to our friends downstairs. Even though they are Papas themselves they have to do their ugly job here in our country.

If they would ever find our Jewish friends here down below they will load them all up on a truck and take them away and because we are hiding them they would take our entire family as well.

First they will put us in the jail here and they will hurt us to make us answer all kinds of questions and then they will send us on a train to Auschwitz in Germany. We will never be able to come back home.

This is not a game son, this is called war. So never, ever tell them anything. If they ask you anything, even if they ask you if youwould like a candy, I am telling you now, you have to start crying and I don't care how loud, please cry because then they will stop asking questions and leave."

Cornelius understood and had a dozen more questions like, "Why do they want to take the friends from below and why would they take us? We are only helping people."

Johanna shook her head and replied, "We are not allowed to help these people. In their eyes we are doing something that is called illegal.

They will punish us for that if we are caught. Our friends below are Jewish people just like I am. If the Germans would find out that I am Jewish too, they would send me along with them when they would catch us.

That's why we don't want to be caught. You know who the Jewish people are, don't you?"

"The people downstairs," Cornelius answered. Johanna smiled, "Yes that is true, but they are much more than that. They are God's people, the people from the Bible. They are from the family of Jesus who died for us to give us life. Now they are taken to lose their lives because Mr. Hitler does not like them."

That had been enough lecturing for the day, Johanna thought, and she let Cornelius slip off her lap. With a loving push she said, "Now you go play and just forget about what I told you."

He never forgot, and in the following days he would have plenty of reasons to remember his mother's story.

Kees had gone down to talk to the "onderduikers," the Dutch word for fugitives in hiding.

They had all come back from under the concrete staircase and were holding each other with great fear in their eyes.

Jacob had suggested to seriously use their singing box and appointed the ones who would participate to take their positions.

When they were all on their spot, all their faces tightly in the holes, Jacob began to pray. Kees watched the situation and even though this was not a time for humor, he looked at the scene and could not resist a smile on his face. "At least they had accomplished something in the midst of all the turmoil."

Chapter Six

THE MESSAGE

—⚡—

That evening a messenger came to the van Rijn residence with a small piece of paper. The message on the paper read, "Tante Riek wants to talk to you."

Kees knew what that meant: a trip to Winterswijk with many German barricades and questions along the way. It meant a long and exhaustive week on a bicycle to the house of Tante Riek and a meeting with other underground leaders to receive instructions.

Usually it meant change; moving people from the city to the country, to wide open farms and haystacks.

Kees would have to ask for a pass from Simowitz, the factory he worked at, making bomb triggers for the Germans. The pass would give him a week to return. It also gave him easier ways to get through the German road blocks.

Tante Riek, (aunt Riek), was the founder and organizer of the Resistance. She was called the "Mother of Hiding Places."

Tens of thousands of hiding places had been created, too many for the Germans to control or even find. The war was still going on, fiercely, now even more severe then ever.

The Hollanders were all Dutch, whether Jewish or not. To the Dutch there was no difference.

Tante Riek's real name was Mrs. Helena Kuipers-Rietberg. A statue commemorating her work and her life has been erected in the city she worked and lived in.

She was a sweet, calm Christian woman who received her strength from the Bible. Her favorite text was in Matthew 22 verses 37 to 39: "Love the Lord your God with all your heart, with all your soul and all your mind. Love your neighbor as yourself."

That is what kept this brave lady going. That scripture is what she had in mind when she asked the underground workers and leaders to come to her home, to give them assurance and comfort, to instruct them how to do what they were doing and to take risks saving the lives of others.

Whether those others were Jewish or Gentiles, they were all children of Almighty God.

Kees planned his trip that evening, even though he had to go to work the next morning and ask the German commander of the factory where he was forced to work three days a week for a pass.

Kees hated to lie, but during war-time and being in the Resistance, one had to lie to be able to deceive the enemy.

He determined to create a letter from a cousin in Winterswijk which would say that his mother was very ill and wanted to see him for the last time because she was dying. He could only use that excuse once, he knew, but he resolved that in the future he would be able to come up with similar pressing reasons.

There was not much Kees could take on this trip. Anything he carried would be subject to a search and most often to confiscation.

The Badge with the Star of David

38

Lately the Germans had been taking even the bicycles from the citizens to make it more difficult for them to move around the country.

Kees's "job" had enabled him to keep his bike, but even that might soon be over.

On the way to Winterswijk he would spend the night at the farms he knew were hiding Jews so he did not have to worry about food. The only thing he took with him was a bottle of cold tea.

He knew the Germans would open the bottle and smell if it was liquor. One time they had laughed at him and emptied the bottle right in front of him.

At his regular time of six o'clock in the morning, he said good-bye to Johanna and Cornelius and went to the Simowitz factory downtown in The Hague.

The bike trip took him just over half an hour. After passing the sentry at the gate, he went straight to the commander's office.

The short, round and burly German in his showy uniform of the Waffen SS looked at him without compassion after reading the letter Kees presented to him.

."Warum?" he said, "She is going to die anyway. Why would you take the time and make the long and dangerous trip to see her? People die every day."

Kees knew it would not be that easy but he replied, "Would you go to see your mother if she was dying?"

With an angry gesture and without giving an answer to Kees's question he signed the pass and threw it at him. "Thank you," Kees said. Even though he could speak German, he refused to do it. That was his Dutch pride

He went directly to the exit gate and began his long trip to Winterswijk. He was excited to visit the farms on the way and see many people he had helped before. At the same time he would receive status reports on their well-being.

The Germans must have been looking for fugitives that morning as he left the city of The Hague.

Before he even reached the countryside, he passed the heavily armed airport where so many brave resistance fighters and the

Boxing troupe of the Resistance had lost their lives in a battle for control of the airport.

He was stopped nine times, frisked four times, and almost lost his bicycle to an ignorant German who refused to accept the validity of his pass.

Finally he was amidst the meadows where an occasional cow was chewing thin grass that was re-appearing after the cold winter of 1943.

Kees did not need a map or road sign, he had ridden his bike to Winterswijk several time before.

Chapter Seven

RESISTANCE AS AN ARTIST

—ɯ—

I n Amsterdam there was a sculptor who had his own gallery. He was a typical artistic person with a straight-forward opinion.

His stubborn attitude saved many lives all over the country. Gerrit van der Veen was his name.

When the Germans had taken over the country and the possessions of the local administrations, some of which had been burned just before the Germans came, they replaced the clerks with collaborators, or "NSB-ers."

The intruders wanted to know everything about everyone, so all the citizens received a letter and a form to fill out. It asked for a person's name, age, gender, address, etc.

At the end of the questionnaire there was a question Gerrit did not like.

That particular question changed him into a fierce opposer of the occupational forces.

The question was about his race, whether he was a Jew or not. "This is wrong, it is bad and it has alternative reasons," he said. "We are all Dutch and that is all there is to it." He determined that he would not accept any of this from the Moffen (Germans.) But that was not all; he reacted by using his skills to fight them.

His favorite words were, "I have not asked them to come here and I don't need anything from them." He came into action immediately, that same hour he ran outside and went from door to door. "Tear it up, don't fill it out. Don't return it," he told all his neighbors. It sounded like a command and Gerrit van der Veen had become a member of the Resistance instantly.

On February 15, 1942, together with some other fighters, he published a manifest against the occupation. Together they delivered it all over the city. The gist of it was, "Do not fill out the questionnaire! The Krauts have alternative reasons!"

The enemy acted that same day and arrested dozens of people, particularly those who signed the manifest. Gerrit van der Veen escaped the arrests and became an "Onderduiker," a person in hiding.

He used his artistic skills and partnered with a printer. Together they experimented to falsify the identity card which everyone had to carry.

It took a lot of effort and skill. It had to have a watermark, a particular kind of paper, the right ink – in short, a completely forged application.

They experimented in a small kitchen on the third floor. Everything was done by hand, the work of artists. Each ID card took about ten hours to make, but what is ten hours of work when compared to a life?

It became one of the largest forgery organizations. They created an estimated 70,000 forged ID's. Gerrit van der Veen and his plan became the largest life-saver for the Jews in hiding.

Kees van Rijn was one of the customers who needed false papers on a daily basis. On his way to Winterswijk, he executed another aspect of the underground war; he carried seven false ID's under his camisole.

Chapter Eight

A NARROW ESCAPE

—ᴍ—

I t was a long trip from The Hague to Utrecht, through all the villages of the Old Rijn River.

Each village had German road-blocks, one at its entrance and one at the exit. It was usually manned by a patrol of six soldiers with a machine gun set up to face the road.

In between the villages, which could be as far apart as 15 miles, there were meadows and farms. Cows were grazing and everything looked as quaint as during peace times.

But the war was going on more severe than ever. One out of five farms had a hiding place somewhere on its property. It could be anywhere on the farm.

Some farmers were hiding two or three people and some larger farms had as many as ten fugitives, "onderduikers," as they called them.

When the farmers went to a village nearby to go shopping, they would have to use food stamps which were issued by the Germans on a weekly basis.

People had to wait and stand in line to receive them at the local town halls.

With the food stamps they would then go to the stores and buy what they were allowed to get – one loaf of bread for a family of three, for example. If they had fugitives at their farm, the Germans would know by the amount of food they had purchased.

Everything had to be done clandestinely and the patrols at the village entrances would meticulously check what they had bought and how much their allowance was. Too much food meant confiscation of all their purchases as a punishment.

People were checked on what they brought into the villages, too. They would even be frisked for contraband or for more food stamps than were allowed.

It was hell going shopping and hell going home from shopping.

At night, however, the countryside came alive. The German patrols went to their barracks because they were too afraid to get shot or even kidnapped at night by one of the roaming "knok ploegen," or boxer gangs.

The farmers would visit each other and swap food with each other.

It was in early in the evening when Kees rode into the city of Tiel.

A German patrol on a motorcycle with a side car carrying two soldiers called out "Halt! Ausweiss!" while riding next to him, and stopped him.

Since it was dark they not only asked him questions, they also pushed him against a wall and began to frisk him.

At first, Kees was shocked; they did not even give him time to produce his pass. He wrestled and tried to pull away from them but that made them even more aggressive.

One of the soldiers blew his whistle; within a minute other soldiers appeared at the scene. Finally, a sergeant barked, "Take him! Arrest him and bring him to the jail."

They took his bicycle, handcuffed him and pushed him on the bed of a truck. With great speed they drove to the town hall of Tiel, where the local jail had been seized to house those who were arrested until the Gestapo came to question them.

When Kees was thrown into the cell, he fell on his knees and prayed for his enemy. "Lord, give them compassion and wisdom. Please let them be humane."

The Gestapo was never humane. They were the types who would

shoot first and then ask questions.

Kees had only one other concern. He had to get rid of the seven fake ID cards he had hidden on his body.

He was grateful that they had not searched him before locking him up.

That was a mistake the Gestapo would have never made.

He looked around his cell, perusing it carefully to see if there was a camera somewhere or a peep hole through which they could be watching him.

He could not find any indication of anything of the kind. Then he began to search for a place to hide the fake ID's or preferably to put them somewhere so he could somehow retrieve them.

All he could see were concrete walls and a wooden cot. There was not even a toilet present in his cell, which was highly unusual. There were no windows or anything in which he could hide his treasure.

The value of the Id's was enormous; many tedious hours of work had been put into them. His dilemma was reason enough for him to break out into a sweat.

How much time would he have to dispose if the ID's?

Then his eye caught a crack in the concrete wall next to the door. He walked over to the spot and tried to feel how deep the crack was.

Apparently it went right through to the hallway. He could look through it! Would it be at all possible to hide his package and pick it up later? He investigated the situation a little closer, trying to picture where he was and where they would take him for questioning. Where was the door to the outside?

He decided not to take a risk, because if they would find it in the crack they would certainly link it to him. Having the fake ID's in his possession could mean instant death. All too often it had occurred when contraband or fake documents were found on underground workers.

At that moment he had an idea. He should take his under shirt off, leave the ID's in it and hide the shirt. He could risk his life that way, but he could also save the lives of six people whose ID he had on his body.

He made the decision the follow his instincts and quickly pull off his shirt and undershirt. He took the ID cards and rolled them up in a very tight roll, wrapped his undershirt neatly around the little roll and casually threw the package in a corner.

He barely had his shirt and coat put back on when he heard the rattle of keys in his cell door.

The man in a black suit who opened the door pulled him roughly out of the cell and pushed him into a room right across the hallway.

He was shoved into a chair. The man in the black suit did not say anything. He just looked at him for a long time, finally saying, "Auschweiss bitte."

The raspy command came quite unexpectedly. Kees did not expect it to go that way. Nervously he produced his ID card but not his pass.

In a state of consternation he had simply forgotten that he had a pass. The Gestapo man looked at his ID and asked him in perfect Dutch, "What are you doing here, all the way from The Hague?"

Finally Kees realized he had not produced his pass. His mind raced, he tried to remember where he had left it. In a little of a panic he thought he might have packed it with the ID's in his undershirt.

Then he remembered! He had held it in his hand when they had arrested him. His mind raced back to the moment of his arrest. Finally calming down at last he felt in his trouser pocket and there it was all crumpled up.

The Gestapo man snapped it out of his hand with a "Wass ist dass (What's that?)" He began to read it.

Hundreds, even thousands of the Dutch Resistance had fallen into traps like Kees had found himself in that night. It would not be the last time for Kees either.

Many had never come out of the jail cell. Most of them had been shot in the backyard of the jail house.

Kees's prayer had saved him this time. The Gestapo man stood up and apologized! He promised to give him his bike back and wished him a safe trip to Winterswijk. "Oh, I forgot my undershirt," Kees simply said as he walked out of the room. He quickly picked it up in the open cell and was guided outside.

All Kees could utter when he hopped on his bike again was, "Thank you Lord."

He only had half a mile to go to reach the farm where he was expected to sleep that night.

It was getting dark when he entered the gates that led to the farm house of farmer Joop Brandwijk. He lived on the farm with his family and their main livestock consisted of 55 milk cows.

Joop and his wife Nel Brandwijk had a 17-year-old son Cor and a daughter Marie, who was nineteen-years-old. Together they ran the farm. They had some chicken, a few pigs and twenty acres of land which supplied sugar beets and hay for the cows in the winter.

The hay stack was a separate structure which had four tall poles and an adjustable roof. Depending on how much hay there was in the fall, farmer Brandwijk would raise or lower the thatched roof of the hay stack.

In the center of the haystack was a staircase about which the Germans did not know. It was at that place where Kees went down that evening.

The hidden staircase led to a basement which had been shrewdly constructed when the war had begun and which now housed an average of fifteen fugitives.

At that time during the war most fugitives were Jews who had escaped the city for the "Razzias," (unexpected house searches), which would be conducted by truck-loads of soldiers who arrested Jews, Jews who had made the mistake of registering themselves in the devious plot of the Germans at the beginning of the war.

They did not know what would be happening in the future until it came. Like a round-up of cattle the Jews were picked up, brought to the railway stations and transported to the death camps in Ravensbrueck, Birkenau, Auswitz and many other concentration camps.

Often the men were separated from their wives and children. Entire families were torn apart and temporarily used as laborers until they had no more strength. Being malnourished, they had to work 20 hours per day and many dropped dead while they were working. Their food rations were so small it made them become walking skeletons in a few weeks.

The women were sometimes used for experimental medical research and if they did not die from the experiments they would be taken to the "showers" where the Germans would release gas instead of water to kill them in large numbers.

Chapter Nine

THE AMBULANCE BUILDERS

—m—

At the airport just outside of The Hague was a hangar where a group of Dutch workers had kept their jobs even after the occupation had begun.

Their job was maintenance and repair of planes and occasionally vehicles which serviced the airport facilities.

The Germans did not let them touch the mechanical parts of the planes. For that particular work they had obviously brought their own engineers.

This group of Dutch workers were also underground workers, actively engaged in the Resistance. The Germans had no clue about their activities.

The vehicles which had been at the airport had been kept in good running order. The German vehicles had just been added to the fleet. Among those vehicles the Germans had brought were three ambulances. The ones the Germans had brought were made of square boxes placed on the chassis of a Mercedes truck. They had been painted green with a huge red cross, in the middle of which was a black swastika.

After the first year of the war it was obvious that the Dutch ambulances would never be used, there were hardly ever any casualties at the Airport.

The accidents that did occur were taken care of by the German

49

ambulances and their drivers.

When the Resistance of the Dutch underground army increased, the Dutch workers at the repair hangar at Ypenburg Airport had joined the secret fighters.

They had been given a specific task which had fit right up their alley.

"Can you create a German ambulance, one or more of them out of the Dutch ones for us?" Those had been the words of Gerrit Jan van der Veen, the former shipbuilder from Amsterdam who had become the legendary activity leader of the country-wide resistance.

The group of workers at the airport had looked at each other and laughed, "We have the perfect place and the models right in our hangar. The German soldiers hardly ever come to visit us other than when they have a dent or some bullet holes in their plane for us to fix. We can separate the job from our normal duties by building a hidden room in the hangar. Yes, we'll see what we can do. Give us a week and we will report what we may be able to accomplish..."

They had gone to work that next morning. They had hauled some corrugated steel sheets from a neighboring hangar which had been bombed and had begun their task.

At first they took a corner which had been filled with a huge stack of parts from planes and moved them forward about thirty meters. Then they had built a separation wall. It took them three days, and during all that time, one of them had to take turns to see if anyone was coming.

Any German visitor had to be distracted in order to not to see what they were doing.

They succeeded with the first part of their mission and after three days they all looked at their handy work. It will work, they all agreed. They sent a messenger to Amsterdam and used one of the German ambulances with the excuse that they had to make a test run.

It took them an additional five weeks to make a perfect replica of a German ambulance. Finally, when the vehicle was finished and ready for a test run, it was a perfect duplicate, clad with the Red Cross and swastika, even the Mercedes emblem on the hood was at its right place.

With a sigh of relief they reported that their mission had been accomplished. A means of transportation for the Jews had been created and was ready for action.

That same evening the first major transport had been scheduled.

On the corner of the Deiman Straat in The Hague a group of German soldiers had been dropped off.

Four men, with their Waffen SS emblem and one in Gestapo uniform, were standing in front of Groenendijk's warehouse when suddenly one of the soldiers fainted and fell on the pavement.

The NSB-ers looking out from their windows saw it happen and wondered what they should do, if anything. Normally the members of the NSB would come into action if anything out of the ordinary would happen.

They were promised rewards in the form of extra food stamps for any tip leading to an arrest. Most of them were unknown neighbors; no one would suspect them during the first few years of the war.

But was this something they would have to report? Probably not. This situation would not lead to an arrest. It happened more often that soldiers would collapse.

After all, even the soldiers hardly had enough food to eat at this time of the war. So the collaborators decided to ignore the situation.

That was exactly what had been anticipated by the group of Germans. They banged on the door of the Groenendijk warehouse and demanded to be let inside so they could wait for an ambulance to pick up the fainted soldier.

It took the Groenendijk people at least five minutes before they could open up because they had been working on the entrance to the next door hiding place at the van Rijn residence.

They had to conceal all evidence that there was such an entrance. With the excuse that they had to move a number of the box-bikes, they were getting away with the lengthy waiting time.

At last they opened up the warehouse door and the group of soldiers carried their comrade into shelter.

It took more than an hour for the ambulance to arrive. The observing NSB-ers had been looking at the warehouse door until they finally saw the ambulance backing up to the large doors. It drove right into the building and took away the view for anyone to observe what was really going on.

The group of soldiers had been very busy while they were in the warehouse. Once inside they had opened up the entrance to the van Rijn hiding place. The six guests had been warned the day before that their transport would be imminent in the next few days, so they gathered their few belongings and went upstairs into the warehouse.

To their shocking surprise, they were greeted by German soldiers who soon revealed that they were Dutch citizens and members of the Resistance.

They had brought clothes and make-up, wigs and hats. In the short hour they had transformed the look of the Jewish people into farm workers.

The Jewish curls of the men had been covered with blond wigs; pictures had been taken and quickly developed for their ID cards.

They had been prepared for a long trip to the south of Holland, to a place close to the German borders but equally close to the Belgium borders.

That would be their starting point to freedom. They were ready when the ambulance arrived and within minutes they had been loaded up, laying flat on their backs with a cover overtop and a gurney with a soldier above them.

In the event that they would be stopped they would not be found because those who stopped them would first read the forged papers the driver would hand to them. When looked inside the ambulance they would see nothing but a wounded officer on his way to his home town in Germany.

In the course of two years thousands of Jews would be transported that way to their freedom. The Germans never discovered the system which had saved so many lives.

The German soldiers marched out of the warehouse after the

ambulance had left, with its sirens blaring it had left to the south of Holland through the heavily bombarded city of Rotterdam.

It was never stopped that time until it reached its temporary destination at the house of Tante Wies in the province of Limburg, in a village called Sevenum.

Tante Wies was one of those many heroes in the Underground of the Second World War.

She had her own motherly methods to take care of people who were in hiding and who needed to get to freedom.

At the end of the war her heroic efforts came to light. With a smile she announced that she had had seven hundred sons, and a hundred daughters.

She must have made a great understatement, considering how many she had helped in her special way.

No one would ever know. Before she began her work something happened that changed the many lives she had helped.

One day her neighbor Piet knocked on her door and told her that two young beggars were looking for her. She said, "Bring them over and I'll see what they need."

They appeared to be two French soldiers who had escaped a camp for prisoners of war in Germany. She immediately realized that they had to disappear quickly or she would be arrested with them.

So she cleaned them up, fed them and gave them civilian clothes. Later in the war when her own supplies had been exhausted, she was demanding clothes, suits and shirts from everyone in the village, even from the mayor of the town. Everyone knew her and knew what she was doing, so they all helped.

After the first two Frenchmen, it became a continual stream of fugitives; French soldiers, English pilots who had been shot down in their planes and of course many Jews who were brought to her to escape to freedom.

The first time they came and were fed and dressed, she called her son Piet and said, "Boy, I want you to take these two to safety. They have wives and children and they need to go home." Her son and his friend rode their bicycles to the Belgian border and showed them which path would bring them to safety.

That path became a route organized by the Resistance of Holland, Belgium and France. It was so well arranged that the fugitives were picked up by some one in every town and village until they reached Switzerland.

No one knows the exact count. The Resistance was everywhere and the Germans would never be able to defeat such a determined people.

Chapter Ten

THE HAY STACK

—m—

W hen Kees came down the ladder inside the hay stack he was welcomed by fifteen anxious people.

Each one of them was hoping to get out of their voluntary imprisonment. Each one of them had a good reason to leave. Each one of them had loved ones somewhere in the midst of this crazy war.

Unfortunately, the leadership of the Resistance had their reasons for choosing who was going to be led to freedom.

For others, there were reasons of safety, reasons which would be of importance for the cause: the ultimate defeat of the enemy. Some were picked by age and others by gender.

There was no argument about it, when people were chosen, it was an unchangeable decision. Four people had been picked to leave the Brandwijk farm. They were picked because one of them was a surgeon, who would be helped to get to London via Switzerland; one of them was a nurse who was the doctor's assistant.

Both of them would be desperately needed in London to help with the many casualties that were caused because of the excessive bombardments on the city.

The other two were Jews who had witnessed an abusive situation in the streets of The Hague. The Germans were told to leave no witnesses and if these two would have been caught it would have meant their instant execution.

The four chosen ones were delighted about their pending departure.

The following days they would undergo a change in appearance, which often meant haircuts or hair coloring, sometimes even a change to make a man look like a woman.

The four would be issued new identities and pictures would be made for their ID cards. Travel documents would be made with passes and reasons why they were traveling and where. Everything was made to look as legal as normal, that way no questions would be asked.

This form of escape was only possible up to the third year of the war. The Germans became more and more suspicious of all travelers and at the end of the third year too many were caught to continue this practice.

For Kees this was a sweet and sour kind of meeting.

He was going to say goodbye to people he had gotten to know as friends, people who had depended on him and loved him for what he had done for them.

On the other hand, it was also hard to leave the others where they were for who knows how long, with the constant threat of being detected.

This uncertainty was often too much for the people and sometimes one had to be sedated in order to keep quiet.

That night Kees remained with his friends deep down in the basement of the hay stack. It was a safe haven for many more to come.

Kees knew that after the four left a new group would quickly replace them. They could be the ones from under his own floor in The Hague.

That evening they all chatted and prayed together for their own safety and for the safety of their families. They prayed for Kees in his dangerous travels and for his family down in the wretched city of The Hague. And they prayed for the all too many people who were trying to escape their impending and unfair death sentence.

Because there were so many safe havens and stations in between their first and last hiding places, and because there were so many people involved in the secret exodus, it was almost impossible for a traitor to include himself in the Underground network.

Yet, a few times it happened. When it did, it would have far-reaching consequences for many, both fugitives and those who were hiding them. Sometimes the Resistance had to do something they did not like to do.

It happened in the city of Utrecht, a city smack in the center of Holland, where a man and a woman had claimed to be Jewish and said they had to go in hiding.

They had found the local hiding place and when they were asked how they had found it, their answers were rather vague.

Despite the suspicion that something might be wrong, they had, however, convinced the host that they were truly fugitives, so he had taken them in.

For two weeks they had stayed in that hiding place when their transportation had come around. Just like the others they were brought to a farm in the country and no one suspected anything.

Meanwhile they had gathered addresses and names, traffic routes and methods on how people were transferred to other places for permanent hiding places or for further transportation to freedom.

During their fourth transport they had disappeared. The only person to blame was the local agent who, for a moment, had forgotten that he could trust no one.

After their disappearance no alarm had been made to the other locations, hence the second mistake had been made. The third mistake caused all hell to break loose.

The agent in charge of the transport went to the local police to ask if he had seen the two. Sometimes the local police would collaborate with the Resistance, but most of the time they were the feared NSB ers who turned people in for food stamps and other favors. This police man was the latter. He immediately called the local Gestapo leader and arrested the transporting agent, leaving the group he had with him in limbo.

Not knowing what they should do, they tried to return to their last hiding place only to find everyone had been arrested and taken away.

That week hundreds of fugitives had been arrested and dozens of hiding places were permanently compromised.

The people who were sheltering fugitives were sent to the death camps together with the ones they had attempted to save from their sentences.

Never was anyone to be trusted again. Mistakes were made and death lured around the corner at all times.

Chapter Eleven

THE SECRET MEETING

—⟋⟍—

K ees had finally arrived at his goal, the City of Winterswijk, after three long days of bicycling and meeting many people on his way.

He was exhausted and ready to take a long rest.

But there was no rest for the very hard working resistance.

At last he was to meet "the Mother of Hiding Places" in Holland, Tante Riek.

Mrs. Kuipers-Rietberg was a motherly, warm, loving woman.

She welcomed Kees as if she had known him for years.

"So nice to finally meet you," she said as she hugged him affectionately. "Come on in and have some coffee. I have just made some soup too if you are hungry."

Kees was pulled inside by his arm and what he saw was nothing extraordinary. It was an everyday family home with a dining table in the center of the room. She poured him his coffee and looked at him expectantly.

Kees took in the atmosphere of peace and tranquility as if no war was going on at all.

Chapter Twelve

THE WAY TO FREEDOM

—ɯɯ—

T he ambulance had to stop at several roadblocks, the expected scene had occurred as was planned. Most soldiers at the roadblocks did not even bother to look into the back of the ambulance. A wounded officer drew their curiosity for just a second and then it gave way for jealousy.

At least this guy was going home to his family, perhaps wounded for life, perhaps only a little handicapped for life. That was no big deal compared to the mess they were in at that point in the war.

It seemed an endless war without a victory. Who was Hitler kidding?

They never won or would ever win. That was the general thought among the German soldiers. Of course there were the Generals and the stories from Poland and Russia. Most of the soldiers had given up on the Third Reich at that time.

"Befehl ist Befehl (a command is a command)," was what they had to live by.

So the ambulance had made it to Sevenum in six hours, which was unheard of during this time of war with all the roadblocks and barricades.

Tante Wies was expecting the new shipment of people and she had left the garage door unlocked so the ambulance could enter quickly and not stir up any curiosity, even though almost all citizens of Sevenum were friends of Tante Wies. They had all supplied her with clothes and even fabric to make clothes. The community began to feel the pressure Tante Wies was creating by taking everything she could get to the fugitives, and helping them getting out of harm's way in Holland, on the way to freedom through Belgium and France to Switzerland.

The Jews in the ambulance came out of their transportation stiffness and were tired, even though they laid down all the way. They did not have a chance to move around or even go to the bathroom. It had been a trying and scary trip for them and when they finally had arrived and tried to stand up out of their prostrate position some of them swayed badly and one of them fainted.

The pressure had been too much to bear for anyone in such a situation.

The oldest of them were the most positive, because they realized that their lives were at stake and it would have ended if they would have been caught on the road somewhere in Holland or in the death camps.

Tante Wies welcomed each one of them with a friendly handshake and showed her usual hospitality when she announced, "There is coffee and sandwiches ready. Come on inside and take a seat at the table, make yourselves comfortable. I would like to hear your stories if you care to tell them to me."

The evening went by so quickly that no one had noticed the clock had passed the hour of twelve midnight.

It was the favorite time for the Nazi's to hold their infamous Razzia. But none of that happened in Sevenum. The last Razzia had not yielded one person, their conclusion had been that there was nothing to catch in Sevenum.

After three days at the house of Tante Wies, all the fugitives had been briefed and updated. They needed to know where to go once in Belgium and France. They also needed to know where not to go, as well as how to contact the agents on the way in case they could not find one or reach a designated place later than was planned.

They had to learn all those facts by heart because anything written could betray them and anyone else in the future. Tante Wies fed them well and made-sure they were dressed for the journey. When the time came for their departure four guides and four bicycles were needed.

Her sons Piet and Jan had friends who had been doing the same trip many times before. They were warned to be ready at the drug store late that evening.

Their decoy place was in fact their store. It was an old-fashioned "Drogisterij," or drugstore where Tante Wies lived and held her escape headquarters.

The store was not conspicuous since many clients even from the surrounding country came in and out all day long.

This time she took some more caution than before. This time there were six people to be taken to the Belgian border and they were all Jews. Many times before that day, Tante Wies had helped pilots and POW camp escapees.

They had to go one by one with an hour in between. She carefully selected who would go first; they were the oldest and slowest ones. The younger and faster ones could catch up with the others.

She urged them not to group together anywhere. A crowd, even a small one, would always attract attention.

Tante Wies operated her rescue home for four years. "One thing I really would like to know," she told her friends, "Did they all make it?" A few did let her know.

Many did not, probably because they never knew where they had been. They had arrived in Sevenum at nights and almost all had left within a few days. They left in the dark at early mornings or late in the evenings and never wrote down a name or an address. Writing down anything was very dangerous in those times of war.

Tante Wies had been one of the blessed ones with the slogan "I am blessed to be a blessing." She was never searched or arrested. She was just a loving mother. Who in the world would want to arrest a mother?

She had saved the lives of at least a thousand people, just like many other mothers all throughout the country. The war had never stopped. Until May 1945.

The successful first trip of the ambulance was followed by many more. So many thousands had to be transported out of the cities of The Hague, Amsterdam and Rotterdam that the mechanics had a full time job in the hangar of the Airport Ypenburg.

The Germans never suspected them of any underground activities and towards the end of the war the mechanics had created seventeen ambulances. They had situated them all over the country, right under the noses of the enemy.

Chapter Thirteen

THE ILLEGAL PRESS

—ɯɯ—

A nother branch of the Resistance, the illegal press, was growing like wild fire. The underground press was urgently needed to publish true news, but more importantly it was needed for the creation of documents.

Perhaps as many as 200,000 people did not have a legal Ausweiss. Anyone on the road during the daytime needed a pass. All these documents were forged in large numbers in the most primitive circumstances – on old-fashioned typewriters and hand presses.

The print shops were hidden in basements, underneath foundations of houses, in attics of abandoned buildings – wherever the Resistance could find a place. A place where the Germans would not think to raid was where illegal presses could be found.

Because of the German decree that every male over the age of seventeen had to be part of the "Arbeits Einsatz," (obligatory labor in the German war Industry), all the printing companies had been closed or some had been taken over by the Germans for their own printing needs.

Many Dutch printers and printing apprentices had been put to work in other types of work for the Nazis at the beginning of the war. As the need for printers for the Underground was increasing greatly, more and more of the professional printers had gone underground to work for the illegal press. When they had quit their "Arbeits Einsatz" jobs they became fugitives, "Onderduikers." If they were caught they were arrested and immediately sent to the concentration camps whether they were Jewish or not.

As the need for information had grown, the Nazis were forbidding the Dutch to have radios and anyone caught carrying newspapers would be in for extensive interrogations and arrest.

However, the truth had to be told and the stubborn Dutch made sure it was done.

Illegal newspapers and a printing press in a haystack

Binnenhof and the Hofpond

Chapter Fourteen

THE MOST SECRET MEETING

—⚡—

In the city of Winterswijk, close to the German border, the gathering of Resistance leaders was growing. Since Kees had arrived several others had come in as well.

After an hour there were more than fifteen people from all parts of the country. The group would have been the catch of a lifetime for the Gestapo.

Before anyone would come as close as three hundred yards from Tante Riek's house they would be spotted. At every street corner there was someone watching the streets and particularly who it was that passed by. If it was anyone unknown it would be reported in a matter of seconds through a chain of people to tante Riek's men in the hallways front and back of the house.

There must have been a hundred helpers who were forming the safety net around the head office of the Resistance. Any German soldier, SS-er or Gestapo man who would be spotted would trigger a chain of events that would immediately disperse and scatter the group of fifteen leaders in Tante Riek's house. No risk was taken by Tante Riek and her men.

Kees knew perhaps five of them, had heard of others and was excited to get to know more of them. All of them were leaders with a similar purpose: To bring fugitives to safety or hide them, feed them and distribute the means to do any of the above.

After an hour of chit-chat and unwinding from an often eventful and exhaustive trip, Tante Riek called the gathering to order.

"Gentlemen and lady," she began, since there was only one other lady present besides Tante Riek, "Thank you all for coming at such short notice. I would like to open this important meeting with a prayer, Please bow your heads." She prayed a short but well-meaning prayer for their safety and for their important mission, for their families and for their enemies.

For those who were non-believers, the last sentence of her prayer sounded ridiculous, but they took her prayer with reverence. Tante Riek was a sincere woman. In fact, to all the people present at that meeting in the house of a simple woman.

Tante Riek was a very special person and if she wanted to bless the enemy, they respected her for it.

"We are all here with the same concerns and you may all have been thinking why we need to be here so urgently. We have had some very disturbing information which needs to be spread throughout our country as fast as possible. We need to take important steps to guard our backs and distrust everyone who seeks our help. First and foremost, I have received credible information from Germany that the so-called work camps are not work camps at all.

The number of people who are entering the camps is far greater than the camps could possibly handle. We have heard that people are gassed to death and that they are incinerated in giant ovens in some camps and in other camps they have seen enormous mass graves in which thousands upon thousands are buried. Some are even buried alive."

It became eerily still in the room of Tante Riek's house and the always astute people present looked at each other in horror. If this was true they could expect a lot of action in their little country by the Sea. Panic could break out and the Germans might go crazy.

"Let me read the letter to you which I have received from a 'camp' in Auschwitz, Germany. Remember this very letter could have been screened by the Germans before they let it go out. This woman by the name of Hannah, a Jewish young lady, is writing this letter to her brother who is still living here in town.

Of course he is Jewish too. When the letter arrived at his home there were three soldiers behind the postman who came to pick him up and arrest him.

The old man Isaac allowed a friend, who was not Jewish, to open the door for him while he was hiding in a closet. The soldiers asked the man who opened the door if he was Isaac Ibranov. The man simply nodded and was immediately taken to the local jail.

He left the letter in the hall way and when they were all gone Isaac came out of the closet, retrieved the letter and immediately came to me here. I was able to hide him and after I read the letter I could hardly believe my eyes at what was written and how it was done.

I will show you the letter, pass it around after I have read it. Please bear with me."

Tante Riek began to read and as she proceeded tears welled up in her eyes. The listeners were holding their breath and you could feel the tension in the room, a silence – the silence of death – filled the room where only the shaking voice of Tante Riek was heard.

"My dear brother,

The trip to this camp in itself was not too bad although we had to stand and lean against each other in the cattle train. For that reason it was not cold. We warmed each other's bodies.

During the journey several people fainted and one of us died from exhaustion. The wagon was sealed too tightly and the air we were breathing became thinner as we went.

When we finally arrived at the camp it was stinking so bad on the train because there was no toilet, of course, and some people could not hold it any longer.

We were unloaded in this terrible camp The soldiers were all very mean and they would shoot at any one not doing exactly what they told them. I saw at least six people die in front of all these people.

After standing on a large field they did a count of all of us and then they told us to take all our belongings and all our clothes and put them on a pile in front of each person. We had to strip naked, they said, because we were going into a large shower all together

It was all very embarrassing to stand there in the cold and being looked at by the Nazi soldiers. Then the soldiers separated the men from the women, as if they could not have done that before we undressed.

The men were pushed to the big hall where we could see the showers overhead while the women were split up by age.

Because I look young (ha, ha) I was taken with the young ones to a sort of clinic where doctors began to examine us one by one. They asked all kind of questions in German, which I could not understand.

I kept saying, 'I don't know, I don't know.'

Then I thought of a word which I hoped would get their attention, I said, 'I have Syphilis.'

My words had caused a shock in the clinic. One of the nurses was sent out of the room but she came back immediately with another doctor.

To my surprise, this man spoke Dutch. He was a nice person, it seemed.

He asked me in Dutch what I had said. I repeated that I had said that I had Syphilis. His response was that I had to be taken to a different examination room.

The Doctor followed the soldiers and me to a private room further down the hallway. When we came into his room he sent the soldiers away and closed the door.

Then he told me quietly, 'I am a Dutchman and I have been put to work here involuntarily. I have been trying to get out of here for more of a civilian kind of duty, but first I have to prove to them that I will come back and that I can be asset to them here in this camp.

What I am about to tell you will startle you, to say the least.

I will help you if you trust me, are you willing to play along with me?'

I really did not know what to think of this but I swallowed hard and said, 'What is this startling news you have to tell me? Tell me now and I'll decide if I will play along with you.'

'This camp here,' he began, 'is not what it seems to be from the

outside.

This camp is a Verniechting camp, a death camp. Whoever arrives here will never leave. All new arrivals are murdered here ,most likely all are gassed to death already.

The doors on the other side open up to huge incinerators where the bodies are cremated. See the smoke coming up from that chimney there?'

I could not believe my ears and I must have looked at him aghast.

'I know this is shocking news to you.' I had turned ashen when he announced this horrible thing and I started to cry.

After a long silence he said, 'I can help you if you will help me. 'Then he continued after a few moments. 'Here is my plan: I will make a report about you having Syphilis and include a proposal to use you here in the experimental clinic to find a cure and a medicine. Do you really have Syphilis? This is important because it is one of the most occurring diseases among German soldiers and the management here would be thrilled to have me work on a solution."

I shook my head and answered his question: "No I don't but I thought it would deter them from using me". He smiled and said: "I thought so, very smart of you to come up with that. I think we can use this situation to benefit both of us.

I already have an idea. I can come up with some medication that might help the Nazis a little. It will be sufficient to keep them away from you and me for quite a while.

Later, when I will announce what my findings have been with you as a guinea pig". I thanked him for the complement with a smile as he went on: "I will have to make false progress reports on your "illness" and then finally show that I have indeed made a head start in the war against Syphilis.

I intend to combine that report with my request for a leave of absence and to be allowed to go on a trip to Holland for two weeks. They will probably send some soldiers along with me to make sure I will come back. Once in Holland I can contact people through the Hospital I used to work and get the news out of what is happening here. Meanwhile you will be protected from any harm or sexual ha-

rassment. Through my collegues I can get information to any one in Holland. You might think of writing a letter to someone there which I can take with me."He had concluded.

This letter I hope will arrive in Winterswijk my brother, and I pray that you are still there when the Doctor or someone else brings it to you. I love you my brother Isaac. Please gat this letter to the Dutch Underground leaders so they can spread the word throughout Holland and please remain in hiding and do not trust the person who brings you this letter. No one can be trusted. All of the people I came here with have perished because they trusted someone.

Pray for me that I might find a way out of here and pray for the Doctor to return to me here in safety.

Good bye and shalom, my brother,

Your sister Hannah.

It was very quiet in the room when Tante Riek had ended her reading of the letter. Some of the listeners were so touched by the letter. Some were swallowing hard to digest what had just been revealed.

Tante Riek, who had read the letter several times before the meeting, was able to keep her composure as she looked around the room at the brave members of the resistance.

It was Kees who broke the silence when he exclaimed, "I knew it! I knew there was something going on there in Germany with all the Jews who had been shipped there. I knew it because how in the world would they have been able to house the millions that were sent there? We've got to do all we can to spread the word. Get it in the news, in all the underground papers and in the Name of Jesus, let us hide more of them even though they don't believe in Him."

His words were followed by many comments from the others until Tante Riek called the gathering to order. "Let us split up in groups of four and make a list of things we need to do. After an hour we will discuss our findings and make a general plan. You should all leave here as soon as possible and do what you have to do."

Chapter Fifteen

LIFE UNDER THE FLOOR

—ɯ—

In The Hague, Johanna had a scare. Jacob, the oldest of the Jewish guests, had come upstairs in broad daylight and told Johanna he wanted to talk to her.

"But Jacob sir," she answered, "you will have to talk to my husband Kees about anything concerning your stay here."

"No madam," he retorted, "I have had enough of this charade and I want to leave now." Johanna could not believe his words, how could this man be so obstinate in this difficult time?

"Sir, please wait until my husband is back, in just a couple of days he will accommodate your wishes without jeopardizing the safety of your friends downstairs."

"I cannot stand this hiding any longer and the lack of hygiene. I cannot sleep and cannot do anything but lay down there ."

He kept coming back with arguments why he should just leave.

"Jacob, once more please. I am telling you if you leave here you will be picked up in minutes by the Gestapo and put on a transport."

"Anything is better than this," he snapped. "I can still work if I have to, this laziness is bad for my body and my soul."

"What if I get you something to read? Would that help you to stay just a few days until Kees is back?"

Johanna had finally found a way to appease him and after he

went back downstairs to the sand and the spiders underneath the house and the stinky compatriots, Johanna made a decision she would later regret.

She took off her apron, she always wore when she was at home, took Cornelius by the hand and said, "Come boy, we are going to the library down the street to see if we can find some Jewish books."

The van Rijn family was made up of Father Kees Mother Johanna, daughter of Dirk Schmall, a Jewish merchant who fled to Holland from Poland after the programs against the Jews had started under Lenin.

He, his wife and four children found refuge in the Netherlands where Christian people had adopted the family and helped them get back on their feet.

Grandpa Dirk was a real merchant who became a true helper for many Dutch farmers once he had become an established trader.

He would buy the entire crop from a farmer's orchard without a blink of an eye and long before the crop was matured. Similarly he would buy the entire stock of big wheels of cheese by just looking at it.

He would make an offer to the farmer which after a handclap was accepted. The farmers loved the old white-headed, bearded man. They could always fall back on Dirk Schmall when in need.

Dirk died two years before the war began and his wife had died four years before that. He was survived by two daughters, Johanna and Lena, and two sons Has and Lenardus.

After the war, only Johanna survived the holocaust and that was by sheer accident. When Johanna and Kees got married the city clerk failed to record her maiden name.

The German administrators had looked through all the city records to find out who the Jews were and where they were living.

Johanna had slipped through the dragnet the Germans had put up at the beginning of the occupation.

That morning she was on her way to the library where she was about to reveal the secret which could jeopardize her identity.

The Germans had occupied the country and at that time they had seized all public buildings, Utilities, radio stations and city administrations.

The libraries were watched by NSB-ers, Dutch citizens who col-laborated with the Germans and were so despised by the true Dutch that they were ear-marked as traitors.

The administrators had to do the dirty work for the Germans and report anything that would relate to the Jewish population.

Johanna did not know the true intentions of the librarian.

She asked if there was a Jewish section in the library. There was, and the lady in charge pointed her to the section she needed to look at.

When Johanna walked in-between the shelves with Cornelius beside her, the librarian made a phone call.

Johanna had found three books by Jewish authors. They were all books on psychology and that fact would become her salvation.

When she went to register the books she was asked to wait in a small room behind the librarian's desk. Within minutes two Gestapo officers walked in and asked her for her Ausweiss. Luckily, it read Johanna van Rijn with her address: Deiman Straat, 396 The Hague.

"Why are you asking for Jewish books Johanna?" one Gestapo interrogator asked. Johanna immediately saw what they were driv-ing at and quickly thought of a right answer.

"I am studying Psychology and my professor, Professor Pierson, recommended Jewish books because they all dealt with Freudian-ism. The interrogators looked at each other and asked some more questions.

They could not find any reason to detain this lady any further and decided to let her go.

At that moment she left with her five-year-old son, and they said to each other, "Let's keep an eye on her and on her home for a while, who knows what may show up there."

Chapter Sixteen

ATTACK ON THE GENERALS

—ᘏᘏᘏ—

I f the walls could talk; the walls of the beautiful, centuries-old center of the Dutch government, the Binnenhof; which had never before been occupied by an enemy.

They were respectful buildings and beautifully decorated for royalty.

If those walls could talk, they would tell of the shameful and frenzied Seiss Inquart.

Inquart was the German Commissary, appointed by Hitler. He was Hitler's slave, his peon, who would dance to Hitler's tune any time he would make a sound.

And what a sound he had made that day! Hitler had sent a delegation directly from Berlin.

They were sitting at the thirty foot conference table where so many Dutch lawmakers had sat and discussed new laws for the country.

Seiss Inquart was shocked by what they were telling him. The Jewish matter could be his downfall, even his death.

A report was handed to him by messengers from Berlin that said the number of Jews which would still be in Holland was way too high.

In fact, only half of the registered Dutch Jews had been captured and transported to the "camps" in Germany.

Where were they all, where were they hiding? Why had they not been captured? The command from Berlin, directly from Himmler and Hitler, was that immediate and measured action had to be taken to capture those in hiding and that those hiding them would also be sentenced to death.

Ridderzaal and Seyss Inquart's entrée

The generals were firm; four of them would stay and oversee what type of measures Seiss Inquart would take to resolve the problem.

It was during the third year of the war that the Germans began to be desperate and behave like madmen.

The meeting was adjourned until the next day. It was time for entertainment and there in the revered halls of the ancient Binnenhof, wild parties were thrown.

In a sense, they desecrated those ancient walls which could not speak. Lots of food, wine and beautiful Dutch girls were brought in.

Those beautiful Dutch girls were the willing ones, often too willing, out to gain the favor of the generals and to get food for their families and money for their services.

The Germans were drinking away their guilt and their "heim-weh," or home-sickness, because most of them were married men and fathers of children they hardly ever saw.

The walls resounded with drunken bar songs, in German of course, and those outside could hear the noise and wondered what they were celebrating.

Not so with the group of men who were dressed in black wet-suits, carefully wading through the large mote which surrounded the Binnenhof. They were moving slowly not to make a sound, even though the noise from the party would kill their quiet movement.

Days before, they had scouted the walls which rose up from the waterline. Their mission was not to destroy the beautiful buildings, but to disturb the party and destroy the generals.

Each of the four men carried two cylinders with tear-gas and each of them carried a smoke bomb in which they had mixed cyanide gas.

These brave men on their destructive mission had never done this kind of attack before. They knew that they could lose their lives by making one little mistake.

When they arrived at the rising wall, they spotted the windows where they would throw the teargas cylinders through. First they had to set the timer of the smoke bombs with their deadly contents.

"Set them on thirty seconds," they were told, "and throw them right after you have thrown the cylinders with the teargas inside."

Only the sound of breaking glass could be heard, not across the pond but inside the building where the rolling cylinders spread the teargas.

At first only a few people noticed the cylinders most of them were too drunk to notice anything rolling on the floor. When the teargas started working, cries of horror, commands and screams could be heard and soldiers with guns came rushing into the room, putting on their gasmasks. Chaos had begun.

And then it became suddenly quiet. The cyanide had taken its sickening, deadly effect. The only ones still standing were the soldiers with their gasmasks.

One huge mistake was made by the Germans. No one was left in command. No one was giving orders. No one was thinking.

Outside, the four men in their dark suits were swimming quickly but silently to the ramp which ran down into the water and where long ago, the horses of the minister's carriages drank.

They slipped quietly into the dark bushes around the moat. No one had seen them, but their mistake would have greater consequences than they had planned.

Finally, ambulances began to arrive at the Binnenhof, the nearby hospital was prepared and many of the party-goers were brought in very sick.

Seiss Inquart and all the generals survived the attack. The mistake the attackers had made was in the dosage of cyanide. It was not enough to kill but plentiful enough to make people sick for a week.

That unfortunate week was followed by a wave of executions. "Grab two citizens in every street in the city of The Hague and shoot them right in front of their houses" had been the command of Rauter, the German general in charge of the German occupation in Holland.

The city sounded like it must have been in the time of Moses, when Pharaoh killed all the first-born in Egypt. The new, hard rules against the population had begun. The attack had been the triggering mechanism.

The Resistance had to be broken, according to the newly-arrived generals.

It never was!

Chapter Seventeen

TROUBLE ON THE WAY BACK

—◊—

T he area around Winterswijk where Kees had attended the important meeting was a rural area.

A lot of farmers had changed part of their land use into growing vegetables, potatoes and sugar beets. The German had taken advantage of the farmers by threatening them with deportations to the "work camps" it they did not give up two thirds of their crops.

The Germans would pay them very little for their products. That is why a lot of farmers cheated on their numbers. A few terrible examples were set by executing some farmers when a group of assigned German inspectors went from place to place counting what was growing and what should be harvested.

The always peaceful, rural landscape had changed into a other kind of war zone.

A different kind of war ensued, a battle of survival for the farming population itself. This battle affected the farmer's regular customers, just as much as it affected the Dutch citizens from the cities.

Kees was riding his bicycle back to The Hague. He was reflecting on those things and situations that had changed the lives of so many millions of people.

How had it been possible that a foreign country would have invaded their peaceful little country? Holland had declared itself neutral just as they had done in the First World War. How could foreigners just take whatever they wanted, including lives?

For what reason?

On his way back, Kees was also thinking of the days ahead and the severe warnings they had received at Tante Riek's meeting.

He had also received his own special assignment: besides hiding and assisting in the transportations of the Jews and other fugitives, Kees was given the task to distribute food stamps for fugitives in the south of Holland which included three provinces.

A dozen or so printing shops in the Hague would be printing thousands of forged food stamps, but Kees would be the one to get them to where ever they were needed, and that was all over Holland.

Kees was enjoying his bike ride back to the city, although his mind was racing. How he was going to do all this? How big would the risk be to be caught with packs of false materials?

The thought of being caught ran a chill through his spine.

The Gestapo would torture him until death to find out where the food stamps came from. No one could see that they had been forged, but which Dutch citizen could have whole packs of them in his possession?

That was enough to be arrested. And what about all the people he was hiding?

Was he spreading himself too thin? As he rode through the serene landscape he reflected on Psalm 23. Was he in the shadow of death? The Psalm went on in his head, "I will fear no evil.... Surely goodness and mercy shall follow me all of my days." It hit him right then and there, "All of my days!"

His demeanor changed in that instant. He began to whistle a song they had sang last time in church. In his mind he repeated over and over "goodness and mercy... all of my days." In that uplifting mood he arrived at the Brandwijk farm halfway home. It was almost dark.

What he saw when he arrived at a visual distance of the farm made him stop whistling. He jumped off his bicycle and threw it in the ditch.

Crawling down in between the Pussy Willows he hid his bicycle first. Then he carefully crawled forward to a point where he could see the farm buildings and the threshing floor.

What was happening there? Half a dozen German army vehicles and twice as many soldiers were standing around the threshing floor. He saw Marie Brandwijk, the voluptuous daughter of the family, talking with the soldiers.

He saw more soldiers walking around the haystack. One of them he saw climbing the ladder. "Lord don't let them find the ladder please," Kees prayed.

Farmer Brandwijk was gesticulating to an officer who in turn called the climbing soldier back.

"Thank God," Kees said aloud, almost startling himself. Apparently they had not discovered the ladder which led down to the basement beneath the hay stack.

It was an excellent hiding place, but Kees could almost feel the anxiety of the people down there. He knew they would be huddled behind the dividing wall which was very hard to find once shut behind them.

The sheer presence of the basement under the hay stack would give enough suspicion to the Germans to question or even arrest Farmer Brandwijk.

The commander of the group called all men together. They were standing in a circle. Kees could not hear what they were saying. He saw the men looking around, towards the stables and the chicken house.

Kees saw him give some kind of command and they all went in different ways into all the buildings on the farm.

After what seemed a long time they began to re-appear. They had things in their hands, armfuls of things.

As Kees looked a little more intensely he saw what they were carrying. They were loading up their trucks with all the extra food the farmer had stocked to sell.

A second group of soldiers was pushing some pigs towards a truck and with four of them they lifted the pigs, one by one, grabbing the pigs by their four legs and throwing them in the bed of the truck. The pigs squealed and with loud thuds they dropped onto the truck, directly followed by a second one, then a third, and a fourth.

"My goodness," Kees thought, "Lord are they taking everything from the farm?" He could see and even hear the farmer protesting

The hypocritical German Governor Seyss Inquart even
comes to say goodbye to the city children on the train

loudly. Kees saw him raising his hand high up in the air and heard him screaming at the commander.

He better watch out, Kees said to himself, and he began to pray for the farmer. "Lord, please let him calm down. They could shoot him if he protested too much."

The Sergeant in charge of the raid – because it was nothing else but a raid – finally gave the command to mount up and leave the farm.

The German vehicles came thundering by the bushes under which Kees had been hiding. When the dust concealed their departure and their view, Kees rose up, jumped on his bicycle and rode to the farm house.

He found the farmer's wife in tears. "Why would they have to be so mean?" she sobbed. "They even wanted to take our daughter but we told them that we would not be able to run the farm without her and that they would have to take us too."

Kees went over to her and put both his hands on her shoulders and tried to comfort her. "Look at it this way, they could have taken her and shot your husband, the way he was protesting could have triggered that easily. And what about your guests in the basement? Don't you think it could have been far worse? Now look at the positive. You can continue to hide people and grow more food and breed more pigs. They did not take any of the cows did they?"

She nodded in agreement and slowly straightened herself up, wiping her tears away. Then farmer Brandwijk came in. He was angry but able to contain his anger saying, "Those Moffen (slang for Germans) were out to find the Jews."

Someone must have been talking, Kees. Can we move them away for a while until things settle down a little?"

Kees shook his head and answered, "Why don't we sit down and talk about that, I have a lot more to tell you and times are getting much worse for us and the ones we are hiding. Come, let's talk right now."

He told the Brandwijk's about the letter from the concentration camp and about the intentions of the Germans to annihilate all the Jews in all their occupied countries.

He told them that the Germans would not only try to arrest them, but they would also not hesitate to shoot those who were helping them.

"Losing your food and livestock is terrible enough," he said. "But losing those you have worked so hard to keep alive is much worse, let alone losing your own life."

Farmer Brandwijk was ready to burst into tears when his son Cor walked into the room. Cor was their only son, a stout young man of 17 years.

He too had to be in hiding because the Germans would take any men over sixteen and put them into their "Arbeits Einsatz," or involuntary work program.

He was in charge of the fugitives who were hiding at the farm's haystack hide-out.

He kept the people fed and cleaned as much as he could. It was he who would take them to other farms, walking through the fields to other farms when new ones were to be arriving. His job was very dangerous and he had a lot of tricks up his sleeve to deceive the aggressors when he was moving people.

One of Cor's tricks was the walking cow he had created. He had taken the hide of a cow, complete with its head and hoofs. When he had to make a dangerous move of people, he and another person would get into the hide and dress up as a live cow.

It was looking so real that even the other cows in the herd would be tricked by the deception. Incognito as a cow, Cor and the person to be moved were followed by the other cows in the herd.

With this form of dress-up he had moved dozens of people from one end of the meadow to the other farm's meadow, until he reached the farm of destination.

Freely and during day-time they had been able to fool the enemy.

But Cor was getting restless at the farm. He wanted to do more against the aggressors. If it was up to him he would join the "Boxers," or the "Knock Ploeg," as the Dutch underground called them. That was more adventurous for farm boy Cor.

His desire became real soon thereafter. Against the will of his parents, he left one day and joined the Boxers. His mother would only see him one more time, before he was shot by a German firing squad.

Kees mounted his bicycle the next morning. The Brandwijks had calmed down after listening for hours to Kees's account of his meeting with Tante Riek and the Resistance leaders.

Early in the morning hours they had taken a couple of hours' nap. Kees had been made ready for his final trip to The Hague. The farmer's wife had packed a lunch and filled his bicycle bags with food, eggs, a chicken and cabbage, a bag of potatoes and two big, home-made loaves of bread.

The canvas baggage carrier behind his seat had been loaded to capacity when Kees said his goodbyes and left for his long ride to the city of The Hague and to his wife and children.

The house in the Deiman Straat. Next to it is the
concrete portico which served as the hiding bunker.

Chapter Eighteen

THE EVACUATION OF CITY CHILDREN

—⟋⟍—

At the train station in The Hague, the hustle and bustle of the crowd made the Germans very nervous. The German soldiers had no idea what was going on that day.

More than two thousand boys and girls were waiting for the next train going to the north of the country.

The farmers in Friesland, a province in the very north of Holland, had come up with a plan to take in thousands of hungry children from the major cities.

All of them had to be at least ten years old and no older than 16. The Germans would take any boy over 16 years of age and put them into "Arbeits Einsatz" to have them work in their factories making war-related products.

The expectations of the children were great. They would be fed and taken care of at the farms, able to do some work and in some places they would even be able to go to school. The latter was a luxury if that was made possible. In the cities of the west of Holland, the schools had been closed for some time.

The male teachers had been put to work for the Germans and the few female teachers were staying home, often helping their husbands in hiding with their underground activities.

The German soldiers were all over the station, checking if any one of the children would be Jewish or older than 16. A group of soldiers in the middle of the crowd were holding a girl and one of the soldiers blew a whistle which prompted the Gestapo contingent to come into action. The girl was around sixteen-years-old, her

"Persoons Bewijs," German-issued ID card, revealed her age. Something was wrong and the Gestapo took the girl out of the crowd to an interrogation office.

Three children of the van Rijn family were also at the station. They were accompanied by their mother Johanna. All four of them had watched the scene of the little girl being taken by the Gestapo.

Mother Johanna looked at her oldest son Jan, who was 13-years old, and said, "Jan, should we do something about that?" Mies, the older sister, interjected, "Mom, why don't you claim her as your niece?"

Johanna shook her head, "Too dangerous, but let us draw closer to the room where they are and see if we can find out who she is. If I claim her as a niece I should at least know her name."

Slowly the four van Rijns walked over, wrestling themselves through the crowd and finally reaching the interrogation room. It was the former office of the Station Manager, now occupied by the dreadful Gestapo.

They sat down right in front of the office; luckily the window was pulled up to allow some fresh air into the sticky room.

"Wohin gehen Sie (where are you going?)" they heard the Gestapo interrogator ask. "I am waiting for my sister to arrive on the next train, her name is Elly Harman and I am Maartje Harman, as you can see on my Ausweiss."

"We are not so sure that that is your real name miss, they heard the Gestapo man say, "Do you have any other proof of your identity?"

Johanna looked around slightly to see the reaction on the girl's face. Obviously she was not very shocked. She was still in trouble, particularly if her so-called sister did not arrive soon. Johanna made a bold decision. She took two steps toward the door of the office and looked in, acting very surprised as if she did not know what was going on and called out in a happy sounding voice, "Maartje! Hey, what are you doing here at the station, are you going to Friesland too?"

The Gestapo man's reaction was one of great surprise. He roughly pulled Johanna inside the office and demanded her Ausweiss. The man in the hated black Gestapo uniform looked at her Ausweiss and asked, "Do you know this young lady? She is Jewish, isn't she?"

Johanna looked him straight in the eyes and began to laugh.

"You've got to be kidding young man. She is as Jewish as you are. We have no Jews in our family and Maartje is my niece, why would you think she would be Jewish?"

Slightly embarrassed, the man barked, "Raush mit Dir (get out of here!)" and he pushed Johanna and Maartje out of the office.

Johanna and her three children, her arm around Maartje walked as far away from the interrogation room as they could.

They tried to keep their distance from the patrolling soldiers as well. Finally Maartje spoke, "Thank you so much for saving me, but why did you do it?"

Johanna thought for a split second and then said "Graag."

It was worth a try, she thought, and Maartje's reaction proved her hunch to be correct. Johanna wanted to know one more thing before the oncoming train entered the station and total chaos would break out. "Tell me one thing Maartje, are you Jewish?"

She nodded, almost unseen, and as she acknowledged the answer she threw herself against Johanna. My whole family is in hiding now. I am the only one still able to travel and work as a messenger. In fact I am expecting someone on the next train to give them an oral message to take to Amsterdam. After that I will be able to go home to my hide out address where my family is in the Drebbel Straat."

Her words caused a shock of surprise to the van Rijn family, the Drebbel Straat was the street right next to their own street.

When they told her where they lived, Maartje's eyes lit up and she said.

"Just last week I was stopped by a German patrol, I was almost arrested because it was at curfew when a man came to my rescue.

He faked to be my father and told the Germans that he had been looking for me. He said he lived in the Deiman Straat and his name was … Kees. The van Rijns all started laughing, and Jan said qui-

93

etly, "So you met my father did you?"

The long-awaited train rolled into the station and came to a halt with a loud screech. The doors were opened and only two people came out of the doors. The German soldiers, used to seeing hundreds of people emerge from the trains, ran over to the arrivals and demanded their Ausweiss.

Meanwhile, the many city children were packing the train. All the seats were taken in a minute and the rest had to find a place were they could hold on to something or they just hung against the other passengers.

Mothers remained on the station's platform. Some were crying, knowing they might never see their children again at such a dangerous time like this.

The three van Rijn Children had found a spot in front of a window and were waving at their mother Johanna. Mies was the only one who cried. Would she ever see her little brother again? Cornelius would be the only one left in the city. He was too young to evacuate to the farms in Friesland.

The people left behind on the platform slowly began to leave the station. The soldiers had left the platform after they had identified the arriving passengers and an eerie peace came over the station.

Johanna was still holding Maartje with her arm over her shoulders as they approached one of the new arrivals.

Maartje quickly exchanged some words with the newly-arrived passenger who then quickly walked over to the waiting room of the station.

Maartje, the little messenger who had accomplished her mission, ran after Johanna on her way out of the station. "Lets walk home together, shall we?" Johanna agreed. Two people together were safer in the city than one by herself.

They had a lot to talk about on their two mile walk back to their home and their hiding place.

Chapter Nineteen

MANY ROADS WHICH LEAD
TO FREEDOM

—ɯ—

At the meeting in Winterswijk, Kees had met Joop Westerweel. Joop was one of those rare, do-it-yourself members of the Resistance. He was a person who, by himself, had brought Jews of any age and profession to Switzerland and Spain.

He had created routes through forests and fields, knowing where and how to avoid the enemy and personally guided thousands of fugitives to their freedom.

Kees was reflecting on his stories when he rode his bicycle back to The Hague that day, the time when Joop Westerweel waited in the Pyrenees Mountains close to the border of Spain. He had made the long journey with seventy Jews and all were huddled together, exhausted and quiet. They all looked at the broad-shouldered Joop who had brought them this far. They had been hiding in an old barn for the last few days and the draft through the dried-up planks made their stay not very comfortable. But at least they were safe and freedom could be seen through the cracks.

Joop wanted to look into each of their eyes and give them a message of hope."You are just a few more days and half a mile away from your freedom. You all will be in a free country and it will be your task to build up your own country in Palestine in remembrance of all those whom you lost. Their memory will be your monument, and it needs to become your strength in your new homeland. Never forget those who gave their lives for that goal. They lost it so you could gain it. This trip was worth it for them."

Joop Westerweel walked back all by himself, hundreds of miles to the old barn where he had left his bicycle and then on to Holland and to the next task: saving more Jewish lives.

Joop's resistance began when he went on a vacation with his wife and three children in the Province of Gelderland in the center of Holland. In the small town where he had planned their vacation, the Germans were nailing posters on the trees and all over the town. They were announcing that all Jews had to report to the town hall within twenty four hours. The Westerweel family could not believe their eyes and knew that all Jews were in grave danger.

The Westerweels felt obliged to get to work against the German evil. They knew a youth home for Jews in a town called Loosdrecht. There were forty nine children in the home and they were in grave danger.

Joop did not have to discuss the matter with his wife Willy. She too felt the urge to help. She was just like Joop. When they came home that evening after the long bike ride from their disrupted vacation, they found two Jewish fugitives in their home.

A friend had attempted to bring them to Belgium but the attempt failed and they had almost been arrested. They had escaped this time, but would they next time?

Since the house was empty and the Westerweels had gone they had made that their home for awhile.

That is how the Westerweels found their task in the Resistance even before they made a specific plan.

The following evening and night, the home with the forty-nine children in Loosdrecht was emptied and abandoned. The children, all forty-nine of them, were spread throughout the entire country. The whole family got involved and five bicycles rode many miles to bring the children to their temporary destinations.

"Group Westerweel" had emerged. During the major part of the war this group worked totally independent, even though it was supported by many.

Kees was on his last stretch, riding his bicycle along the banks of the old Rhijn. He was really enjoying the ride and the beautiful nature when a German Patrol boat came racing by on the river. He saw the soldiers looking at him, being the only bicycle rider by the river. Kees had chosen this route because he could avoid the German roadblocks. He had not expected any trouble this time.

The boat was turning around and approached the river bank. A soldier at the bow of the boat called out something he could not hear. He saw the soldier raising his gun and he heard the sound of a bullet hissing by.

This was serious, he thought, and he quickly rolled his bike into the ditch on the other side of the river bank.

The boat was now even closer. He heard German voices and shouts, "Halt, Ausweiss!" Kees came up from the ditch "Haende hoch (hands up!)" he heard. As Kees raised both his hands in the air, two soldiers who had jumped on shore came running toward him. They grabbed him by the arms and began to handcuff him.

Kees did not say a word but calmly let them do their job. He knew that sooner or later a Sergeant would show up and ask him the question, "What are you doing here? I see your Ausweiss but where is your travel pass?"

Finally Kees spoke, "It is in my inner pocket. If you take off my handcuffs I can show it to you. The Sergeant barked an order and they quickly unlocked his handcuffs. "Heande Hoch," they said, repeating the earlier command. Kees looked at the Sergeant and said, "How can I get my pass if I have to keep my hands up?" The Sergeant barked again and the soldiers began to frisk him. Finally they found his pass and handed it to the Sergeant.

"So you came all the way from Winterswijk?" the Sergeant asked him, and Kees nodded. "Yes sir, a long trip and a great break from work."

"I see you work for Simowitz in The Hague. You have to report tomorrow. I will make sure that you do. What do you have in those side bags of the bicycle?"

Kees had been hoping they would not ask that question, but now he could only tell the truth. One of the soldiers went to get his bike and when he came up the bank of the river he had a big smile on his face, "Contraband food, Sergeant," he said. With Kees watching them empty the bags, he explained, "The food I bought on the way from a farmer."

That was a double problem if they would pursue his answer. Kees could get farmer Brandwijk in trouble if he told them where he got it.

Apparently the food was more important to the Germans at this time. The Sergeant yelled "Confiscated!" and they cleaned out his bags. Even his sandwich was taken.

With a "report to the factory tomorrow," they left. In a way Kees felt sorry for them. They must be hungry too, he thought to himself. "Lord bless them," he spoke aloud as he went on his way.

Kees forgot to dwell any further about the heroic endeavors of Joop Westerweel. The rest of his trip he was wondering what to tell Johanna when he got home and how he was going to feed his four children in the coming days.

He did not know that three of his children had left for Friesland, a place where there was more food and less war.

Kees would be very busy in the coming weeks. His new assignment from Tante Wies was still fresh on his mind.

Chapter Twenty

AT HOME IN THE HAGUE

—〰—

W hen Kees Finally arrived at his home in the Deiman Straat, he was surprised to find only his youngest son, Cornelius and his wife Johanna in the house.

Normally all four children would come running at him after his trips. Not only to greet him, but more to see what he had brought for them to eat. Hunger was rapidly becoming a daily word in every household in the cities.

This time the house was quiet, and while Johanna embraced him firmly, little Cornelius held him by clinging onto his legs. The boy called out, "Papa, what happened to you? We were supposed to go on a trip together, you promised days ago. Where were you?"

After the first spontaneous embrace, Johanna did not waste any time. "Kees, we have to have a long talk about a lot of things which have happened while you were gone. Let's sit down in the front room. Cornelius, you go play outside. You still have an hour before it is dark."

"But Mom, it is so windy outside, and I don't like to play in the wind," he answered.

"Go anyway, it will be good for you and it will blow the lice out of your hair."

Johanna was reminded daily how bad the lice problem was in the city among the children. There was no soap or shampoo, nor was there any medication available against the head lice that had infected almost every child in the cities.

Cornelius went outside and found a group of kids playing ball games. There used to be many young children in the street, but after the Jewish kids had been deported to the concentration camps, and the kids of ten and older had gone to the farms in the North, only the young ones were left to play in the streets.

Sometimes the ball was kicked over the fence of one of the neighbors, and one of the kids would have to go ask if he could pick it up in the backyard. One neighbor, an older man, was always very nasty to the kids. He would cut the ball in two pieces and then throw it back onto the street. Another neighbor was the barber on the corner. When the ball went over his fence, he was always very friendly and nice about it.

Cornelius had received a warning about the barber from his dad. "The Barber is an NSB-er," his dad told him. Cornelius had heard that word and wanted to know what that word meant.

His dad told him that NSB-ers were traitors who would betray their fellow citizens to the Germans when they did something illegal like hiding Jews. The Barber was something else which Cornelius did not understand. They called him a "homo" and his Dad had told him that he could never accept any favors from the barber and that he could never go with him or be alone with him!

That day as he played with the boys, the ball went over the barber's fence into his backyard. It was Cornelius' fault, so he was the one who had to go ask the barber for it. The boys pressed him to go inside the barber shop but because of his dad's warnings he could not do that.

The other boys began to tease him and called him a "sissy." "You're afraid to go into the shop, you Sissy!" Despite the peer pressure, he did not budge. With his father's warning still fresh in his ears, he could not tell the others why he finally sent an older boy to get the ball.

Five minutes later, the boy came back triumphantly with the ball under his arm and a lollipop in his mouth. He said, "See, there is nothing to be scared about. I even got a lollipop. The barber was so friendly, he asked me all kinds of questions, like where my house was and who else lived with us...So next time any one of you can go get the ball, he is a nice guy, he even gave me a hug when I left."

Johanna and Kees were in a deep conversation and were venting their experiences of the last five days. Johanna had told him what had expired with Jacob Ibranof, how he had come upstairs in broad daylight and had demanded to be allowed to leave the hiding place.

She told him that she had warned him, that he would compromise the hiding place and put all the people in danger of being arrested and deported. She said that she had finally persuaded him to stay on the promise that she would get him some books from the library.

She told him that when she had taken Cornelius and had gone to the library, the Gestapo had come to interrogate her. Kees frowned and said, "But Johanna, how could you do that and even ask for the Jewish section? Didn't you know that the library was manned with NSB-ers?"

"Honey, I did not know that and after I had asked the librarian I had a feeling something was wrong. Anyhow, they let me go!"

Kees was not so sure that the library visit would not have any further consequences for them.

At that point in the conversation Kees said, "Let's bring Jacob up here and have a straight talk with him. After all, he does not know about the camps in Germany. Perhaps we will need to tell him the truth and see how much he wants to go having gained what we know now. We better close the curtains of the front windows so no one can see us with him here tonight." Kees stood up from his chair while Johanna closed the heavy velvet curtains. Facing the front of the house, she saw Cornelius play with the neighborhood boys. At least he has some entertainment, she thought.

Kees walked over to the narrow hallway and disappeared in to the closet. You could hear something sliding inside and then there was silence. Kees had climbed down the narrow ladder which brought him to the literal underground of the house.

The twenty guests were all doing something. One of the few ladies was fervently knitting something. Another one was writing on a tablet. Twelve of them were lost with their faces into the singing box.

Not a sound could be heard. From their body language you could see that they were discussing something or perhaps they might have been praying.

He looked around the box to determine which body was that of Jacob. The Jewish man could easily be recognized by his clothes. He always wore black pants, suspenders, and of course, the prayer strings. When Kees had found him he gently put his hand on his shoulders and tapped Jacob lightly.

It took a minute before Jacob reacted. Apparently he had to finish his conversation or his prayer and also warn the others to be quiet and withdraw their heads without making a noise – all at the same time.

"Sorry sir," Jacob began to say, but Kees waved his hand and put a finger to his lip. He pointed upstairs and led the way up the ladder.

When they came on the ground floor of the house, Kees said softly, "I have to talk to you alone for a while. I have information which will not only blow your mind, it will also change your entire outlook on this miserable life which you are living."

Jacob Ibranof was an orthodox Jew. He wore the traditional Orthodox clothing and the customary long hair, complete with ringlets coming to his shoulders. His beard was reaching to his chest because he had vowed never to cut it.

A person like him would not last very long on the streets of The Hague. Within minutes the Germans would capture him, if only because of his appearance. He would be spotted by one or more of the NSB-ers first, if he was lucky, and in minutes he would be gone.

Jacob Ibranof held a Doctorate in Psychology and had his own practice in city of The Hague. On one unfortunate, horrible evening his wife Rachel had been taken by the Germans when she was shopping at the local Greengrocer.

She had searched for kosher foods and apparently the Nazis had been watching that section of the store for anyone buying kosher foods.

That day had been devastating for him because it had given him a warning to get out of his house, abandon his office and go underground immediately.

She was gone for eight months and he had never heard from her. He could not ask the Germans or they would grab him too. The uncertainty about his wife's whereabouts drove him crazy. He missed her terribly.

Then one day in late November 1943, he received a message through one of his clients who had made regular visits at Jacob's practice before Rachel had disappeared.

"Get out sir. You will have to leave this place right now, because I have information that the Nazis will hold a Razzia in this neighborhood tonight.

You are on their hit list to be arrested. You will have ten minutes to gather some important possessions and clothes. Get out now, Sir."

Stubbornly, Jacob had hesitated for a full five minutes but he did heed the warning and had followed the messenger to his house two streets to the North.

Then they had heard the sound of the coming trucks and motorcycles and they saw them barricade the streets just beyond the house they were waiting.

That had been Jacob's narrow escape and from that moment on, his life had changed from being a prosperous doctor to a hunted fugitive.

Two months later he had been brought to the Deiman Straat in a baker's box tricycle and through Groenendijk's warehouse he had literally gone underground at the van Rijn's residence waiting for further transportation to eventually get to freedom.

As a rule, people were brought to the van Rijn residence to stay only for a short time. This time it had lasted a few weeks longer, partly because of Kees' busy schedule and partly because of Kees' trip to Winterswijk. Only Kees could transfer a person to the chain of hiding places which eventually led to freedom.

Jacob became restless waiting for Kees to begin telling him what he had on his mind. Trained psychologists did not like to wait for answers. He would pry it out of his patients. Not so this time. Besides, Kees was not a client.

Finally he asked, "Kees, when can I get out of here? If you don't take me to a different place I will go by myself."

Kees had to be tactful but firm at the same time. "Please, Jacob. I know you are worried about your wife Rachel. I also will need time to arrange a place where you can go. I can do that tomorrow afternoon.

I have to report to Simowitz tomorrow and I will be home at three in the afternoon. Don't jeopardize the safety of all the others and of my family."

Jacob answered him passionately, "I understand but please make it short and fast. I've got to get out of here and I don't want to go dressed like a woman. I may be a proud Jew but I am still able to work any kind of job and if the Germans take me. I am sure they'll put me to work with my kind of knowledge."

Kees shook his head. "Jacob I just came from a meeting where I learned something hardly anybody knows about yet, something that will shock you and our whole country when the news of it is spread. Please hear me out and brace yourself for some very bad news."

He began to tell Jacob about the letter from the doctor in Winterswijk who had come from a concentration camp in Auschwitz. He told Jacob what was really happening there and in all the other concentration camps in Germany "You mean they are actually killing my people who went there?" Kees nodded. "That has been proven by now. How could it be possible for a camp which houses 200,000 people, to keep the millions and millions they have send there?"

Jacob could not believe what he had just heard; he slumped over on the table top and just cried, thinking of his beloved wife who must have been murdered there.

When Jacob finally lifted up his head and wiped his face he spoke with a hoarse, raspy voice. "I'll do whatever I have to do. I see the significance now to stay alive. I'll do it for my beloved Rachel and for my entire race and with your help, we must save whomever we can save."

Chapter Twenty One

THE CITY CHILDREN

—〜〜—

T he train had stopped many times on its way to the Province of Friesland. The little passengers, all children between the ages of ten and sixteen, were excited and sometimes a little rowdy. Those who had brought some food had eaten it a long time ago. Some of them had even shared their food with less fortunate children who had not brought anything.

Every time the train stopped soldiers came on board. They were acting as if they were train conductors. They went from carriage to carriage, checked the kid's tickets and name tags. They seemed to be looking for something or someone in particular.

Asking for the children's tickets was apparently not the only motive for their search. One of them was carrying a list of names of all who were on the train and if anyone was not on it, that person was taken some where else.

Each one of the children had to show their Ausweiss and the soldiers kept checking their names with the list. In the end more than twenty five children had been taken away to a separate carriage. The remaining little passengers never saw them come back.

Sometimes the train would just stop and stood there waiting for another train, one with cattle wagons, which came thundering by. In the waiting train the little passengers did not know that the passing, thundering train was full of doomed citizens on their way to the many death camps in Germany and Poland and a certain "final solution," as the Germans called their filthy activity.

At the station in Leeuwarden, the capitol of the Province of Friesland, hundreds of people were anxiously waiting for the arrival of the city children. An atmosphere of great expectation hung over the train station.

The people of Friesland were a proud people who spoke their own language. Most of the waiting people were farmers who had rode their bicycles or their horse and carriages which were now waiting outside the station with a farm hand.

The German soldiers felt uneasy in this crowd of determined farmers and farmer's wives. Each waiting person was holding a large card with a name on it. This had been organized in advance with great care and many volunteers so that everyone knew who was going to stay with them.

In the train which was finally about to arrive, a similar sense of excitement was growing. Each child had a badge attached on a string around their neck. It clearly showed their first name and their last name in smaller print, as well as their address of origination.

With a loud whistle and screeching brakes the train full of city children came to a stop at the station. The German soldiers were wise enough to stay at the back of the crowd this time. Even though they carried their guns they knew the Friesian farmers could disarm them in no time and clobber them to death.

The city children began to pour out of the train as soon as the doors were opened and on the platform all hands were raised holding the name cards. It was as though someone had given the command "raise cards" when they all went up at the same time.

The people began to search for a matching name tag while the children looked up at the name card to find their match. It was a hilarious madhouse, but soon the matching began to take effect. Total strangers to each other, they matched up and introduced themselves, holding small-talk as they began leaving the station.

It was interesting to see how people who had never seen each other mixed and got acquainted without having seen one another's picture.

The van Rijn children tried to stay together while searching for their foster parents. David was the first one to find his matching name tag and when they had introduced each other, they found out that Mies van Rijn, David's sister, was also going to stay with the same family.

They had introduced themselves as Mr. and Mrs. Jaap Wielenga. Johannes, the third Van Rijn child, was still looking for his name tag match. He stayed close to his brother and sister until finally a neighbor of the Wielenga's came to claim him. "Good," Jaap said. "At least you kids can visit each other since we live so close together." A neighbor in the wide-open country of Friesland could be close by and yet seven miles apart.

To break the ice, Jaap held out both his hands toward the two van Rijn children and said jovially, "Come here you two, I have been waiting long enough to meet you. Come and give me a big hug!" Mies was the first one to go. Reluctantly, David followed.

It took at least an hour until every child was matched up with a temporary foster parent. There were at least twenty foster parents who were puzzled why they could not find their dedicated child. There was no one to ask for assistance and when they had waited until the entire crowd had gone, they looked disappointedly at the train to see if some had remained inside. This small group of about twenty five came together and talked to each other, asking each other what had gone wrong.

Finally when they began to leave, they could see a group of soldiers emerge from the very front carriage. They were surrounding a group of children and held up their guns toward the children as they pushed them to the station building. They could hear some of them crying. They all wondered what that was about.

One of the departing farmers took a bold step toward the building where the children had entered. His wife began to pull him back by his arm, but he broke loose and went inside the building.

Loud screams could be heard inside, first in Friesian and then in German. Then a shot sounded and screams from many children. Then, silence. A deadly silence followed. The wife of the farmers knew what had happened and began to cry. The other people began to comfort her. Angry voices could be heard. Soldiers came running over to the group and one of them yelled, "Raush mit Dir gehen Sie zu Hause, sofort!"

The van Rijn children had to get used to Jaap's joviality. "You may call me Pake and my wife is Beppe," Jaap said as they walked out of the station toward their horse and Briek (Dutch word for Buggy.) The children were both repeating the strange names they had to call their foster parents with. David said to his sister, "I hope we will get some food soon, I am so hungry. I could eat a horse! But if I do that we won't be able to get to the farm!" Mies laughed. Even at a time like this the van Rijn children kept their sense of humor.

When Beppe spoke, their wish instantly came true. "Come quickly on the carriage, I have some sandwiches and milk for you two."

They did not like to be separated from Johannes but they were obliged to follow Pake and Beppe. Johannes, the oldest of the three, called after them. "I will be fine, don't worry about me! I'll come and see you soon. We're only next door to each other." Little did he know about the seven mile distance which would be between them.

Johannes looked up at his host who had introduced herself as Tante Netty. "I am the sister of the local pastor. I live with him and take care of him. He is not married but he insisted upon getting a city child to come and stay with him. He could not come but you will meet him when we get home. Are you hungry?" He nodded.

"I thought so. Well, let's go quickly so I can make you some sandwiches at home. You'll have to sit on the back of my bicycle and hold your bag in your lap, okay?"

In The Hague, the city was dark and quiet. The absence of lots of children was clearly noticeable. Johanna was thinking about her three children far north in Friesland. Would they be all right? She was already missing them. She felt confident that they were in good hands and that they would be well-fed. There would have to be no fear of bombs either.

Chapter Twenty Two

THE SUFFERING OF THE JEWS

—ᘉ—

T he Nazi preparations were so detailed and so devious that even the most educated Jew did not grasp what was happening to them. The Jewish Council was actually helping the Germans gather the helpless, young and old, male and female and children were all at first invited to report at the railroad station in The Hague.

The underground Christian newspaper Trouw reported the following article on June 3, 1943.

"The Germans have taken an intensified interest in the Dutch Jewish population, this in accord with the communication of the Reich's Commissary, Seys Inquart, who announced the statement the other day that 'this very year' the Jewish question here would be solved.

The campaign exploded again when, after the call for Jews to report at the central station in The Hague on May 20, only 980 of the 14,000 who had been invited, showed up. New measures clamped down on those in possession of a Sperstempel (a special stamp on one's ID card exempting the bearer from deportation) as a result of their work for the Jewish Council. Half of the exemptions from deportation were withdrawn, including those Jews who were from German Descent, residing in The Netherlands.

A new order to report was issued; it did not yield the desired result either. Whereupon, the Nazi maniacs began their hunt on the night of May 23rd and it continued several days thereafter.

The streets where many Jews resided were cordoned off with soldiers and barricades. Even the passing streetcars were shut and locked in order to pass by. The hunt had begun, all hell broke loose, from door to door, and the soldiers entered and chased them outside and into the waiting trucks. The suffering of the Jews had become indescribable.

The satanic rage was never-ending. In Camp Westerbork one hundred Jews from mixed marriages, with or without children, were put to the choice: either Auschwitz or sterilization. Forty-seven of the one hundred chose Auschwitz. The other fifty three chose what in our opinion was worse: sterilization.

When in addition we consider this measure, promulgated in defiance of earlier promises, the Nazis directed those Jews who had become Christians also to Westerbork. We saw even more Jews suffering in an unfathomable way.

Deeply troubled, we watch this entire evil take place in our Christian Holland.

To what judgment will they have to submit themselves, who still call themselves Dutchmen and who are taking part in the atrocities?"

All they could bring was one bag per family and some blankets!

When Kees read the article, who could not resist crying? He also cried out to the Lord, "How long do we have to deal with this monstrosity of an enemy?"

He was determined to increase his activities to hide and transport the innocent and helpless Jews even more. With tears still in his eyes he went down below the house where eighteen Jews were waiting to be brought to a farm. He brought the illegal newspaper with him and gave it to the day leader to read.

It was a hard decision to have them read it but how else would they hear about the severity of their predicament? Kees asked for all to be silent and to sit down "Please prepare yourselves for a very disturbing reading of a newspaper article.

110

A few Jewish families who did report to the train station.
They had to wait for hours and did not seem very anxious.

Before you read it, Sam, let us have a moment of prayer. We all serve the same God, whom we will ask to give us grace and mercy, even understanding, though I don't know how." Kees began to pray and while he did, he could hear several people begin to cry, the moment was so intense.

Chapter Twenty Three

OPERATION ISOLATION

—w—

When the Nazis understood that they would never win from the stubborn Dutch, they began to implement "Operation Isolation."

Anything which would keep the Dutch from isolation from the rest of the world would be removed. The first action was to shut down all the news agencies, then all the newspapers. When they were all shut down a new era of information began. Propaganda was the word. The newspapers which would collaborate were given NSB editors who had to go through all the articles and eliminate anything against the Nazis.

Seyss Inquart stimulated national football games and anything in sport and culture was coming back, he promised. It did come back, but not before it was converted into propaganda.

No one can tell how many Dutch people fell for the new approach. The theaters were full and the concert halls were sold out, However, the majority of the audiences were Germans and NSB-ers.

Advertising began to explode with propaganda and posters were hung everywhere promoting Nazi-ism. Very few participated and the national football games (soccer) were shunned by the spectators, even though the national team was forced to play. Winning had become an issue because you could not let the enemy win a game.

Dirty practices evolved on the playing fields. Football players were even threatened by the Gestapo. If they did not perform, they would be sent to the Westerbork Camp. Everyone knew, once in Westerbork you were on your way to a Nazi camp in Germany or Poland.

The lack of information led people to their radios, listening to the BBC would give them real information. News and rumors about a pending invasion by the allies began as early as 1942. It had to take three years before the allies finally made their move. It was hope and determination which kept the citizens alive in The Netherlands.

Kees had a small radio and he would listen to "Radio Free Holland" until as early as 1942, a new order was issued by Seyss Inquart.

Radio:

"It is prohibited to have a Radio. All radios have to be handed in at your local police station. Radios which are found in the houses will be confiscated and the owner will be arrested. Anyone caught listening will be arrested.

-Seyss Inquart

The Dutch protested by hiding their radios and by listening to the BBC anyway. They would listen underneath beds and in closets. The hope grew even bigger now that the news became more sporadic.

The Underground used their radios for encoded messages from the government in exile. They could not be without their radios. In fact, thousands of radios literally went underground and listening to the BBC was a must for their instructions.

Kees had his friend Frans build-in his Radio into a Psalm book.

When he listened to the news from England he would get encoded messages like:

"Bram has to go the hills."

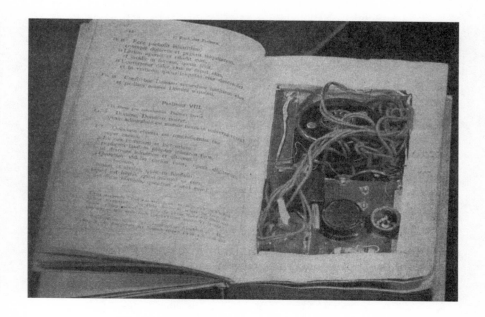

This meant that the oldest Jews in his hiding place were going to be transported to Switzerland soon. Then he would listen the next day for the date and time:

"Bram will go to the hospital with his mother at four."

This message entailed that the oldest couple was going to be picked up at 4:00 on day four, which is Wednesday, in an ambulance.

Kees would thus be able to get the people ready and packed for that day and time for their trip to freedom. The preparations could mean that disguises might have to be applied, hair might be cut and a False ID had to be created. Even though the people transported in an ambulance were hidden beneath the floor of the truck, they had to lay down and a double floor was placed over top of them.

Precautions were taken in case treason had caused the ambulance to be searched or in case they ran into road blocks or an accident.

Kees did not like to send an ambulance with the capacity of seven fugitives for transport to have to make the long trip with only two people. So he went to his underground colleagues and discussed who else needed to go to Switzerland.

One of the fugitives to be transported had to be a fake German soldier who would be wrapped in bandages and strapped to the gurney on top of the double floor.

That role was usually played by a person who was in the Underground and whose ID had been compromised, or a pilot or agent from a neighboring country. It could be a spy who needed to bring messages to England. The role of wounded soldier was never played by a Jewish person – they all thought that would be too risky.

The illegal press reacted to the demand to seize all radios by placing ads in the underground newspapers, and by creating hundreds of thousands of illegal pamphlets which were spread throughout the country by the courier networks.

One of those pamphlets read:

"No Radio? Yes, Radio!
Do not follow the advice to turn
in 'your old appliances'
the Nazis do not want you to have.
We deny the enemy the right to
seize personal property based on
article 46 of the Geneva Convention,
which says, 'Private property
cannot be confiscated.'
If you have a radio, do not
display it. Hide it in such a way
that you can continue to listen to it.
Accept the watch word: not a
single radio for the enemy.

Chapter Twenty Four

THE LITTLE SPY

—∿∿—

Cornelius had found himself a second job. Frans had asked him one day, "Cornelius, I want you to go look at the barricade around the corner. Just go and look at the weapons they have. See if they have machine guns and also how many people are guarding the barricade... do you think you can do that?"

He had liked the assignment and went to the "Versperrung" Right away. His first assignment was easy and he liked it. He went close to the soldiers and began to talk to them. They thought it was cute to have the interested little guy look at their guns. They demonstrated how they loaded them. He asked about the machine guns, how many bullets could it shoot and how fast. They were delighted to show him. After all, life at a barricade was not very exciting. They would rather participate in a Razzia, when people were trying to run and they could shoot.

When Cornelius went home he felt great. He had liked the soldiers and they had been very friendly. He reported to Frans like a professional spy. "There are fifteen soldiers and one of them is a captain. They have two machine guns and they can shoot fifty bullets in a minute. They all have two guns, one pistol and one rifle and they have a sort of tank with a cannon. They would not tell me about it, they said, because it was new."

"Very good job," Frans told him. "Whenever you go with your

Dad I want you to do the same thing, find out what they have and where it is , tell your Dad about it and let him write it down in code so he can tell me about it in case you forget."

Cornelius liked his new role, it gave him a sense of importance. "You can count on me," said the young little spy as he left Frans' home in the Drebbel Straat.

Cornelius spying on a tank with German soldiers.

Chapter Twenty Five
MOVING THE DRIVEN
AND THE DISLODGED

—ɯ—

T he hunted-down Jews received the news about the fate of their
families, of those who had been deported to the concentration camps. The horrible news was hand-delivered fast, often by the
mouth of young messengers,

The illegal press created pamphlets which were spread quickly,
but which came into the hands of the enemy as well. Many arrests
were made. Anyone having a handful of pamphlets was arrested and
sometimes tortured in order to find out where the pamphlets had
been printed.

The Jews became much more aware of the gravity of their exis-
tence. The Underground became more alert and on the look-out for
traitors, and NSB-ers were watched and possibly deceived in many
ways.

No hiding place was safe for long. The transportations of Jews
became more dangerous every day.

The imitation ambulances kept doing their job. They were probably the safest for transportation of the Jews. The Ypenburg hangar
remained one of the best-kept secrets of the Underground. The place
where the duplicate ambulances were stationed was in overtime
gear. Their runs were made more frequently than ever before.

The forgery presses too were working overtime. Some were
manned twenty hours to create the necessary passes and transport

orders for "wounded German soldiers" who were no soldiers at all.

Never was anyone caught posing as a wounded German soldier. The ambulances were able to bring people to the Holland borders for further transport through Belgium and France to freedom in either Switzerland, or through the Pyrenees to Spain.

Many good doctors were involved in the creation of wounded German soldiers with medical reports and bandages applied in many inventive ways.

The entire country became a large network in which many people worked together to hide the Jews and other hunted people and bring them to safety.

The measures taken by the Germans were calculated from the beginning. To lure the Jews into their dragnet they had first created the Jewish Council with promises they would not keep. When the Jewish Council made an announcement it was readily accepted by the Jews until it became known what their role really was.

The main active leaders were Dr. David Cohen and Dr. A. Asscher. The two were so active they even went to the railroad station to greet the departing Jews. They are seen in the picture below. Both are wearing their Star of David proudly. This picture was taken at the station in The Hague.

The continual messages they published in their weekly magazine all had to do with obedience to the Nazis. Below is the translation of one of those notorious articles.

> De Joodsche Raad voor Amsterdam maakt er alle Joden
> nogmaals met nadruk op attent, dat het noodzakelijk is om
> voortdurend op de hoogte te wezen van de mededeelingen,
> maatregelen en bepalingen, die voor hen van belang zijn.
> Deze worden steeds in het officieel orgaan van den Joodschen
> Raad voor Amsterdam gepubliceerd.
> Een ieder dient dus in zijn welbegrepen eigenbelang ervoor
> te zorgen, dat hij wekelijks kennis neemt van de in „Het
> Joodsche Weekblad" gepubliceerde officieele berichten.
> Op de lezers van dit blad rust de plicht, deze mededeeling
> zooveel mogelijk te verbreiden.
>
> De voorzitters van den Joodschen
> Raad voor Amsterdam:
> A. ASSCHER.
> Prof. dr. D. COHEN.

"The Jewish Council for Amsterdam is making known to all Jews that it is very important to remain familiarized with all the rules and regulations, for their own benefit. These rules and regulations will be published in our official Jewish Weekly.

The readers have an obligation to make these announcements known to all.

The Chairman of the
Jewish Council for Amsterdam
A.Assher
Professor Dr. D. Cohen"

Other more discriminating measures were imposed on the Jewish population.

The regular ID every Dutchman had to get was enhanced with a big red 'J,' meaning Jewish, of course. On the bottom of the Jewish ID an extra stamp was placed which read, *"From Saturday afternoons, 3 O'clock until Monday mornings, 6 am Invalid."*

The Nazis made sure that on the weekends the Jewish population stayed home so they could be picked up! They were told the reason for that stamp was so they could worship, but Jews don't go to their synagogues on Sundays.

The Jewish Council accepted all these extra measures; they did everything to appease the Germans.

The next measure was even bolder in the face of the Jewish community. *"A Certificate to have come forward,"* clad with the Star of David, the signature of Mr. A. Asscher, and a stamp reading *"Joodse Raad for Amsterdam,"* completed the certificate.

To top off the entire act of discrimination, the Jewish Council made an announcement in their weekly publication:

BEWIJS VAN AANMELDING,

als bedoeld in artikel 9, eerste lid, van de Verordening No. 6/1941 van den Rijks-commissaris voor het bezette Nederlandsche gebied, betreffende den aanmeldingsplicht van personen van geheel of gedeeltelijk JOODSCHE BLOEDE voor AMSTERDAM

*

De ondergeteekende, ambtenaar voor de aanmelding, verklaart dat de aan keer-zijde aangeduide persoon, opgenomen in het Bevolkingsregister dezer gemeente, heeft voldaan aan de verplichting tot aanmelding volgens de bovengenoemde Verordening.

Afgegeven op 9 APR. 1941

in Gemeente AMSTERDAM

voor den Burgemeester,
De Administrateur
afd. Bev.register en Verkiezingen,

...cht van den Beauftragte van den Rijkscommissaris voor ...dam is ieder te Amsterdam woonachtige Jood, die zijn (resp. persoonsbewijs) op verlangen moet vertoonen, ...ht **het bewijs van aanmelding als Jood** tezamen met zijn (resp. persoonsbewijs) bij zich te dragen en het op ver-aartoe bevoegde autoriteiten te toonen.

De Joodsche Raad voor Amsterdam,

A. ASSCHER ⎱ Voorzitters.
Prof. Dr. D. COHEN ⎰

"According to the order from the Reich's Commissary, Seys Inquart, every Jew living in Amsterdam (and any other city in the Netherlands) who has an ID card and is asked to show it to the authorities is obliged to show his or her 'Certificate to have come forward' at the same time.

The Jewish Council
A. Asscher
Prof. Dr. D. Cohen"

Chapter Twenty Six
THE FACTORIES OF THE WAR MACHINE

—m—

Kees was always busy doing something or other the minute he came home from Simowitz.

He needed more time for his underground activities, so he had applied for a nightshift.

The war machine needed a constant stream of ammunition, bomb triggers and many other military supplies. The Simowitz factory in The Hague was producing 24 hours-a-day, 7 days-a-week.

The forced laborers were brought in by truck-loads. The factory was run by a military detachment headed by a Gestapo unit under a captain.

Mixed in with the forced laborers were voluntary NSB-ers. They were planted among the forced laborers in order to spy on them and betray them.

No one knew the exact number of NSB-ers or who they were. That could be harmful to them, which made sabotage very difficult and most dangerous.

Even though the forced laborers made daily efforts to slow down the production. The danger of it was instant execution. Anyone caught doing illegal activities was shot on sight.

Kees often had come home angry and shaken because someone had been caught and shot.

The Dutch collaborators were the traitors who would play to be forced laborers but their constant surveillance led to many deaths.

Yet despite the dangers and all that went on in the factory, Kees was able to bring home little shiny presents for Cornelius to play with. The boy loved the shiny parts of glossy brass. He made all kinds of toys with them.

His father never told him that the shiny, interesting looking parts he brought home to him would save the lives of many people. Whenever a bomb trigger failed or a gun jammed or a gas mask would leak, it could have been the result of a missing part Cornelius had received from his Dad.

Kees's request for a nightshift position had been granted; he had to work from twelve midnight until eight in the morning four days-a-week.

With two hours of sleep, Kees was able to work his underground duties and activities all day every day and evening. He was able to go on three day trips on the weekends.

Having a reputation for punctuality, the young Doctor Ypma, who had had his furlough to go back to Holland, had come back to the concentration camp just as he had promised.

His mind was in great turmoil because he had made the decision to rescue as many people as he could from this death camp.

His little experimental clinic was becoming too small now that 17 beds had been filled with "patients." He planned to save more than that number. He did not know how, exactly. Gradually a plan began to form in his mind.

Tante Riek had given him numerous ideas for a pending escape. He wondered if he had the guts to do it.

She had given him many options, lots of contact names and several routes to go through France, to Switzerland, and through the Pyrenees to Spain. She had made him learn all the names, places and routes by heart. Nothing could be written down, she had assured him. Nothing, never!

The doctor was an analytical person, not a hero. His heart raced when he thought of the bold and courageous plan he had made.

Hannah came to his office in the little clinic that bright fall morning. She thanked him profusely. "Doctor Ypma!"

"Call me Henk," he interrupted.

"Doctor Henk," she began, "I so appreciate you coming back here, I never expected it. I was so scared here without you. I would not have known what to do if you had not come back. You are risking your life for us. Thank you, thank you and thank you. And thank you so much for bringing my letter to my brother in Winterswijk. That in itself was a courageous act and it will save thousands of lives."

He looked at her in his compassionate way and realized how beautiful she was with her dark eyes and her raven-black curly hair. She alone would be worth it to risk his life. To get her saved from her undeserved death sentence would be his most rewarding accomplishment.

At that moment he made a decision. "I'll do it! I will plan to take all seventeen of the girls, now I know how!"

His research was already a scam, a way for himself to survive the brutal Nazis. But if they would find out about his fake information they would shoot him in an instant. So what did he have to lose?

The seventeen young Jewish ladies had been selected by him with the help of sweet Hannah. None of them had Syphilis. None of them were sick. On the contrary, they were healthier than any other person in the camp. He had faked all his research and had increased the health of the young ladies.

In his fake reports, even the medicine he prescribed to the males in the next ward had been phony.

Of course they had seen some improvements, simple Aspirin would help somewhat, particularly when mixed with some antibiotics. He knew it would never cure them.

That very fact went against his ethical professionalism, the oath he once made to heal and help. Easing the pain of patients stood in his way to keep doing what he was doing. But this was war-time and the enemies were Nazis.

All the girls in his clinic were in the know of his scam. He knew he could trust them! Now he had to confide his plan with them. Would they agree? They would never betray him, he knew that for certain. But any misstep and hint of the truth would kill them all.

They had been transported to this death camp for only one reason: *"Vernichtung,"* or "The Final Solution," as Himmler had called it.

Their death was imminent and as soon as he could pronounce total success with his research and a perfect cure for the disease they would not be needed anymore, which meant execution by means of the dreadful gas chambers.

He needed more time to think. He needed help to plan. He needed advice, but from whom?

His plan was to begin to play on his superiors without raising any suspicion. He turned to Hannah and said, "My dear young lady, I have the plan in detail now, a plan to get you all out of here really soon.

Would you please help me to think this through?" Hannah's dark black eyes grew brighter as he spoke those words.

"Of course I will," she answered. "I will lay out your plans before you and see if there are any flaws. When we have no questions left I will inform the others and ask them for input, if they have any, until we know without a doubt that it is going to work."

Henk finally gave her the details. "There is a much larger 'human research' facility down in the Swartzwalt. There they are doing downright dirty research on human beings, Jewish for the most part. People who go there die from incurred illnesses and from operations unheard of.

If I would report that I found the perfect cure for Syphilis, they would want to transfer all of you to their facility for further experiments which would include infecting you with the disease to see if it can be healed. And you and I know that that would be catastrophic."

"I am listening and getting more afraid of it by the minute," Hannah remarked, "but go on."

"The location of that facility is close to the Swiss border," he said.

"Oh, I am getting your drift," said Hannah.

"I am going to announce the cure soon and I will then volunteer to bring you all to the other place. I will tell them that I will need to continue my research for the sake of mankind and that with all I have discovered, they will need me there. They will assign me a truck with a driver, hopefully only one. Because you are harmless women they would not expect any danger of escape with me riding along too. Of course, the truck will be a secured one which will be locked on the outside. I will make them feel good about the move, all for the benefit of The Reich.

I will tell my superiors that you all agree with the transfer and that you are cooperating for the sake of science.

I have studied the map of the area where the research facility is and I was told that there is a border crossing, a dirt road into Switzerland where no Nazi patrol ever goes. The Dutch resistance uses the crossing all the time without ever having had a problem

Just before we reach the road which leads to the research facility we will have to create a diversion in order to make the driver stop the truck. We can do that somewhere on a quiet road."

"Yes. We'll begin to scream and call you to say that someone is dying," Hannah interjected, now getting into the plan with great enthusiasm. "Then you must act annoyed about it and you make him open the back of the truck against your will."

"That's a good one," Henk said. "How did you come up with that?"

"When he opens the back of the truck we will all jump on him, all seventeen of us. He'll have no chance to even pull his gun. Let's make sure you get us a few rolls of masking tape and that we have them in the back with us. We'll tape the sucker up so completely that he won't be able to use his hands, feet or mouth to get help. We'll just leave him there in the woods."

"No, no. We can't do that," Henk said. "First of all, if someone finds him sooner than we cross over the border, he'll betray us all.

Secondly, we don't need to murder him. He has not done us any wrong. No, we will just take him with us and leave him in the truck while we cross the border. I will bring a German uniform and change into it so I will be the driver in case we get stopped. You can all watch him in the back of the truck. As far as I have been told, the border with Switzerland is only eight kilometers further down the road and if a German patrol stops us, I'll simply say that I got lost on my way to the facility."

The plan sounded feasible. Implementing it would be the final challenge.

The doctor had worked for days on his news-breaking report. He had planned it in such a way that the Generals and the staff of the concentration camp would feel that it was their breakthrough and achievement as well as a major accomplishment.

He wrote it so it could be used as a headline in a newspaper. He formulated the wording as if they had been the initiators. That the generals were being fooled never crossed their minds. They saw fame for themselves and it blinded them.

In order to prove his "break-through" even more convincingly, he asked for a dozen Syphilis-infected men, carefully avoiding the word "soldiers." He aimed to get a dozen of the interned men from the camp, men he could talk to and whom he could even save from the gas chambers.

After the camp leadership had sent him seven soldiers, he carefully objected by stating that if they were subjected to any risk in using the new medication he did not want to be blamed for their possible death.

"The Reich needs its soldiers, why not get some prisoners?"

That argument was fully acceptable for the Generals and they even praised him for his suggestion.

The doctor's respectability was rising. They told him to go into the barracks and find his candidates himself.

The next day he rose very early and began his search for suitable "patients." At first, he went straight to the point by walking into the barracks where hundreds of young men were waiting for their new day of hard labor. They were housed in triple bunk beds without mattresses but they were still infested with lice.

His appearance made the men fear him. His white doctor's coat and armband with a swastika made them as un-cooperative as they could afford to be.

When he asked them if there were men with Syphilis, there was no answer. Then he asked them who would be willing to help him with a medical experiment. Two hands were raised.

Reluctantly, they asked him what the research would entail. He did not answer but wrote down their serial numbers and left. The young doctor with his good intentions had to visit several barracks to find his volunteers.

The meeting went well. When they had arrived at the clinic by order of the Ward Sergeant, he had treated them respectfully and with dignity. He had told them just a part of his plan and that they would have to act as if they were Syphilis patients. He assured them that he would not give them any harmful medications, but he needed to make them look as though they were very sick from the dreadful disease. Then he would stage a gradual healing process and then make them look fully-healed.

He did not make them any promises of freedom, but he hinted that primarily their reward would be a temporary stay of their pending execution. All he could promise was an extension of their lives until further notice.

Chapter Twenty Seven
DISTRIBUTION OF FOOD STAMPS

—⁓—

C ornelius was excited that fall morning in 1943. His father Kees was taking him on a trip to the farms, a three day trip he promised him. Cornelius could hardly sleep from the excitement. Finally he was going out of the city to the open air and the smell of the farms.

They were hungry that morning. The food supply had dwindled to nothing and although they had thousands of food stamps they could not get any food.

The stores in the city were empty; their inventory had not been replenished by order of Seiss Inquart. He was following the command of the generals and ultimately Hitler to starve the city people until they would give up all the people they were hiding.

The German soldiers had taken most of the food from the stores for themselves because they too were hungry. In the streets of the cities of The Hague, Rotterdam and Amsterdam, people were dying. Daily people were dropping dead in the streets. They were the lonely ones or the older ones who lived alone and had no one to care for them.

The German squad in charge of the streets drove their trucks through the city and loaded the corpses onto a dump truck to be buried in a mass grave.

The people of the Resistance did not give up. Hollanders are undefeatable. They went to the farms and brought contraband food to the cities. Others such as Kees rode their bicycles for hundreds of miles per-day to distribute forged food stamps.

Johanna was dressing Cornelius that morning. He was a skinny boy when he came out of his bed but by the time he was dressed he was rather chunky. His underwear was knitted out of old woolen sweaters which his mother had carefully pulled apart and re-knitted.

It was warm but a little itchy. Cornelius had become used to the itchy feeling. Knowing that he was going to the farms to get food made him submit to anything. The next layer Cornelius was being dressed with were packs and packs of food stamps. The night before Kees had gone to several print shops and collected thousands of carefully hand-pressed food stamps.

They were made so authentically that no one could tell they were fakes. Therefore, they were readily accepted by the shop owners and food distribution centers.

After the packs of food stamps were placed on Cornelius' body his mother wrapped him in strips of bed sheets she had cut. She was using them like an extra-wide bandage and covered his body from head to toe wherever he had food stamps hidden. Finally Cornelius was dressed, clad in pants and a shirt and a sweater over which went an anorak with a hood.

The first time they had dressed him this way they had laughed so much because it was hilarious to see a small boy become fatter and fatter. Kees had made a seat on the back of his bicycle with foot-rest and a back-rest. It was a comfortable place to be behind his father's broad back and when the wind blew hard he could hide his face against him.

This particular morning the weather was nice and crisp. Cornelius knew he would not be cold with all the stuff on his body.

When Kees had put him in his seat he had said, "Now remember, your task is to cry when we are stopped. Cry hard so the soldiers will let us go quickly." He knew his assignment and was determined not to lose his dad or their life-saving bicycle.

The first farm they always went to was the Brandwijk farm. Cornelius liked it there. His mind was already made up, when he was grown-up he would buy that farm and be a farmer. Every time they went there he had learned something new about farming.

Mrs. Brandwijk was such a kind and compassionate person. Cornelius was always fascinated with her.

The trip this time was soon interrupted by the hated German words that sounded in the crisp morning just before the Hornbrug. The Hornbrug was a bridge that would take them over the river the Vliet and along the river on a bicycle path to the country and farms.

"Halt, Auf steigen, Ausweiss!" It sounded so mean but sometimes the soldiers could be friendly.

The soldiers took his father's identity card and studied it. "Ah, Sie arbeiten fuer Simowitz, wohin fahren Sie jetz? (You work at Simowitz where are you going?)"

When Kees began to talk, Cornelius began to cry. He cried at the top of his lungs until a soldier said the releasing words, "Oh Gehen Sie mahl."

This time the stop was easy, but that did not last very long. Two miles along down the road they were stopped by a motorcycle with side car and two soldiers. These two were nasty. They had to search Kees who had to take of his coat and jacket. They went through every pocket and found a bag of seed at which they looked very suspiciously. Cornelius thought he would give them a good crying show this time and began like the sound of a siren went off.

"Wass ist Loss mit der Jungen? (What's the matter with that boy?)" they asked Kees. He answered them that he was taking him to a doctor in Gouda because he was having severe stomach pains.

One of the soldiers came over to Cornelius and stroked his hair. "Ich habe einer Jungen wie du zu Hause."

Cornelius cried even louder when he talked to him. The other soldier had given Kees his bag of spinach seeds back and made the gesture to move on. That was the second stop today and they were only on their way for less than two hours. "What is this country coming to and how many will have to die before this ordeal is over?" Kees thought to himself.

"You did a great job son, crying like you did. I would have hated to have lost the bag of seed I had bought for the Brandwijk's."

Now let's hope there will be no more interruptions this beautiful morning."

The river was still. Where normally tug boats and barks would come by, traffic had ceased to exist. The farmers who used to bring their vegetables to the auctions had nothing to auction. Every time a crop of something would be ripe for harvest the Germans would come and harvest it for them without paying for it. Yet all the farmers kept growing their crops. Seed time and harvest will never cease, it says in the Bible, and the farmers were proving the truth of that text.

Most of the farmers had hidden patches of land. Far away in the fields hidden by brambles of Pussy Willow trees they would grow small amounts for their own use and for their guest. On one out of every five farms there were guests hidden somewhere. The Germans knew it but failed to find the hide-outs almost every time.

For their guests they grew some of the food. Other foods which they could not grow had to be bought in the villages or had to be traded with the other farmers. For the purchased items they needed food stamps for all their guests. Kees and Cornelius would supply them most of the time.

Cornelius, the five-year-old son, was the decoy of the Resistance and the carrier of the merchandise.

When they were on the road riding their precious bicycle, the biggest risk was to lose their bicycle.

Only one time that had happened, when soldiers were in need of one, and perhaps they were drunk. They had pulled Cornelius from his seat and rode away with their so very important means of transportation.

The two of them had to walk back home and it had taken them two days and many kilometers of walking. At that point Kees had instructed Cornelius about his crying routine. It had worked every time Cornelius was with him. Thus Cornelius had become one of the youngest members of the Resistance.

Their arrival, even though it was expected, was always a joyful experience. The Brandwijk family was waiting on the driveway in front of their house. Kees and Cornelius had to get off the bike and open the iron gate of the long driveway which led to the farmhouse

The Farm

and the other farm buildings.

The two of them walked the rest of the way, with Kees holding his bike in a balancing act at his right hand. Cornelius could not wait for his dad and ran towards the waiting family. He went straight for the 19-year-old daughter of the family, who was his favorite. She received Cornelius with open arms and almost fell over backwards when he jumped up into her arms."So good to see you my little big boy!" she said as she hugged him. Then he went to Mrs.Brandwijk and then Mr. Brandwijk, but someone was missing. The son Cor was not there. At that time Kees had caught up with his son and began to greet them. Both Kees and his son said at the same time in unison, "Where is Cor?" No one answered, and when Kees asked the question again Mr. Brandwijk answered, "Cor had to join the Knock Ploeg in Amsterdam and we have not heard from him for weeks."

Kees thought for a moment, searching for words to say. "That is a noble cause but very dangerous."

"We agree and we would not have allowed him to go until one night he went without our consent. His work here at the farm was important, but I guess he wanted the adventure and excitement of a fight."

Cornelius did not understand why his friend was gone. He used to have such good times with him on the farm. They all went inside and there on the thrashing floor was a big surprise for the big and small visitors. At a long table were fifteen old friends of Kees and Cornelius. The Jews which had first stayed at their house in the Deiman Straat in The Hague had come out of their shelter beneath the hay stack and where having breakfast on the thrashing floor.

This occasion was a joyful break for them as well, and normally their food was brought to them by Cor but lately it was brought by Marie. There was a risk to be there. If a German patrol would come it would take them several minutes to disappear, having to climb up on the haystack and down the ladder to the basement.

Farmer Brandwijk had made an exception with the warning, "You will have to be fast after the bell rings, very fast, and whoever is still in sight will have to face the consequences of interrogations and deportation to a concentration camp. But whatever happens you will be responsible yourselves and you must promise never to tell what is going on here, even if you are tortured."

They all agreed. This event would be worth it, it would give them a little taste of freedom.

After the first greetings they all sat down and talked. The warning bell which farmer Brandwijk had installed on the gate never rang that morning and for once there was happiness in the large assembly. They talked about things of the war and what they had learned from Kees at his last visit. A temporary sadness fell over the entire group when they mentioned their family members who had gone to the concentration camps and who had most likely perished. The memories lingered over the group for a while until Kees stood up and told them that the allied forces were making plans for an invasion.

Meanwhile, Mrs. Brandwijk had taken Cornelius to her bedroom where she had removed part of the food stamps he was carrying on his body. She had prepared him some great slices of bread which she always cut with a knife while holding the bread against her bosom. Cornelius was always fascinated by the way she cut the bread and feared that one day she would cut herself. Here, a little chit-chat gave him a chance to wolf-down the great meal she had made for him. In his mind this was the feast he had longed for, even though it was just bread and butter. Nothing else was better than bread and butter if you are rationed only half a slice per day.

After his meal he asked her if he could go to the chicken pen and collect the eggs they had laid. He had always loved to do that and it seemed as if the chicken knew him when he walked into their domain. He collected a basket-full of eggs. Mrs. Brandwijk immediately offered to cook four of them, two for his dad and two for him. Cornelius thought that perhaps he had become a little too bold when he asked, "What about two for my mom?" Not even surprised she answered him, "Of course I will cook two for your mom, and I am proud of you that you thought of her."

When Marie Brandwijk came outside, Cornelius was elated because they were going to sow the spinach seeds his dad had brought.

Behind the drinking pond was a row of blackberries with heavy thorns on them. The Brandwijk's had created their own private stock of vegetables there. When the Germans had come in the past they had always overlooked their private garden and even though it was not enough to sell or barter with, it yielded sufficiently for their own family and their guests. Of course you could not always eat the same thing, and there was only a little variety.

They took a rake and a hoe and walked over to the patch of land which had been prepared for the spinach seed. It was early fall and spinach normally was sowed in the spring, Marie explained to him. "When we sow seed in the fall the leaves will be thicker and more coarse, but that will be healthier and more loaded with vitamins," she said.

They were looking at the patch of soil and Marie told him to rake the top layer of it with his little hands. He really could not control the raking very well. Marie took over the job and showed him how the rake could just disturb only the top two inches of the soil. She made ridges of six inches apart and finally sowed the seed inside the ridges, after which she filled them in with the soil.

"Now," she said, "We need to cover the whole patch with a cloth so that the seed will quickly germinate. That way it won't be eaten by the birds or the rabbits. The next time you come we will be able to eat the spinach. That is, if you will come in about four weeks. After that, the spinach will begin to grow seed and then you cannot eat it anymore." Cornelius was learning a lot that morning and he loved every moment of it.

"The next thing we need to do this morning is to feed the pigs, do you think we can handle that?" Marie and Cornelius walked over to the pig sty. When they passed the house she heard the alarm bell of the front gate go off. "Oh, Cornelius, look at who is coming into the gate quickly, please?"

Cornelius ran around the house just in time to see a German motorcycle with two soldiers who were opening the gate. He ran back to Marie and excitedly told her what he had seen. Marie ran into the house and screamed "Germans coming, hurry, hurry!"

The Jews who lived in the haystack dwelling far underneath the hay had already taken action and several had already climbed up to the top of the hay when they heard the motorcycle stop in front of the farm house. Kees had to go into hiding as well because he was at the farm illegally, and that could be detrimental to his underground work.

Farmer Brandwijk had held his composure and slowly walked outside towards the dismounting soldiers.

"Good morning, Gentlemen," he said in a friendly tone. "What brings you to our little farm this morning?" The two soldiers looked at each other and smiled, saying, "Wir suchen etwas zum essen (we are looking for something to eat.)"

"Please come inside," farmer Brandwijk said. "I will get my wife to make you some food." Apparently these two soldiers were friendly and intended no harm to any of them, but it was better to be careful because if the soldiers saw something unusual, they could use that against them at a later date, Brandwijk thought.

He avoided going through the threshing floor into the house, because the Jews might have left some clues of their presence there. Instead he walked in front of the soldiers toward the upper room in the front of the house, thus giving his Jewish guests a chance to get to their hiding place unseen.

They had not panicked when the alarm bell rang; the oldest had taken the lead and had walked through the backdoor of the thrashing floor towards the adjoining haystack. One by one they climbed up the steep ladder and at the top of the hay down again into their basement hiding place.

Kees had hidden himself in the horse stable where he could watch his Jewish friends go up the ladder and disappear. He had timed their flight from the thrashing floor until the last person was out of sight.

It had taken them a total of four minutes. He decided to tell Brandwijk about that and he made a decision to tell the Jewish people too. They would have to train their disappearance more thoroughly to cut down the time to two minutes.

The Brandwijk's were both busy feeding the two soldiers when Marie walked into the upper room. The two soldiers were pleasantly surprised when they saw her. The farmer saw the look in their eyes and thought, "If I play this right I can take advantage of the way they are looking at my daughter." The two soldiers could not keep their eyes off Marie, so the farmer asked, "Are you two married or single?"

One soldier tried to speak Dutch and with a heavy accent he said "No sir, but I would like to be and I have someone in mind." He looked at Marie and had a twinkle in his eye.

Brandwijk spoke. "Now you boys behave yourselves, my daughter is too young and very much needed at this farm. But when this war is over, you may come back and ask for her hand. That might be all you will get from her. I hope you will agree that this time and both our situations are not suitable for anyone to get married." They all laughed and the atmosphere in the upper room began to relax.

"Dad," said Marie, "Me and Cornelius are going to feed the pigs right now so you can stay and talk with these gentlemen. Is that okay? Her dad nodded and gave her wink. They understood each other very well.

As Marie walked out of the room she said to the two soldiers, "Nice to have met you two... I hope when you come back you will come in peace." Marie walked out and felt great. She thought she had made good public relations today, and with the enemy no less!

Cornelius followed Marie and slipped his hand into Marie's hand. "Are the pigs more important than the Germans?" he asked.

"No, but a relationship with them is very important. If we make them our friends they will not come and steal things from us and we will be able to take all suspicions of our farm out of their minds. Then we can freely help our Jewish friends."

The pigs were squealing when they entered the pig sty. They had only three pigs left and Marie told him what had happened a few weeks before, how the Germans had stolen all of the other pigs.

She also told him that two of the pigs were pregnant and that they would soon have two dozen new piglets again. And if the Germans became their friends they would never steal them again.

Cornelius was watching when Marie filled the trough with food and tried to imitate the squealing. He was becoming a good imitator, and Marie commented him on his efforts.

"What are you trying to do? Become a family member of them and speak their language?"

They both laughed, and once the pigs began to slobber up their food they stopped making their noise. Cornelius did not like the smell of them and walked outside. Along the wall of the pigsty was a flower bed full of big Marigolds.

Cornelius liked those flowers and particularly their scent.

He asked what they were called.

"Marigolds, named after me," she said. He repeated the word twice, "Marigolds, Marigolds." He would remember that name for the rest of his life. Marie showed him how the seed could be collected from the Marigolds. "Look, you take a flower which is fully bloomed out and totally dried up." She picked one off a plant and showed him. "You pull out the whole bloom from this green tube, and then you can see the seed, these little black and white-striped sticks, hundreds of them. They are the seeds, and they will each make a whole new plant."

Cornelius asked if he could pick some more seeds of the Marigolds. "Sure," said Marie. "Take as many as you want."

Chapter Twenty Eight

A TRIP TO FREEDOM

—⟋⟍—

A safely-secured truck was waiting at, the gates no one leaves through, to open. The dreaded gates of concentration camp Auschwitz had seen many trucks enter and many train-loads of people roll in, but they had hardly ever seen a truck-load of people leave.

The truck had been carefully loaded up with seventeen young Jewish women. They had been packed up with their little belongings and even had been able to dress themselves from anything they could pick in a huge warehouse with thousands of clothes racks full of used clothing.

The young ladies had been highly favored by the German commanders for their services to the Reich, because of their assistance to a Dutch doctor who had been interned himself. His knowledge of venereal diseases had been noticed when his file was read and at first, under armed control, he had been allowed to conduct some medical tests on patients who had some type of venereal disease.

When he had proven himself to the commanders of the camp, he had become a trustworthy doctor in the experimental clinic of Auschwitz. He had proposed to conduct a more elaborate testing program with Syphilis patients in order to find a cure for the thousands of German soldiers infected with the disease. Syphilis had almost decimated the army and the fatalities from it could become much higher if no cure was found quickly.

The doctor had reported his findings to the commanders of the camp who in turn had reported the breakthrough to the High Command in Berlin.

Congratulations had been sent to the camp, and an order was issued to allow the doctor more freedom and anything he would need for further research since his work was deemed outstanding and of great benefit to the Reich.

Just weeks after the breakthrough had been made known to the higher authorities, the doctor had issued another report in which he had recommended to take all his patients to a more sophisticated experimental facility in the German Alps. At first the camp commanders had looked at his request with suspicion, but the High Command's advice had prevailed and an order for the transport had been granted.

The truck which was waiting at the gate was finally led through. The soldier who was driving the vehicle had received his travel orders back from the sentry at the gate. He was a young man who did not like to fight and who hated guns yet he had been issued a pistol the day before.

He liked these kinds of assignments. They gave him some kind of freedom and avoidance of having to fight.

He had studied his army maps and knew the route he was going to take. He had figured how to make the trip in seven hours and return to Auschwitz the next day. His companion in the cab of the truck was a young doctor who introduced himself with a handshake, saying, "I am Doctor Henk Ypma, you may call me Herr Doctor. I hope we will have a pleasant trip today. I brought two food packages from the officer's mess room, packed especially for the trip.

The girls in the back of the truck won't need anything so we can stay on the road the whole time."

They did not talk very much the entire trip. The simple uneducated German soldier and the highly educated Dutch Doctor had nothing in common. So the trip was quite dull. The girls in the rear had been quiet, for a long time until it happened.

All hell seemed to have broken lose in the back of the truck.

Loud screams and banging on the front board were heard. "What is going on with them in the back?" the doctor said after a long time and the screaming would not cease.

The German driver asked what they should do. The doctor shrugged his shoulders, and asked, "What do you suggest, can't we just wait until we get there? We should be there pretty soon, should we not?"

The German soldier took the bait and pulled over to the side of the road. It was a rural road which had practically no traffic. Henk had it all planned that way. The only uncertainty was how the driver would react. He stopped in the grass on the side of the road. Next to the road were trees, lots of pine trees, which went on for a few miles.

On-coming traffic was non-existent.

When the soldier stepped out of the cabin he said to the doctor,

"Let me just ask what is going on, please stay here until I find out."

It could not have gone any better. The soldier reacted exactly as Hannah and Henk had predicted. He walked over to the back of the truck and called out, "What is going on with you girls?"

The screaming stopped for a moment and a few voices from the inside called out, "One of us is dying! Please hurry and get the doctor!" The driver walked back to the cabin of the truck and told Henk what they had said and why they had been making all the noise.

Henk asked the soldier what he could do, and the soldier responded with fatal words. "We better open up and check them out. I'd hate to deliver a dead body to the research facility, especially one of these important ladies. How do you propose we do that?" Henk asked. He was playing the game in such a way that the driver felt he was in charge of the operation.

The driver took the initiative and walked to the rear of the truck pulled his keys from his pocket and began to unlock the doors. "As soon as I open the doors, I want you to go inside and see what needs to be done. I will wait here and perhaps lock you inside so no one can escape."

"That sounds like a good plan," Henk said as he stepped sideways, waiting for the doors to swing open.

And swing open they did, with the kind of vengeance that only women react with. The minute they heard the latch release all seventeen women pushed at the doors. They had put all their weight against the doors and literally fell out of the truck on top of the driver, who did not know what was happening to him until he found himself on the ground all-taped up, unable to talk.

Henk walked over to the man and said, "Sorry boy, but we need to take you for a ride to the border of Switzerland. OK ladies, let's lift him onto the truck bed. You all get in quickly and I'll close the door, I'll even lock it so it does not give any suspicion to anyone who would catch up with us. It will take us only ten minutes to get this rig to the border and to total freedom. Maybe Heinrich here might want to come with us and say bye-bye to Herr Hitler."

Chapter Twenty Nine

A SECOND TRUCK

—⚏—

S ix hours after the first truck left through the gates that never opened for anyone to leave, another truck, sealed and loaded, was waiting for the sentry to return his papers and open the gate.

In the cabin were a soldier as driver and a second soldier. They had been instructed to make sure their cargo would reach its destination without accidents or incidents.

"You will be close to the Swiss border when you reach the facility. It is a very quiet area, so you should not have any problems. For no reason at all should you unlock and open the back of the truck."

The two soldiers had a determination to make the trip a success and when the gate opened at last they went on their merry way expecting no trouble whatsoever.

The men in the back of the truck were all Jewish young men in ages between nineteen and twenty eight. They had been put to work in the concentration camp moving dirt out of deep trenches. They saw many people die doing the heavy labor and when they were chosen for the medical experiments, they didn't care, they knew they were going to die soon. Their days were numbered, so they might as well do something easier to bear than hauling dirt.

The Dutch doctor who had hand-picked them out of the barracks had told them that their period of experimentation would not last for very long. He had told them that he would see if he could get them

149

out of Auschwitz and perhaps even to freedom.

They had worked with him whole-heartedly and felt good about it. When the doctor finally came and told them about his plan to get them to freedom by crossing the border of Switzerland, they could not believe their ears.

The doctor had shown them his orders to take them all to a research facility in the Alps, and he showed them how he planned to get them out of their truck during an attack. They promised to help him and take the risk of getting shot. "We'll do anything. You tell us when the time is ripe," they had said.

Henk had quickly put on a soldier's uniform he had brought and was driving the final kilometers to the Swiss border crossing. He drove the truck as far as a hundred yards from the border and pulled it off the road into the woods. He found a place where he could turn the truck and parked it with the cab facing the road.

The girls were all ready and waiting to make their last run to freedom when he opened the doors of the truck. Hannah was radiant and looked at her rescuer with such joy when she passed him, that he could not resist taking her in his arms and kissing her.

The other girls coming out of the truck were not even surprised, they had heard how loving he had been and Hannah had been talking about him all the time. They all knew that these two would become lovers.

The last hundred yards were like an exhilarating sprint to freedom. No one was there to stop them and no one could have if they had tried. About two hundred yards on the safe side of the border, they came to a stop together. They made one big circle and Henk told them to hold hands.

"Now ladies," he began. "Let us pray and thank God for this wonderful escape." His prayer was short and to the point. "Lord, we thank you for letting us enter this land of freedom. Please direct our path as we go on with the new lease you have given on our lives." Then he prayed for something the girls had not expected. "We pray for the German soldier we left in the truck, that he may be found and be blessed for the rest of his life. We also pray for the next truck which is going to come this way that no one will get hurt and that they too will find this place of freedom without any casualties. Amen."

There was a moment of silence when Henk had finished his prayer, then they all applauded. Henk raised his hand for silence and spoke. "Ladies, as you all know, now that you are here in Switzerland you will be on your own. Walk on and follow this road and in about two miles you will find a village. Once there you will go to the local bakery shop. The owners will help you to a shelter where there will be food and a place to sleep. Tomorrow other people will come to help you and bring you to the city of Zürich, where the Israeli committee will help you to go to several places of your choice. You will be able to go to Palestine, Canada or the United States. Many have gone before you and others will follow. Good luck and God bless you."

They were all surprised to hear his little speech, and it was Hannah who asked, "Are you not coming with us?"

"Come here, Hannah." He held his arms out to her. Hannah ran into his arms. "My sweet Hannah, I love you with all my heart and I am asking you to wait for me in the next village.

I am going to have to do one important mission and then I will join you as soon as I have accomplished my task." She had tears in her eyes and he kissed her tears away. "Go now and lead your friends to peace and a future. May God be with you." Henk turned around and walked into the woods.

The girls all left and Henk never saw them again, except for Hannah.

One mile back, on the same road they had come on, a pair of binoculars reflected the sunlight which shone into its lenses. The man behind the binoculars was camouflaged with branches and wore a camouflage uniform, his face was all blackened and if he had not had the reflections of the sun on his binoculars no one would ever notice him. Behind the man were four others clad in the same type of camouflage. They were waiting for a sign, and they were waiting for a man. His name was Henk, a doctor from Auschwitz, they were told, and he was saving a large number of their people.

Further up on the road going north, a hitch-hiker was standing on the side of the road waiting for a vehicle to pass and pick him up. He had been there for at least half an hour but no one had passed yet. He was told to play the hitchhiker but in fact he was part of the group down the road who would have him warn them when an army truck passed him. "Play the hitch-hiker and when it has passed, shake your fist at them as if you are mad at them for not picking you up."

Half a mile south of the group of camouflaged people was the truck in which the girls had arrived. Henk had placed it in such a way that it would roll onto the road when he released the hand break. He would jump out and let the truck roll. He had rigged it so it would come to a stop right in the middle of the road, blocking its entire width.

The group in the middle was waiting for the sign. They had strict orders just to rescue and not to shoot. "This operation has to be silent. We don't want any distraction or a visit from a bunch of soldiers who are hearing shots."

Everyone was in position and on-edge when the sound of a truck engine was heard coming from the north. The hitch-hiker could be seen standing on the edge of the tarmac and holding his thumb out, requesting a ride. The two soldiers laughed at him when they passed and they could see him get angry behind them. They slowed down a little to give the hitch-hiker the impression they would stop.

Then they speeded up going even faster than before. They did not notice the camouflaged group of people in the bushes. The driver kept looking at the hitch-hiker in his mirror. "He's really mad," he told his companion, when all of a sudden an army truck came rolling out of the woods. The driver saw it too late and the co-driver screamed, "Stop!"His second scream was blurred by the loud bang of the hit when it plowed into the truck which had rolled onto the road.

Both soldiers were thrown forward against the windshield and passed out. The roaring engine was still spluttering and then there was total silence.

Out of the woods the men in camouflage dress and painted faces came running silently towards the back of the truck. They screamed to the men inside, "Stand back, we're going to shoot the lock open!"

Two shots coming from a hand gun with a silencer did the job. At that moment everything seemed to become totally silent, no voices, just the shuffling of feet could be heard. The twelve young Jewish men saw their comrades, their fellow Jews from Switzerland who had freed them.

Then Henk showed up at the scene. He had checked on the one soldier in his own truck, who was still alive and well but perhaps a little shaken from the collision. He had also checked on the two soldiers in the crashed truck and had found that the crash had unfortunately taken their life.

He reported his findings to the Jewish man who seemed to be the leader of the group.

"Sorry, but fine," was his short answer. "We need to go fast now sir!" He gestured at the others and the newly-rescued men. He took the lead and began to run toward the border, the same spot were a few hours earlier the seventeen young ladies had entered their freedom.

They ran at least one mile past the border when the leader stopped. Henk was exhausted and not in very good condition, having been in a stationary job at the Auschwitz clinic. He dropped on the ground and lay there prostrate in the grass, when a gentle hand stroked his neck. At first he began to feel angry, what man in his right mind would touch him like that at a time like this? There were only men around him when he had dropped. Then he heard a voice, a soft and sweet voice. With a shock of joy and surprise he tried to grasp his composure. He heard Hannah say, "You did it my darling, you sweet man. You saved twenty nine people today from a certain death. You are my hero."

She fell down next to him and kissed his face and stroked his back, and then... he passed out.

Chapter Thirty

FROM FARM TO FARM

—⁂—

C ornelius had climbed on top of the haystack and descended into the basement underneath.

He felt so free there at the farm and having the ability to see all his friends made all the ongoing war activities into nothing. Cornelius had learned a lot that day. He had learned to squeal like a pig, sow seeds and pick seeds from Marigolds. He had also learned about the threat when soldiers came to a farm and how one could make them into friends by being nice to the enemy.

When he opened the door of the basement they all greeted him happily. "Hi Cornelius! Are you having a good time here on the farm? We are jealous of you because you can be outside and play while we have to sit here and hardly get any fresh air." He was hugged by several of them and said, "I am having to go now. My dad and I have to go to two more farms before we can go back home and my mom is all by herself, except…. Well, you know."

He had almost told them about the friends under the floor but then he realized that they had been there themselves. "So I came to say goodbye to all of you. We will come back in a month, my dad said, and you might not be here anymore. So really, goodbye for always."

He had tears in his eyes and when he climbed up the ladder inside the haystack he had felt a knot in his stomach. Would he ever

155

see these people again? Would they get caught by the Germans some day? Or would they go to those camps in Germany? They were all questions which remained on his mind even when he said goodbye to the Brandwijk's and to Marie. He felt he had so many friends he could so easily lose forever.

Mrs. Brandwijk, this sweet motherly lady had given him another slice of bread and a little package with two boiled eggs in it. "For your mother, Cornelius. See? I did not forget." He laughed and blew her a kiss as his dad put his feet to the pedals and began to ride his bicycle.

Farmer Brandwijk was running in front of them and called to Kees, "Slow down, I want to open the gate for you!" Just as they arrived at the gate, the farmer had opened it so they could keep riding and take the road to the next farm and many other people they both knew.

The next town they had to go to was called Zoeterwoude. It was a beautiful village with farms spread-out along a river. The farm they were heading to was on the other side of the village, which meant that they would have to go through barricades and be subject to questions and possibly a search.

Cornelius knew what to do. His act of crying had become a fun task for him. He was getting really good at his way of creating a scene of diversion and irritation – it had become a routine.

When they entered the village the barricade was manned by more soldiers than usual and there were even Gestapo and NSB-ers there. Kees thought for a moment to turn around but that would be a clear sign for the soldiers who would immediately follow him and order him to come back.

Kees said to Cornelius, "Are you ready for an extra good act son?" Enthusiastically Cornelius replied, "Yes dad, I can do it really well."

The hated words sounded as nasty as ever, "Halt Ausweiss, Aufsteigen!" They did not even say "Bitte," Kees noticed. What was going on with all these people here? Kees stepped next to his bicycle but left Cornelius sitting in his seat.

The Nazis were really aggressive this time. With guns pointed at

Kees they commanded him to stick up his hands, but Kees was holding the bicycle with Cornelius on it. Kees said "Let me put the bicycle against the wall so I can do what you want me to." He walked over to the nearest wall, placed the bicycle against it and walked back to the barricade. Cornelius thought this was the right moment to begin his act because his dad was walking away from him. When he started to bawl all eyes were turned to him. A mother with two children came to him and started talking, trying to comfort him, but no one could.

Meanwhile, Kees was getting a third-degree interrogation. After a thorough frisking, they put their attention on his papers. Kees had free-reign to travel and he was not that far from his home. They were studying his Ausweiss. "Perhaps this is a fake one," he heard a soldier say to a sergeant. "We need to check his factory."

"Was machen wir mit den Jungen?" he heard another soldier say."Lass est mahl, Nein wir suchen einem Vertraeter." They were all discussing what they should do with him when a staff Mercedes came to a stop at the barricade and a Gestapo captain stepped out.

The soldiers went into attention and saluted. The captain walked over to Kees and looked at him intently and shook his head."Nicht Ihm," he said and with a wave of his hand he said, "Lass mahl Gehen."

Kees knew what that meant and began to walk away. After ten steps a voice called after him, "Du, Herr van Rijn." It sounded like Kees was called, so he turned around. The soldier was holding up his Auweiss and said, "Vergessen sie nicht etwas?"

When they were riding away safely on their bicycle Kees said softly under his breath, "Vervloekte Moffen," which means "Damn Krauts." It was an expression not customarily used by Kees. In his heart he was furious. He did not want to show that to his son so he looked for words to calm himself. Then he said, "Son, the Lord has brought us through hell again. You did a good job, praise the Lord."

His anger had subsided but not until he came to the other end of the town and through the barricade to exit.

The next farm they went to was fifteen miles away. Kees wanted

157

to avoid any other villages and barricades. They had lost so much time at every stop that it would be worthwhile to circumvent any other villages. Kees decided to follow the Ringvaart, a river heavily used for transportation of sand, dirt, gravel and farm supplies. Along the Ringvaart was a narrow path which was usually used for horses to pull the barks on the river. One person would lead the horse and a second person would steer the boat by its rudder

There was no village along the Ringvaart so there would be no barricades and road blocks. During the war, many horses had to be slaughtered for food so the number of pulling horses had been diminished drastically.

Kees was looking around and enjoyed nature. He loved the meadows and the fields, it made him think of the place he grew up called Oud Beierland. An occasional Orchard broke the flow of meadows. The usual number of cows had also diminished. The German occupation had cost the farmers a large number of their livestock. Kees pedaled along, gradually losing his anger.

His trip had been uneventful. Kees looked forward to sitting on a regular chair instead of on the painful saddle.

His work as a resistance fighter meant riding many kilometers every time he went on a trip. Still, after seven hours it became painful. Cornelius and Kees had sung together as they traveled and all seemed as if for a while there was no war.

The farm in Abbenes was owned by Gilles Verhaar, an older farmer who ran a mixed farm where he grew both vegetables and had livestock. The day Kees arrived was a day of happiness at the farm. A horse had birthed a foal and two cows had given him calves.

Kees and Cornelius were welcomed by the entire family and they had to see the new arrivals first.

"We have to hide the young animals because the Germans will take them so soon that they would be too young to be on their own. Besides, they would eat them as young animals which would be a shame.

Would you two help me bring these animals to a shack I have about a mile away in a Bramble site, where the Germans would never come, Kees?"

Cornelius thought this was the best adventure of his life, to guide the mothers and baby animals to a hiding place and to do that under a cover of darkness.

The attic of the shack they took the animals to was covered with hay, and nine Jewish guests were in hiding there for a period of time. Kees knew two of them and they greeted him with enthusiasm.

"Mr. van Rijn and Cornelius, they both said when they entered the building 'we have not seen you for so long.' Are you bringing more people or are you coming to pick us up?"

Kees shook his head. "No, today I am on a food stamp tour and I still have to go to one more place tomorrow before I can go back to The Hague. How have you been, are you going to introduce me to these other people?"

Introductions were made and Kees asked where they all had come from. "We are Jews from Amsterdam," said a man who introduced himself as Mordichai Rosen. "We all used to live in the Jordaan and the Germans chased us out of there before they sealed our neighborhood. We don't know what has happened to the others. I think they have all been taken away. The last I heard is that the Nazis had looted the whole area and stolen all our belongings."

Kees became very serious and invited them all to sit down in the hay and listen to him. "My dear friends," he began. "Most of you don't know me, two of you do. I am from the Resistance in The Hague and what I do is take care of fugitives by using my house as a central point for further transportation to the farms. You all know that from the farms many people are brought to the borders with Belgium and then led to Switzerland or Spain. Well that is going to change drastically. We have received most disturbing news from the concentration camps in Germany. Please hear me out and strengthen yourselves to hear the latest news."

It had become very silent in the attic of that small and rustic cow shack in the middle of a bramble bush, way out in the fields of the Haarlemmermeer. The peoples' eyes were watching every movement of Kees' lips and could not wait to hear what was going to be said.

"Your people – I'm sorry, *our* people of Jewish descent are all

159

being murdered in those so-called 'camps' in Germany. We now have reports from Birkenou, Auschwitz, Bergen Belsen and several more that they are systematically killing the people who arrive there, sometimes upon arrival and sometimes days or weeks later."

The silence was broken by muffled cries and gasps, and tears were rolling freely from the cheeks of men and women. At last, some one dared to interrupt the silence and asked the question, "How, and why?"

Kees could not answer the question and more people wanted answers. Kees did not know how to comfort the broken people, he was at a loss for words himself. Finally someone asked a question he was able to answer. "How and when will we be transported out of the country?"

Kees was relieved that he would be able to talk again and said, "It will be a long time before we can move any people. The danger of being caught is getter much greater. If you are safe where you are it will be better if you stay where you are. As long as the Nazis are frantically searching, you better stay put here."

"But this is no way to live and how are we going to get fed and how long will that be? Will there be any end to this situation?" Many were asking questions and many of them could not be answered.

Kees interrupted the many people who were asking questions at the same time. "As I said before, the Nazis have become too thorough to risk any transportations. As for food, I have brought a lot of food stamps and your guardian here will make sure you get fed. It may be for a short time, it could be for a long time, but at least you will stay alive. Please don't do anything which could jeopardize your hosts and your fellow fugitives here and at other farms. Lastly, pray a lot."

Kees got up and was walking to the ladder which led to the stable down below to join the farmer and his son. He walked the long mile through the wet grass, arriving at the farm house when it had become pitch dark.

The Jews in the shack were all talking to each other about the news which had hit them so severely.

They too were in total darkness. The clouds in the night sky would not let any moonlight or starlight through. They could not light a light themselves. The night was so pitch dark that they could only hear each other. They were all thinking about their relatives who had been taken away to the dreaded camps in Germany. Would they ever see each other again?

Chapter Thirty One

THE SOURCE OF RESISTANCE

—∼∽—

C or Brandwijk had found his calling in Amsterdam. He had heard of a resistance group under Gerrit Jan van der Veen, an ex-fire fighter, sculptor and really brave Hollander.

Gerrit had shown his courageousness and willingness to risk his life in exchange for any type of blow he could administer to the Nazis. The occupation had taken possession of all the public administration offices in the country. One of the largest was the Office for Labor in Amsterdam. Everyone in this country had been registered for slave labor in Germany. The Nazis could just go to their homes and pick them up.

"And the the Jews, they are in there too. We need to do something about that," he had said one day. It was good idea and it was do-able. "Let's put it on fire," he told his group of underground fighters. Cor Brandwijk had joined them and was in full agreement with the plan. This was what he had been looking for, a chance to give the Nazis something to think about.

They had prepared the plan real well. Gerrit, Cor and two others would pose as German inspectors who were going to report to the security entrance of the building and say that they needed to get inside to inspect security measures.

On February 11, 1943 they went into action. They were able to get inside, subdued and tied-up the night watch and began preparations to set the building on fire.

They had made one tiny mistake; the tied-up night watch was afraid of fire and did not want to burn to death. He was able to sound an alarm. German sentries ran to the building and found the perpetrators doing their destructive work. They called the Fire Brigade.

The little fire they had started did not do much damage but the group was able to escape.

The group of fighters began to make a better plan, one which could do even more harm to the Nazis.

On March 27, 1943, only seven weeks later, one of the most glorious and successful nights would occur for the Underground fighters. This time they had prepared themselves much better. Gerrit van der Veen and his group had rehearsed it many times.

They knew it would be dangerous but compared to the Office of Labor, it became small fries compared to their new target: The Administration Office of the Citizens of Amsterdam.

They know it will be a big one and that the building is secured by many soldiers. They also know that everyone who lives in Amsterdam is registered there. Not only those who would be able to work as slaves in the factories but also all of the Jewish population.

They take their time, because this will be a huge operation. Gerrit van der Veen and Willem Arondeus will dress themselves up as officers of the State Police.

Cor Brandwijk and six others will come as detectives of the police, dressed in civilian clothes.

Their first attempt failed. They could not bluff themselves inside and when an alarm had been triggered they all ran. Luckily no one was hurt and they all got away.

Then one day later, they show up with nine of them, and a huge dose of determination. They are in front of the building where two sentries are on-guard from the outside. They jump to attention when they see their superiors approaching.

Gerrit announces to the two sentries, "We have come to inspect this building, follow us right now." The two men follow obediently but once inside they are taken out of commission. The same happens to the two watchmen on the inside.

They administer all four an injection which will put them asleep for two hours. Two of the Resistance fighters take the uniforms of the sentries and take their positions outside. The other seven get to work. They make piles of the papers they had pulled from the drawers and pull over book racks and shelves made of wood. "They burn real well," Cor remarked as he dumped some more books on top of the pile.

They work really hard. They are all sweating. Was it from their hard work or from fear? No one said a word.

The two imposters outside were able to deviate other Germans away from the building. Automatic fuses and triggers are placed in the piles of fuel and out they go. But before they ignite the triggers, they pull the captives outside into the backyard of the building. Unfortunately, they did not bring them far enough outside and they were never found. When they were safely away from their target and to their hiding places the explosions began. The night sky turned red and the explosions kept sounding and could be heard throughout the entire city.

That evening became known to the entire population as one of the bravest occasions for the Resistance.

The fire fighters who came to fight the fire do a great job, they make sure that they do their work as slowly as possible and that the water they hose into the building finishes the job. Nothing is useable and the building gets completely destroyed.

The NSB-ers are put to work to find out who did the job. Soon the joy of success is replaced by tears. Many people were arrested, even a large number who had nothing to do with the attack.

The NSB-ers are promised rewards of thousands of Guilders. Gerrit van der Veen is able to escape the retributions and by sheer luck is able to leave the city just in time.

Three months later, fifteen men are brought to the Dunes in Scheveningen. The fire squad sounds upon a harsh command and seventeen brave people who had probably saved the lives of thousands of Jews and many other citizens drop to the ground on their way to heaven.

Gerrit van der Veen came back to the city and found Cor Brandwijk who had also escaped the wrath of the Nazis.

Chapter Thirty Two

THE HUNGER WINTER

—ww—

J ohanna was crying. She was cold and did not have any money for coal. She did not have any food in the house and there was no more firewood either. Kees had come home without any food except three big sugar beets.

It would take time to clean, grate and cook those sugar beets. It would not give them much food nutrients, but it did make some filler. Cornelius was begging her for milk. She did not have any. She could not buy any. "Mom, please give me some milk," he would ask every ten minutes. What could she do? Desperation was getting on her. Thank God the three other children were away at the farms. Kees was at work at the factory. "Mom, I am hungry, I am so hungry I can eat a newspaper." Cornelius was begging her for food again and again.

She had to find a solution tonight. When Kees came home she would talk to him and send him on a search for food and for anything that could heat their house.

It was early winter in 1943. The German command had made a plan. Their planning was to root-out the hidden Jews and to find the "onderduikers" (people in hiding). They had calculated that there must be at least forty thousand Jews out there. They had to be found. If they would tighten the food supply they would either die or come in to the open. The citizens would also starve so they would give up

167

the ones who were in hiding. In theory, it would work, but they did not know the determination of the Dutch.

The Hollanders were inventive, they would get through this hunger winter somehow or another. The first thing the Nazis had done was to cut off the fuel supply. Every house in the Netherlands was heated with one or more potbelly stoves. Every oven, if they had one, was heated with coal. There were no water heaters, so water was heated on the stoves. They could not wash with hot water, or bathe with hot water. They could not even cook on their potbelly stoves.

A general desperation had set in, but the Dutch would find ways!

The curfew at night prohibited anyone from being outside after seven p.m. Nightlife had become non-existent. However, there were more people outside at night in the pitch dark than the Germans would ever know. The nights were for scavenging, for barter and for raids.

In order to keep themselves alive the Dutch were cutting trees, breaking down wood fences, shacks – anything made of wood. They went into the bombed houses and ripped out planks and beams for fuel. They did not have chain saws, nor could they use hammers. The Nazis would hear their hammering, and because they would break curfew the scavengers would be arrested.

The Dutch found ways to survive, sometimes in great dangers, often spending a night in jail for theft and scavenging. The Resistance became stronger by the day. "This can't go on forever," they said. "We will have to get these Germans to become scared of us."

In the Canals through Amsterdam, hundreds of German soldiers were drowned. The *Knok ploegen* would grab any soldier, knock him out and dump him in the canals. Every night half a dozen soldiers disappeared into the canals. The Germans began to be afraid to be outside in the evenings. They began to patrol more on motorcycles and in groups of four when they walked through the streets of Amsterdam. The *knok ploegen* did not relent. They came in larger gangs if they had to.

The Germans began to shoot before they called out their infamous words, "Halt Ausweiss." Many Dutch citizens who were just out to find food or fuel were shot because the soldiers mistakenly thought they were from the *Knok ploegen.*

In the other cities the Resistance flourished too. Each city had its own methods of fighting back and scaring the Germans.

The German command in The Hague issued more orders, more commands to shoot and more commands to cut down on the food supplies for the citizens.

In all the cities the hunger became so severe that people were found dead in the streets. Daily, the NSB-ers had to go out with the soldiers to pick up the corpses. At first they were the elderly and those living alone, people with handicaps and those who could barely walk. Then there were children who had lost their parents.

Interestingly, the Jews were spared from that lot because they were often in basements where the cold was bearable or they had been transported to the farms where food was still available in some degree and where the farmers had fuel in the form of dried-up cow dung.

God's chosen people were protected in some measure. The trains to the destructive camps were less loaded. The jails were now filled with people from the Resistance, fighters who had gotten caught.

Many churches had begun to serve soup for anyone who would come to their daily soup kitchens. Often the Germans came and demanded the first batch of soup, under protest of the waiting citizens the Nazis would shove the people aside and filled their pots and pans with the soup. Several times the hungry citizens could not keep their temper. The soldiers could be very dangerous at times, particularly when people began scolding them.

In the church on the Goeverneurlaan in The Hague the pastor was helping the people .He himself filled the soup canisters the people were bringing. He was a stout and courageous man. He always had an encouraging word for everyone.

One day during the winter of 1944, the pastor had been scooping soup for at least an hour. The huge cooking pots were beginning to show the bottoms. A lot of commotion made him look up from his task. Three soldiers were pushing his people aside so they could get to the front of the line. The pastor saw what was happening and walked over to the three soldiers. In a friendly tone of voice he told the soldiers that if they did not stay in line, he would refuse them any soup.

"You are just as any of these people," he said, "and God loves them as much as he does you. So please wait your turn or I will refuse you any soup at all." The soldier he had spoken to turned to the others. One of them turned around and slapped the pastor in his face. The incident could have stopped right there but when one of the church members saw what was happening he jumped in front of the soldier and said, "You do that to me if you dare."

The soldier reacted like a little boy and slapped the man twice. When the pastor intervened things were getting out of hand. Others joined in the fight, which until then had been a fist-fight. Suddenly a shot sounded and the pastor fell dead on the ground. All the parishioners who were waiting for their soup joined together, disarmed the soldiers and attacked them by stabbing them repeatedly with their knives. They clobbered them with their pots and pans until the three were dead on the street.

The soldiers were left dead on the street; the people took the Pastor inside the church. Two hours after the incident, the church was set a fire by the Nazis. Several church members had been locked inside the church and were burned alive.

Hunger had taken its toll in ways other than hunger itself. The toll was much higher than the value of the soup. The pride of the Dutch was much greater than their respect for the enemy.

From that day the Germans never joined the soup lines, a command from Rauter was given to avoid the soup kichens. Sometimes during the war even the Nazis had come to their senses.

Chapter Thirty Three

THE DUTCH AND THE DUTCH JEWS

—ɷ—

I n the Netherlands, that little watery country which is at some places as much as seven yards below sea level, Jews have been a major part of the population. They had been there for centuries and they were real Dutch. Ask any Dutchman if he knows any Jews, and he might say, "What do you mean," or "who do you mean? I only know Dutch people."

So much were Jews part of the population that no one knew who was Jewish or who was not.

So when the Germans came, their first goal was to separate the Dutch from Jews and non Jews which was not easy because no one had told them the German's motive. When the Nazis sent everyone a questionnaire to fill out and return, many people began to refuse to participate.

Why would they tell the Germans if they were Aryans or Jews anyway? They were all Dutch that was all that mattered. Many non-thinking Dutch filled the questionnaire out and lots of Jews did too, not knowing what the Germans would use their information for.

Even when, as a result of their own information, they had been given the command to wear the Star of David the Jewish and the Dutch participated. Some Jews were proud to be wearing the badge, who would not be proud of their own origin?

The occupying Nazis had their program and followed it accu-

171

rately as much as the citizens were co-operating. The separation was planned and happening.

Every Dutchman who declared that he was not Jewish was unknowingly helping the Nazis.

The family of Silverschmidt, for instance, lived close by Cornelius. They had two pretty daughters with whom he played in the street. They were twins and real cute. Cornelius walked with them to the children's choir on Saturdays and he loved the girls. Their pretty dresses and their little white socks and black lacquer shoes stood out and attracted him so much. They had never told him they were Jewish until then. All of a sudden they came living underneath his floor and were hiding from the Germans together with their father and mother.

Cornelius could not understand why pretty girls like that would have to be hiding from the Germans or why they could be transported to a camp, even get killed there as his father Kees had explained one day. He only spoke about Jews when he read the Bible and he respected the Jews because they were God's chosen people, he always said.

Cornelius went to the girls' home one day to ask if they would like to play outside. They did not want to come to the door. When Cornelius went inside the house the girls were crying. Their mother had sewed a big yellow star on their pretty dresses and jackets. They did not understand why they had to wear that ugly star and did not want to go outside with them.

From then on Cornelius went to play inside with them, until they moved in with him beneath the floor.

The Nazis kept coming up with ways to make life unbearable for the Jewish population. One day General Mussert had sent his crooks into the streets of the cities just to harass the Jews.

Armed with sticks and chains the criminals went into the cafés and restaurants and attacked the Jews who were present , forcing them to leave. They beat the owners up if they would not place a sign reading, *"No Jews allowed"* in their windows. Many nasty fights occurred and many citizens were arrested.

For weeks the German-induced riots went on. The Nazis even

stopped the streetcars and forced the Jewish to get off. Windows of Jewish homes and Jewish shops were broken with bricks wrapped in papers which said *"Verdamte Jude."*

The citizens did not accept the cruelty and harassment of the Jews. During the Razzias ,some called them pogroms. The German trucks would drive into a neighborhood, men were grabbed from their beds, and they were hit and kicked and loaded into the trucks. Children were grabbed from their mother's arms and pushed onto the trucks and if they held on to their father, the Nazis would hit them with the butt of their gun. The city became so angry that "we won't take this any longer" became the general consensus.

The working class came together and decided to use the only weapon they knew how to use. A city-wide strike was announced. Unfortunately, the leaders of the strike were Communists.

The general strike spread to other cities and towns and within days the entire country was brought to an economic halt. The Slogan of all people and the purpose of the strike was "Keep your hand off our Jews." Everyone took to the streets huge crowds filled the streets of the cities. The Germans stayed away for a while. They would not be safe on the streets, even with their guns. In the end they would be clobbered to death by the crowd which became more angry by the hour. The crowds were able to refute the Germans openly, the strike had become the mighty expression of power without German interference. The strike became known as one of the biggest protests of the war, a protest by all the Hollanders against the Nazis, the people-hunters, and in favor of the Jews.

It took the Germans days to come out with a counter-attack on the crowds, something which would hurt the entire population.

Germans would ride tanks directly into the crowds killing hundreds. They would brutally roll their tanks over the people, destroying their bodies. The crowds diffused and the strike ended.

These massacreing actions woke up many citizens and many went into the underground .Thousands opened their homes for the Jews and those of the Resistance who were sought by the Nazis.

People came into harmony, a harmony which oppression creates, and with one accord all Dutch began to think the same. They thought the same and began to act and talk the same. "They will never win," everyone proclaimed.

Everyone except for the NSB-ers. Those who sympathized with the Germans for personal gain had to become more secretive and became even more traitorous. They were promised higher rewards for the arrest of Resistance fighters and Jews.

Hundreds of the Resistance were thrown into the jails. Three of the Resistance leaders were shot to death at a public place. The NSB-ers received their Judas rewards. Below, a receipt which was given by the Germans for each person they betrayed.

Der Befehlshaber der .... am
Sicherheitspolizei und des SD
für die besetzten nied. Gebiete

Aussenstelle:.....................

Q u i t t u n g

Dem niederl. Staatsangehörigen...

geb. am .... in......................wurde eine Belohnung in
Höhe von
.... hfl.

ausgezahlt, weil er den Fluchtjuden (Strafjuden)...........................

geb. am.............. in .... zuletzt wohnhaft in
.............................der deutschen Sicherheitspolizei über-
gab, so dass eine Festnahme erfolgen konnte.

....

(Name und Dienstgrad)

A receipt which read: "Receipt, The Dutch Citizen (name) Born on (date) in (city) is herewith paid a reward in the amount of (xxx) for bringing information to the German security service which led to the arrest of aflight Jew,(convicted Jew) by the name of (so and so) Signed by......... (Name and rank)"

On Sunday the van Rijn family went to church just one kilometer away. When they came close to the church they noticed a number of German Trucks parked close to the church. Kees did not suspect that anything could happen while they were in church. The church service was in a community building which had a stage with a curtain in front of it. Behind the curtain was a baptismal font which could be opened with a hatch in the stage floor.

The water had been drained from the baptismal font just because it would get dirty if it was not used every week. Algae would grow in it. Not many babies were born during the war and likewise not many baptisms were held.

No sooner had the service began than a loud noise was heard and some sixty soldiers marched into the church. People panicked because there was absolutely no way out. The soldiers took every man of eighteen years-of-age and older. The Arbeit Einsatz had taken its toll before when any workable men had been picked up from all the streets in the city. The Germans worked systematically to keep any man from resisting them by taking their time of day and putting them to work in the war industry. After a thorough inspection of the men present and their Ausweiss checked, more than twenty seven men were taken out of the sanctuary.

Kees had done the collection just half a minute before the soldiers entered the church. He had taken the money to a back room together with three female deacons. They were sitting at a table counting the money. When Kees had heard the noise of the disturbing group of Germans he had quickly hid himself in a closet. Minutes later three soldiers entered the room where the money was being counted. The three girls looked up and made a shriek when they saw the soldiers. The soldiers looked around the room and shook their heads. "Nothing here," one of them said. Before he turned around to leave the room he grabbed a big handful of the money. The oldest deacon yelled, "That is God's money sir! Do you think you will be blessed by that?" Madly he threw the money on the floor and they all left.

When Kees came out of the closet he was shocked and pale. "Do you think the Lord is protecting me?" he asked with a shaking voice. The three ladies nodded, and one of them said, "You must have a special task to fulfill, Kees."

The Germans had left the building, the church service was resumed and from then on the workable men were listening to the sermon down in the basement with the baptismal hatch wide open behind the curtains.

That afternoon no men were walking home from the church. The van Rijn family had added a woman to their walk home. Kees had changed and was now clad in a skirt with nylons and a shawl over his head.

Even though he already worked for the Arbeitz Einsatz, he knew they would re-assign him if he had been caught. At the present time he had lots of work to finish.

At the van Rijn residence, a surprise was waiting for the family. When they entered the house, they walked into a wall of smoke. The sugar beets Johanna had grated and had put in a large pot on the potbelly stove in the living room had boiled over. The syrup had run on the stove which in turn had began to burn and smoke. The smell of it was atrocious, they all gagged. Kees opened the back door to air out the curtain of smoke.

The sugar beets were the only food they had in the house that day. Their next issue of food would be on Monday. Johanna would have to stand in line at the gymnasium of the school and hope there would be enough food left when her turn came. She had food stamps for six people. In reality she had used the food stamps up more than a week before. She went to every food distribution center with the same number of food stamps. After all, she had to get food for twenty six people. It was always a scary moment to give the NSB-er in charge her forged food stamps but they never noticed anything illegal.

Johanna carefully dressed herself each time as different as possible in order to not be recognized. She avoided talking when she was waiting in line or with the people who issued the food. Better safe than sorry, she had determined. The food supply had been cut back deliberately by the Germans. They had determined that in order to starve the Dutch population they systematically had to lower the calorie intake. It had begun after the great strike. As a retribution, the Germans had announced that no one would be able to get more than twelve hundred calories per day. That was not enough to live on, but it wouldn't be fatal either.

Many civil servants had secretly created additional food supplies but the supply gradually diminished and the extra stock dwindled quickly. Two months later the daily supply had gone down to five hundred and fifty calories per day for a person.

After two more months only three hundred and forty calories per day were allowed and then two hundred and thirty. After that, the food supply was gone. There was literally nothing available.

The Germans never won the war, because the Dutch were invincible. The hunger was their last attack and even that they could not win. Cornelius, Kees and Johanna were very inventive.

Mother Johanna made pancakes out of grated sugar beets. She made syrup out of the same batches of beets and Kees made suckers out of the syrup. Cornelius found a continual supply of pigeon eggs He had talked to the Pigeon breeder who lived above their home on the third floor. Cornelius had asked the man all kinds of questions like, "How often a pigeon does lay its eggs?" He found out that as long as the bird has one egg in its nest it will keep laying eggs.

So next door on the roof of the Groenendijk warehouse was a ridge on both sides and hundreds of pigeons nestled there on that ridge. Cornelius had stumbled on the ridge of bird nests when he had gone on top of the roof to play and also to peek into the tiny toilet where the pig lived. He had seen the eggs and taken some to the pigeon breeder upstairs. "Yes my boy," the man said, "you can certainly eat these provided you get them out of the nests on time. You must go there every day, always leaving one egg in the nest. You must also mark each egg so it never gets older than three days. If the egg is in the nest longer than three days, the baby bird will start to form and then you can't eat it anymore."

Cornelius had gone to work systematically. He had taken a pencil and while he removed the eggs out of all the nests he had made a mark near the nest so he knew when he had taken all the eggs out of the nests. The eggs he had removed were thrown away on the advice of the Pigeon breeder who had said that most of them would not be good.

The next day Cornelius had gone back on the roof and had found eight new eggs in the nests. Carefully he made a little mark on each of them. When he came downstairs and into him Mom's kitchen, he announced, "From now on we will have at least two eggs for each of

us every day." Johanna had laughed, "Boy you have a great imagi-
nation. How do you get that into your head? Is the hunger affecting
your brain already?"

Cornelius had laughed too, but he knew more than Johanna
needed to know at that time. "You wait and see Mom," he said and
walked away to go visit the guests downstairs.

They were hungry too, but they had just received the news from
Kees that five of them were going to be picked up for transport, the
news had been received with great joy for those who were leaving
and with sadness for those who had to stay. Kees had not announced
in what way they were going to leave, only who and that they would
have to be ready at five o'clock in the morning.

Kees had received a message an hour before that an ambulance
would be there at the Deiman Straat at five the next morning. Because of the dwindling food supply the number of Jews who should
be moved out of the cities had to increase and sped up.

Cornelius sat down with the Jewish friends and reflected on the
pending departure. Odd, he thought, that the two pretty girls and her
parents stayed and the old people went to leave first. He determined
to ask his dad why that was. He loved the little girls but that could
not be the reason why they stayed.

They had come before the ones who were to leave. Was that an
honest decision?

The people who were going to leave were very excited; they
were talking loudly when the alarm board cracked. Within half a
minute they were behind the concrete wall they had taken Cornelius
along. There would not be enough time for him to go upstairs or he
might betray the hiding place.

They were all listening intensely, and then a shot broke the silence, then another shot and a third. They could not hear what was
going on upstairs except that they knew that there must be Germans
in the house upstairs.

Kees was in discussion with the three soldiers who had demanded to enter the house. "Why have you come here?" he asked. "We
are no Jews and I work in the Arbeits Einsatz here in The Hague."
They had told him that they had received information that he had

Jews in hiding in his house. Kees denied that and proposed that they look around. "We have no room for anybody here in this little house, please see for yourself." The shots the soldiers had fired had been aimed at a wall where they had suspected there could be a double wall, but no sound had followed the shots. One of the soldiers walked over to the wall and began knocking on it. It sounded hollow so he raised his gun and shot through the wall five more times.

If anyone would be in there he would have heard a scream, he reasoned. He stuck his finger into one of the holes when suddenly a part of the wall gave way, opening the wall section. Kees had not even been aware of a double wall at that spot but when the soldier pulled it open he saw what was behind it. All the pipes going to the upstairs apartments were hidden behind the wall and one of those pipes was gushing water in between the space.

It was enough damage for the soldiers. They left for a third time in two months without finding their prey.

"Those NSB-ers in the neighborhood must have seen or heard something," Kees said to a pale Johanna.

He walked to the hallway and pressed the cracking board twice, saying, "Is Cornelius down there with them?" Johanna nodded and looked at him. "When will there be an end to this crazy war?" she pleaded. "We can never survive with all these problems. Soon we will not be able to get any more food. Little Cornelius is becoming weird too. Today he announced that we will have two eggs a day each starting tomorrow. Is he getting sick and delirious?" Then with her head against his shoulder she began to cry." We need to get the Jews out of here soon. I don't want them to die here from malnutrition. Then we will be guilty of their deaths, but we can't let them down either. Oh what can we do Kees?"

That kind of desperation was heard throughout the provinces of Holland, a despair which even had led people to suicide. Kees had made a decision, his family would not starve, no matter what he had to do.

A day later he had thought of a solution, and so had his son.

Kees went into his shack in the backyard, where he found small pieces of board which he had saved from the potbelly stoves. He constructed a box of the same size as the seat Cornelius sat on at the back of his bicycle. The box was big enough to contain ten pounds of potatoes or a twenty five pound bag of flour. Then he took some soft cloth and covered the seat putting in some filler from an old pillow inside. Then he reconstructed the seat which was on the bicycle, taking off the regular seat but leaving the feet rests and the back rest intact.

He re-attached the whole assembly to his bike. Now he had a secret container on his bike and with Cornelius sitting on top of it, no one would ever suspect it.

Kees intended to try it out that very day. He called Cornelius and lifted him into the seat. "We are going to make a surprise visit to the Brandwijk farm today," he told his son. "We need food my boy, don't you agree?"

"But Dad, I have to first go get some eggs. I have to, please get me off the bike." Kees did not understand what the little boy was talking about but he was curious to find out. Cornelius was lifted off his special seat and ran to the backyard. He climbed on the fence, then on to the ledge and went up on the roof. This would be his first day of harvesting pigeon eggs , he would not want to miss it for any trip. This had to be done on the scheduled time or he would have to throw them away again and start all over

He found lots of eggs that day. In eight nests he found just one egg. He had learned to leave one egg in the nest so he marked them. In seven other nests he found two eggs. He danced from excitement. His mom and dad would be so surprised! He had forgotten one little detail: how was he going to get them down? He needed a small bucket on a rope or something. Cornelius went down the same way, the ledge, the fence and a jump onto the patio. His mom saw him coming and looked at him expectantly. "Not yet Mom," he said. "I need a bucket and a rope." She let him find it by himself and he quickly tied the rope to the handle, stuck the other end of the rope in his belt and climbed back on the roof again. Just minutes later he had pulled up the bucket, put the eggs in it and lowered it down to the patio where an astonished Johanna and his dad were looking in the bucket to see seven pigeon eggs. "Well, I'll be," yelled Kees.

"Quiet," said Johanna.

"Let's keep this our secret," said Cornelius. "From now on I'll have some every day."

They were small, those pigeon eggs, but they were nutritious!

Cornelius had more plans to help feed his family and his Jewish friends!

The road to the Brandwijk farm was not easy that morning. They had to pass several road blocks, or "Versperrungen," as the Germans called them. Kees was frisked every time. He had his Ausweiss and his travel pass ready but each time he was questioned as to why he was riding his bike.

Cornelius was allowed to stay on the bicycle every time which gave Kees some assurance that his hidden secret storage was going to work. Cornelius had to cry only one time when Kees had given him the sign to do so. Every time an inspection was becoming awkward Kees would give Cornelius a sign by scratching on his nose with his left hand. Cornelius was very alert when his father was inspected because he knew trouble could be occurring any moment.

When they arrived at the Brandwijk farm he found a surprised family. They always loved to see Kees because he always brought them some news or some documents.

After an exchange of hugs and friendly greetings they all went into the farmhouse. "What brings you to our humble farm today Kees?" the farmer asked at last. "We need something to eat, my friends, and we cannot get any more food in the city. We are moving five of our guests tomorrow for the same reason. I still have fourteen people under my floor. That makes seventeen hungry bellies in total every day. Is there anything you could supply? I would have to come almost every two days because I can only carry and hide a small amount. People are dying by the hundreds in the streets of The Hague. I have decided not to allow that to happen to my family or my guests.

The Brandwijk's agreed with Kees' statement. They knew what Kees believed, he had often quoted a verse to them from the Bible, "As for me and my house we will serve the Lord, and whoever serves the Lord will not perish, not by the sword nor by famine," Kees had always added.

They discussed what he could take. "We have just gone to the miller with five sacks of grain. The flour is wheat flower which makes great bread, provided you can put some eggs in it. So we we'll give you a bag of flour and six eggs today. If you come back tomorrow or the day after you can fill your container with potatoes and some brussel sprouts. After that we will see what we can do.

The Germans have not been back here to raid and plunder our farm since we feed a few of them every few days. They have become very friendly because of that. Sometimes we make interesting conversations. Most of those Germans have families too and practically all of them want to go back home. They too disagree with this war but they are forced into it, just like we are.

Meanwhile Cornelius was roaming the farm, who was working in the garden behind the Brambles. "Marie," he had said, "I need more lessons in sowing seeds and picking the seeds from the plants, can you help me please?" Marie had raised her eyebrows, wondering what he was up to. "I want to begin growing vegetables in our back yard in The Hague My mom said I can do what I want there. The Germans hardly ever come there and if I have seed I can grow something for our Jewish friends." That is a good idea Cornelius, I think we could find some lettuce seed right now, a few plants here have grown too long and then you can't eat them anymore because they taste bitter. Here, let's look at them and see if the seeds are ripe. Every plant has different ways and times to make seed , yes our lettuce will give us some." She showed him how to pick the little seed pots and told him that he had to dry them for a week or so and then the tiny black seeds would come out by themselves.

"There are some other ways to grow food and we are just at the right time to help you with that too. All cabbage plants have to be sown in our little hot beds under glass. We are about to plant them in our little beds. If you will help me, I will show you but we must first prepare the soil. Remember how we do that?" Cornelius did, he picked up the rake and began to rake the soil.

"Wait a minute," said Marie. "You have to first pull out the weeds and some other stuff, make it clean first then you can rake. Together they prepared the patch of soil and then Marie planted the different types of cabbage seedling. "The reddish ones are red cabbage and the green ones will become green cabbage. There are different kinds of green ones they are cauliflower, you can see the difference in the shape of leaves, they are a little rounder."

Together they had planted six long rows of the different seedlings. It looked real nice. Then Cornelius saw all the leftover seedlings and said, "So you won't be needing those there?"

They packed a bundle of twenty plants of each kind with a little rope around it. Three bundles of twenty plants, sixty in total. That would be a lot of cabbage and cauliflower. Cornelius could not wait to get his plants planted in the backyard of his city home.

"When are they ready to eat?" he asked, his anxiety clearly showing. "Will I have some cabbage at Christmas?"

"No you silly boy. It will take until the spring before the cabbages appear, it does not grow like the spinach we sowed the other day. "They went home that day in a happy mood. Flower and eggs were hidden underneath the seat on which Cornelius sat, under his shirt and jacket he had sixty cabbage plants and a bag of lettuce seed was in his pocket. Marie told him when he could sow lettuce and how. If he could find an old window he could make a hot bed. When he sowed the lettuce in that, they could be eating lettuce in February. Without the hot bed he could not sow it until the end of March. Cornelius was determined to find an old window and build the hotbed.

The road blocks were easy this time, going into the city was usually easier than leaving it. Yet they were stopped several times. That sort of tension would never cease until the war would be over.

Cornelius could not wait to get to work in his garden, the minute he walked into the house he ran to the backyard and found a rake and started. It was heavy labor, and in the late afternoon of fall he was sweating. His mother called him, "Corrie, I have something to drink for you, what on earth are you doing?"

"Mom, I am going to make sure we will have plenty of vegetables In March next year and I will have Lettuce in January."

"But my dear boy, where did you learn all about that?"

"I have had a lesson from Marie Brandwijk today and now I

know how to do that. Next spring I am also going to grow Marigolds and Tulips," Cornelius said proudly.

Johanna pushed her tears back. She did not want to show her son how moved she was. What had this war all come to, with four year-old children growing gardens and inventing ways to supply food, even eggs.

Chapter Thirty Four

THE JEWISH COUNCIL

—⚍—

"The Final Solution," as the Germans called it, was targeted to annihilate all the Jews in Europe. They had planned this as early as 1932. The system was, that in every country a Jewish council was erected with members of the highest elite in the Jewish community. When the Nazis occupied Holland they had experience in setting up the Jewish Council.

It was the biggest deception because all the Jews looked up to the members of the Council. The Council would issue communiqués to the Jewish community telling them to follow the Nazi commands and orders carefully, not to offend them – in short, to "do what they say."

The Council was given some measure of authority but that was only a formality. As a result, Jewish people who received a letter to be at a certain place with their entire family to be deported duly came like lambs being brought to the slaughter house.

They went with great expectations, waited for hours and were loaded up in cattle trains. Destination: death camp.

In 1941 the Jewish Council was already functioning. The president was a diamond dealer by the name of Abraham Asscher; his vice president was a professor of history, David Cohen.

In addition, twenty others were given the "privilege" to become members of the Council. All of them were only there to save their own hide and they knew it in their hearts. Their constant urging to follow the German rules punctually caused almost one hundred thousand Dutch Jews to be killed in the death camps of Auschwitz, Birkenau and other camps.

They reasoned that disobedience to Nazi rule would lead to harsher action. Could anything be harsher than death by gas chamber?

The Council even published the Nazi rules and regulations in their official magazine, thus playing right into the hand of the German plans. They tried to keep some Jews from the deportation list by picking out the names of more prominent Jews who were willing to pay for the services of the Jewish Council.

The Star of David had been used as far back as the eighteenth century. Therefore, when the Germans introduced their system of recognizing the Jews with the yellow star on a piece of cloth, the Jewish Council saw it as an honor to distribute it to their members throughout the entire country. The Nazis did not give them much time lest they would begin to question the measure. They had three days to cover all their members with a supply of the yellow Star of David. It was short notice but the Jewish Council managed it. Their authority and determination to make all Jews safe with the measure was undertaken like a coup de grace. They even made the people pay for the piece of cloth, four pieces were sent per person over the age of four years and they received them on time. The Germans had set a final date or they would start arresting those without the Star. Ironically that was their goal after all.

The official, and authorized by the Germans, press began to justify the measure. One of them reported, "It looks like a field of buttercups out there."Other papers called it "collaborating with the enemy." The Dutch population reacted differently. You would see Dutch people tip their hat when they would see the Star and others even began to wear the Star as well. Some papers complained that certain Jews were just pinning the Star to their jacket so they could remove it quickly when they needed to. The Nazis made an announcement that the Star would have to be sewed on and if not, they threatened them with immediate arrests. The so-called "Final

Solution" was getting closer to its finalization with the help of the victims themselves.

Alas in the end, the entire Council was also deported including Asscher and Cohen. Thus the Jewish Council had been dismantled. During the deportations Professor Cohen came to the railway station to see his fellow Jews off. On that day fifty five hundred Jews had been deported.

Professor Cohen was later deported to Camp Theresien Stadt and by some miracle he came back to Amsterdam after the war. He got away from the death camps, but in 1947, the newly-erected Jewish Honor Council stripped him from any function he could hold in the Jewish community. His buddy Asscher was murdered in one of the Nazi gas chambers.

Despite the advice of the Jewish council and against their wishes, many Dutch citizens hid Jews until the end of the war. Kees and Johanna van Rijn were able to save many and so did lots of other Dutch non-Jews.

Chapter Thirty Five

A DANGEROUS MONK

—⟋⟍—

Kees van Rijn was often called to help prisoners in the prison of The Hague. The people called it "Het Oranje Hotel, the Hotel of the House of Orange. They were faithful to the Queen of Holland, those who were imprisoned there. The queen was from the House of Orange.

Kees had been asked to visit people in the prison. The Nazis thought that Kees would make them soft for their interrogation. On the contrary, in reality Kees prayed with them to receive strength during the torturous interrogations, often lasting as long as twenty four hours without water or food and being deprived of sleep. The interrogations were mainly directed to force names of co-workers in the Resistance out of the prisoners. They succeeded sometimes. But the Nazis under-estimated the stubborn Dutch who, once they had been caught, could and would count on being shot quickly, even if they would reveal names.

This time Kees was asked to visit a Monk by the name of Titus Brandsma. "Just a Monk who is talking against The Reich," they had said. "Please bring him to his senses.

"The Nazis had picked him up in the city of Nijmegen by just knocking on the doors of the monastery. The Monk opened the door and the five soldiers who had been sent to arrest him did not even draw their guns. The Monk was never armed, anyway.

189

They had taken him to The Hague by train and had dropped him off at the dreadful gates of the Oranje Hotel. The first day of interrogations had delivered nothing. The Gestapo interrogators had promised him he would have to stay only one day. Tomorrow, he would be able to go home.

When Kees made his visit to the Monk he only prayed for strength and wisdom. Kees had to be careful what he said because the Nazis could be listening. When he began to advise the Monk he winked at him and said the word "Graag," meaning he was from the Resistance and would not mean a word he was saying as he went on. "Mr. Brandsma, please answer the question truthfully and this ordeal will be over quickly. There is not much to hide from you, they know everything, wink, wink." Please do what I say and you will be appreciated by the Germans, you'll see." Wink, wink.

The Monk Titus Brandsma had been one of those advocates who would not allow the untruthful propaganda of the enemy to be accepted by the Dutch. In addition he had defended the position of his church against the aggressors. Was that a crime? The skinny, tiny Monk did not think so.

When the Germans told him he would have to stay only one day, they must have thought that this little skinny guy could be broken in minutes.

The defenseless Monk was dangerous in the eyes of the Nazis because of his words and the truth he preached. He would obey God before he would the Germans. This man would say no to anything that would be against his conscience. He would tell that everywhere he could. He would openly tell his listeners to say no as well. The Nazi and Gestapo interrogators underestimated this stubborn Dutchman. He was dangerous with his words. He would never be free again.

The Monk had travelled all over the country preaching his truth and it was not what the Nazis appreciated. On the contrary, this was outright resistance and instigation of the population and it had to end.

Kees had done what he could as a Christian; the rest was up to God who would give this Monk the power to resist the enemy. He was shipped to the Death camp of Dachau, where he was once again tortured and humiliated. He arrived there and received the number 30492, which was tattooed on his arm. He had only a few weeks to live and he knew it and regarded his pending death as a reward for his resistance.

Titus Brandsma went through the camp as a shepherd, comforting people and telling them that their redemption would be close and it would be a reward for their labors against The Reich.

He died in the camp from hunger and from the hundreds of wounds he had received through his continual torture. In his will, he had requested to be buried in his Monk's robe. The Germans did not care about anyone's last will, and they burned him in their incinerators, dropping his ashes in a deep hole dug by the laborers he had ministered to until the last day he lived.

A stone marks the place now called, "The Grave of Thousands of Unknown."

Kees rode his bicycle home, crying out in his heart to God. "How long Lord can we resist this madness?" He received an answer from God too, "I have always delivered my people, haven't I."

Kees pondered the answer for weeks after that.

"The Jews below were getting a treat that day. There were fifteen people left and Cornelius had gathered fifteen pigeon eggs. His mother had baked bread with the flour from the Brandwijk farm. It smelled so good that Cornelius was excited to bring the treat downstairs. They had boiled the pigeon eggs. They were small but very tasty he had approvingly said. It was close to the Jewish holiday of Hanukkah.

He had the tray with thirty slices of bread, the eggs in the center, ready to bring down stairs when the doorbell rang. The regular routine was immediately performed: the crack board was first then a minute of waiting as the people down below did their routine. Then they went slowly to the door and juggled with the four latches which had been installed solely for delays. Johanna finally opened the door with a smile and the two men who had interrogated her in the library pushed themselves into the house. Johanna backed up a little but not further than the door to the "Mooie Kamer," or "pretty

191

room," which they only used for visitors. The men took the hint and sat down at the table without being asked.

Meanwhile Cornelius was busy hiding the sandwiches and the eggs he had so carefully arranged on the tray to surprise the friends below for their celebration of Hanukkah.

"We wanted to come back to see you about the Jewish books you took from the library two weeks ago. Where are they, can we see them?" One of them began. It was a trick! Johanna kept her composure because she had taken them upstairs just a couple of days before. "Sure," she said. "I have them right here in this closet. I was planning to bring them back soon, is there anything wrong with that?"

The two men looked at each other. This was not what they had expected. They had hoped she would have panicked and would have to go look for them in a hiding place they had never been able to find in the van Rijn residence. They tried another way. "Have you made a report on this study you have been doing with these books?" Another trick, Johanna thought, but she was prepared for this one too. She had made some remarks and notes about the contents, some page numbers and names and had deliberately left them in one of the books. "Here," she said as she opened the wrong book to find them. She leafed through the book and played a dummy, knowing the papers were in the other book. "Oh, they must be in the other book," she said as she put the first one down. Wrong hunch, she could almost see the Gestapo men thinking, "We are wasting our time." Johanna had found the notes and handed them to the men.

They left. "Hope this was the last time of their search about these blasted books," Johanna said, sighing. She was becoming more careful and suspicious by the day.

Cornelius had finally delivered his tray with the treat for his friends down below. He asked them what Hanukkah meant, and they explained it. Cornelius asked, "Are you looking forward to celebrating Hanukkah in your own country?"

His dad had explained to him that all the Jews were praying to go to Israel and live in their own country and that that was the reason they all wanted to go there, particularly now that the Nazis were trying to destroy them. Cornelius felt real happy that afternoon because they were doing something for a people who had almost no future and they were helping them to keep them alive and eventually they would be helped to go to their own country.

He said to his mother when he came upstairs, "Mom, I am so happy and I don't know why." She looked at him and thought, "My son is understanding the concept of giving and of sowing and reaping, he is such a special boy."

Cornelius went to the backyard to look at his plants they had already established, and the lettuce seed was already germinating. From the building next door he heard a strange sound. It came from the side of the building where the toilet was. Whenever he climbed on the roof next door he stepped on the ledge of a window he could look through. He wanted to know what the sound was which came out of the building. He soon did. Standing with his feet on the ledge, he peeped through the little window which was slightly open. What he smelled was familiar, and he could not believe what he saw – a small piglet was walking inside what had apparently been a toilet.

What was Mr. Groenendijk up to? Cornelius remembered how he had imitated the sound of pigs and tried it out. The piglet looked up when he made the sound. He would have to tease the animal so he could find out if the sound was correct. He picked up a thin pole which was lying on the roof and tried to poke the animal. It worked! The pig gave a squeal; he tried to imitate it several times. Then he poked the pig again and tried it again. He thought he was really getting good at it. At the same time he had no idea he would be able to save the piglet's life one day.

Mr. Groenendijk had traded the piglet for the use of a box tricycle. I have lots of food for a pig," he had told the barter partner. "I can probably feed it to be a fat one in no time flat. Where do you get all that food here?" the man had asked. "If you have too much I'll be happy to take it off your hands," he had laughed.

Groenendijk had told him, "Every day the bakers, the fish mongers and the green grocers bring back their box trikes with refuge on it. I have to clean the junk and most of the time it is edible for pigs. They eat fish guts and cauliflower leaves, breadcrumbs and sour milk, don't they?"

He nodded and said, "You bet you, and the way things are going we might even eat that kind of stuff ourselves."

The pig had found a home, a bale of straw had been brought, and soon it would clearly smell like a pig-sty in Cornelius' back yard, unless he closed the window.

The attack on the jail was very well prepared. In the jail are too many people who no longer have a lease on life. Their time is running out and they are all our friends who fought with us for so long, we cannot leave them there. The jail is like a lion's den, the animal of prey has its bounty there. It's also the prime target. Almost an impossible project. In the past two attempts had failed. This time it cannot fail. Too many people's lives are at stake. They prepare the attack as if they are making a Swiss clock. Meticulously the parts are put together until it all fits.

At last Gerrit van der Veen had become a member of the Council of Resistance. Cor Brandwijk had his own department in the attack to attract other Resistance cells. It needs to be done with great secrecy. If one NSB-er has imbedded himself in a Resistance cell the whole plan will fail and could cause many casualties.

They take their time even though time is of the essence.

Cor talks to one of the prison guards, a man by the name of van Welsum. He agreed to help and he would open doors just before they arrive. They have discussions in groups of five to brainstorm the procedure. The big question remains: will we be able to break out seventy people?

The next day van Welsum noticed an abnormality at the jail. One of the Dutch NSB-ers and an SS man at the same time had brought a watchdog. He had never done that before. Is there any correlation with regards to their plan? If so, who is talking?

Gerrit van der Veen proposes to wait a week to see if the dog is going to stay or if it is just a temporary measure.

The day of the attack everyone gathers at a dedicated place, watches are synchronized. At the appointed time van Welsum opens some cell doors and tells the inhabitants to stay put and that their freedom draws near. A minute later the officer of the front deposits his key on the keyboard in the guard room and goes home. That was the moment van Welsum had waited for. He waits until he hears the officer leave and quickly opens the outside entrance doors.

Then he crossed over the lawn on the inside of the prison and opened two more doors. At that point in time four doors are open for the attackers to come in. Silently they open the gates and door. They are dressed in black and are almost invisible in the dark. When van Welsum turns off the outdoor lights no one can be seen. Everyone had been warned about the watch dog but it was nowhere in sight.

In a split second fifteen men had entered the jail ready to open more doors and lead the prisoners to freedom.

The dog was waiting for a sign from its keeper. They had not forgotten the warning but they thought it could be handled. When the dog was released it attacked Gerrit van der Veen. He pulled his gun and two shots were heard. The dog was dead but the attack had already failed.

An alarm went off and from every side the watch appeared with rifles and handguns. The attackers did not have a chance. Gerrit was shot in the back and was instantly paralyzed. Cor was shot in his leg and was trying to haul his body through the outside gate. Five men of the Resistance died that night. Three were caught and put in a cell at the very jail they wanted to release so many from.

Without a judge or jury three men were brought to the dunes. Gerrit had been carried on a gurney. In the dunes twelve soldiers were getting ready, two of Gerrit's friends lift him up from the gurney. Hanging on his friends shoulders but standing like men, they hear the shots.

The farmer and his wife Brandwijk, who had seen their son only once since he had left the farm, took the simple letter the jail commandant sent them with courage. "He was a good citizen and a brave man." They did not even see his body again. It had been buried in a mass grave which had been dug by their countrymen and to which bodies were added almost every day.

Who gave those Nazis such power over life and death? Surely no one other than the Devil himself. It would take more than one more year before the Holocaust ended.

Kees went to the Brandwijk farm two weeks later and heard the news about Cor. He consoled his friends and told them that their son was a hero. Sometimes words are not enough. They understood that they had to go forward in saving lives until the very end.

It was bitter cold in the house on the Deiman Straat. There was nothing left to burn; people were roaming the streets to break down fences, cut trees or loot from bombed buildings. When a tree was cut it would attract dozens of people and sometimes fights would break out over one limb. The weakest went home with the thinnest branches.

Anything which could burn even if it was for just an hour.

In the midst of this mess the German police would often disperse all people, which was the least type of force they would employ. Often they would arrest a few people which led to the others to run for their lives. But their lives were also extended with the material from the tree. Just like hyenas with their prey, chased away by a lion, so the people returned to the tree until the entire tree was gone.

Their lives had been extended for a few more days.

Cornelius had many friends as young as he was he had friends all over the country. He helped people, brought them food or little things he knew they needed. In The Hague lived an elderly man who was a tailor.

His name was Mr. Epker. This man was Jewish. He could not walk. He was born lame and so he had learned to be a tailor who, in those times, sat on top of a table with criss-crossed legs doing his sowing. Mr. Epker had a collection of pictures so big that Cornelius would go to visit and look at the pictures for hours. He had pasted the pictures which he had cut from magazines and from newspapers on cardboard backings and filed them in boxes and boxes and boxes all over his two room apartment.

They were filed by category so you could look at landscapes for hours or windmills by the hundreds even cars and horses and all the animals of the world. Cornelius loved to go to Mr. Epker, to just be there as friends, a four-year-old and a forty-year-old. They enjoyed their time together.

The last time Cornelius went he had helped Mr. Epker to make tea for both of them but when it came to sugar the man did not have any. He did not even have a sugar pot. This time Cornelius had taken his mother's sugar pot and forced it in the pocket of his jacket.

Before he had gone up the stairs to Mr. Epkers's apartment he had wrapped the sugar pot in a piece of paper he had brought. He was planning to give it to Mr. Epker the moment he had made the tea. When that moment had come he triumphantly produced his present.

The tailor was so surprised and happy that he promised Cornelius he could take home five of the pictures he had and he could pick out whichever one he chose. At home later that day Johanna was looking for her sugar pot, but she could not find it. She really wondered what had happened to it for a long time.

So Cornelius had made friends everywhere by giving, by asking questions and by helping people. He was a little skinny boy full of life, and he was destined to survive the war.

Kees was preparing another transport to leave his house to a farm in the South in the Province of Zeeland. The place was a long way from home and Kees was thinking how he was going to get this transport of four people to their destination. He called Mr. Rosenzweig from below and asked him how he expected to solve the problem of the transport. "Bear in mind, Mr. Rosenzweig, it is about eighty kilometers and we will have to pass at least fifteen barricades on the way."

"Whatever you do I do not want to change my appearance," Mr. Rosenzweig told him time and again.

"But sir," Kees said, getting desperate with this man's attitude. "Do you want to arrive alive at your destination or just get a transfer to Auschwitz right here?"

"God will protect me no matter what or how I go so I might as well go as a Jew because that is what I am," Mr. Rosenzweig said.

Kees did not know what to do until the doorbell rang. It was a single ring which meant it was a friend. The Germans always rang many times and shouted with it.

When he opened the door he saw his answer standing in front of him, if he could just persuade him. "Come on in Harry, I was just thinking of you. Come and have a cup of Surro with us."

Surro was an abbreviation of the word "surrogate" which in turn was the word for surrogate coffee. There was no coffee in the country except that which had been seized by the generals for their personal use. A substitute for coffee had been put on the market. It tasted a little like coffee, perhaps a little more bitter.

As Harry came in, Kees poured the surro and introduced Mr. Rosenzweig. Harry was safe to Kees's guests. Time after time Harry, who was a local undertaker, had taken people in his horse-drawn hearse to the farms. This time he was the answer to Kees's dilemma with Mr. Rosenzweig.

"Well Mr. Rosenzweig," Kees said, carefully avoiding Harry's occupation. "This man will take you as you are, as Jewish-looking as you want, to your destination without any problem. Meet your rescuer. Harry, here is your next assignment. Tomorrow morning at five, I want you to be loading up four people for transport to Kwadendamme in Zeeland. Can you be ready for this?"

"Short notice," Harry replied. "I will have to see if I don't have any other appointments."Here was a man who really had appointments with the dead. He was very punctual about it too. "I will have to take at least two long days going and coming as well. Let me go see my agenda, I will be right back." Harry said as he jumped up and walked out the front door to his stable just one block away.

Meanwhile, Mr. Rosenzweig inquired as to what kind of transport Harry did, so Kees told him. "He is the undertaker."

"Oh, no, no, no. I will not tolerate an undertaker to take me, and I cannot fake to be dead. That is against my religion," Rosenzweig said. " Oh, yes, yes ,yes," mimed Kees. "You will go because this is the only way we can get you to Zeeland."

Kees had a plan and he did not tell Mr. Rosenzweig. He would go willingly without saying a word. Kees had done it before and with this stubborn Jew there was no further arguing. "Mr. Rosenzweig, please go downstairs and get your things ready, and tell the other three too. Tomorrow at five, yes.?"

Kees gestured for him to go and he went like a beaten dog with its tail between its legs.

When Harry came back he confirmed that he could do it, "but I will need some food for underway and papers for a dead man by the name of, whatever, can you get it this late Kees?" Kees nodded and said, "I already have one from the last time when we did not use it, remember? So five o'clock then and food, okay?"

Harry was a man of short sentences. He made a plan and did it without discussion. Harry was the kind of man whom Kees liked a lot.

That evening Kees stayed up until 2:00 a.m. and then he went downstairs and woke up Mr. Rosenzweig, not by shaking or calling but by the sharp prick of a hypodermic needle. He woke up hours later like a zombie. Not saying a word he was ushered through the warehouse exit where Harry was waiting with his twin span horses and hearse. Four people were loaded up in the bottom of the carriage. The sides of the space they were laying in had tine cuts in the planks so plenty of fresh air could reach the passengers. On top came a set of planks and on top of that, a coffin. In the coffin was a dummy dead body used many a time before. The Germans never looked inside a coffin. They thought it would bring them bad luck. Good for them, even better for the Jews who had made regular use of this form of transportation.

Sadly, Harry and Kees had never thought that the Germans would ever use dogs to sniff at a coffin and get onto a hearse. This trip ended just four miles from Kwadendamme, its final destination.

Five people were arrested and sent directly to Auschwitz. Without any orders or a verdict from a judge, Harry and his four passengers were never seen or heard of since they left The Hague.

Kees had to become even smarter with his transportations. He had always out-smarted the Nazis and he could not forgive himself for his own ignorance. There was a next time and there were transports in hearses. There would also be distractions for dogs on the same transports.

Chapter Thirty Six

HOW THEY KEPT GOING

—⁓—

People like Kees and Johanna van Rijn were taking a huge risk in hiding and transporting Jewish Dutch people. What kept them going was firstly their faith in God. Kees married a Jewish girl who had become a Christian when she was a little girl. Johanna's father had come from Poland. He had received help from a Christian family who had helped his whole family become established Dutch citizens.

When Kees married Johanna, her family, the Schmall family, had become fairly wealthy. Her father Jitzu Dirk Schmall was a professional craftsman and had his own Blacksmithery on the edge of The Hague. Their marriage was held in Oud Beyerland, a small town in the south of Holland where the grandfather of Kees had a successful cheese wholesale.

The local clerk of the city administration had made a change in Johanna's last name by writing her last name as "Small" instead of the Jewish version "Schmall." That little error had saved Johanna's life during the Holocaust.

There were three ways the Jews could get out of deportation during the first year of the round-up: by marriage, by going into hiding, or by suicide. The latter was happening increasingly after it had become known that their trip to the camps was a one-way trip to their deaths. During the last two years of the war, which was during 1943 and 1944, more than 2two thousand Jews chose the suicide escape.

Kees and Johanna were very aware of this problem and with all the safety and secrecy measures they took, they never had to deal with a suicide case.

The Deiman Straat had become a safe haven for hundreds because Kees was in the Resistance. He received help from Resistance organizations financially, with food, with false papers and with the transportations.

The bravest of the brave, yet humble, Kees and Johanna lived the entire war in great fear. But it was another kind of fear, the fear of the Lord, which kept them going.

One of Kees' specialties was to find others who could provide temporary hiding places. Through his colleagues in the Resistance he knew many people who were solid enough to hide Jews. Many Jews went to other cities close by. One of them was the city of Leiden. This old city was home to the oldest university in Europe, a university which had been founded in the fourteenth century by Willem of Orange from England. The city had many big houses with lots of hiding places in them – attics, personnel doors to quarters in the houses which had not been used for years… the inventive Leidenaars were able to create hiding places the Germans could never find.

The risk however was great and the punishment for those in hiding was immediate death in several cases.

There was a house smack next door to the city's concert hall, where the Germans and NSB-ers held their "upsweeping meeting." Often the Jews in hiding could hear the propaganda and negative words about their race in loud speeches, right next door.

In the beginning of the Holocaust, the Jewish citizens were simply receiving letters from the city administration – invitations!

As early as the middle of 1942 Jews were called to report at a certain location. They were told to be there and were even advised on what to bring. The reasoning in the invitation was "to participate in research about their health, in order to participate in a program to provide them with more jobs!"

The lie did not fly. Out of ten thousand invitations only five hundred would actually come. Those five hundred were put on a train immediately and sent to a camp in The Netherlands where, supposedly, they would be preselected for what kind of job would be best for them. The unbelievable fact that even their children could come along for this "research project" made it even more suspicious.

The poisonous Jewish Council had advised all Jews to obey every call and measure that the Nazis would come up with. The Dutch camp called Westerbork became the fastest stepping board for the Nazis to get people to the death camps.

When the invitations did not work well enough the Germans began the Razzias.

Entire sections of cities were surrounded and closed off with barbed wire fences. Then the Nazis went from door to door, demanding people to open up. If they didn't the soldiers forced themselves into the houses and literally took the Jews from their beds. They were shoved into trucks and sent directly to Westerbork.

The Roman Catholic Church leadership had sent a letter to the German commanders Inquart, Rauter and Mussert in protest of the persecution of the Jews. At that time no one knew that the Jews would be annihilated in gas chambers by the millions.

Inquart ordered an immediate arrest of all Catholic Jews as an answer to the protest letter.

Chapter Thirty Seven
ORPHANAGES FOR JEWISH CHILDREN

—ɱ—

W henever new Jewish people had been picked up and when they had been deported, their children had often not been at home or had simply been overlooked by the Nazis. The Resistance workers who were notified by their friends when Jews had been taken out of their homes always took the children to several Orphanages.

Kees had often brought a child to the Orphanage. With dread and in horror he had seen children being kicked and whipped into the trucks which would take them to Westerbork, the stepping-stone to the death camps. On a day in 1943 Kees had found a three-year-old child in front of his house. The child was able to tell him that her parents had been loaded onto a truck while she was hiding under the staircase in their home.

After the Germans had left, she had stayed in the house until the next morning, hoping her parents would return. Finally she had gone outside and had walked for hours in ever greater circles until she had sat down in front of Kees and Johanna's house in the Deiman Straat. Johanna had brought the crying child inside, fed her and comforted her until Kees had come home. His immediate advice was to bring the child to a Jewish Orphanage. They stripped the Star of David from her clothes and Kees was on his bicycle en route to a Jewish house he had brought other children to before.

That was the first time he met a young lady by the name of Reina Prinsen. She was only twenty-years-old. As young as she was she was probably the bravest girl her age. Reina became a courier and transported handguns, illegal documents, false food stamps and even hand-grenades for the Resistance.

Reina was one of the youngest heroes of the Resistance. At one time she proclaimed, "I want to help the Jewish children. There are so many of them and all the ones in the Orphanages will one day soon be picked up as well. As long as the Nazis have their hands full picking up adults they will probably leave the children alone. I will not wait until that dreadful day comes."

Reina had begun to make a list of addresses of Jewish Orphanages in the whole country. She had hid the list and knew it by heart. She travelled from one city to the other and talked to the leaders of the houses.

She taught them how to hide the children and to prepare them for an evacuation. Reina was a visionary at her young age. She also prepared addresses for the children to go to in the event of an evacuation.

When Kees met her for the first time he had heard from her in the circles of Resistance workers. Reina had an alias, they called her "Leentje," this girl with her brown hair and her big blue eyes. It almost sounded as if she had put Kees in his place, saying with a sound of accusation, "Why are you bringing this child here, don't you know that this address is known by the Nazis and that they take children to the death camps as well?"

Kees was shocked by the compassion in the girl's speech. He had known and had always wondered why these Jewish children could stay in the Orphanage for all this time.

Ashamed of his ignorance, he had taken the child back home. They had discussed together where they would bring the child. A Christian family from their church had taken the child.

Stripped from her Jewishness, she survived the war.

Kees had expressed to Reina his concerns about her. "How can you survive this with all the risks you are taking?" Kees had gone back an hour later and had asked to talk and pray with her. He had told her that he had found a good family for the child and that he was willing to help Reina find more addresses where single children could be brought.

It was the last time he had seen Reina. Two days later she had been arrested and taken to a prison in the center of the city. Later an illegal resistance worker wrote in a letter:

"Most of my fellow prisoners were shocked when we saw Reina Prinsen coming by our cell. We were shocked. That young innocent face was almost unrecognizable, blue from torturous hits, swollen and beaten like a criminal. Her legs were bandaged she was carried by two Siegerheits policemen (SD-ers) with revengeful looking faces."

Her parents found out about her arrest in the newspaper. It mentioned that she was caught with a revolver in her purse. For two years they never knew what had happened to their daughter, when at last after the war was ended they discovered that she was executed by a firing squad in Oranienburg.

There is a street named after her in Amsterdam. A rose is growing down below the street sign, donated by Prins Bernard. The rose was planted by a three-year-old Jewish girl who was named after Reina Prinsen.

How many children she saved no one will ever know – at least Two hundred, estimated the co-workers in the Resistance.

Jewish Orphanage

Cornelius waiting at
the soup kitchen

Chapter Thirty Eight
SAVING LIVES AND SAVING THE PIG

—〜〜—

T here were soldiers everywhere when Kees woke up one morning around Christmas in 1943.

"They must have come by the thousands," Kees exclaimed to Johanna. "I'll sound the crack board quickly, you better get up and be prepared for a big Razzia." As he said those words, a loud knock on the door announced that he was right.

Kees knew that the Jews downstairs were quickly doing their routine and getting from the hiding place to their under-the-concrete bullet-proof shelter. Just one minute later they would lock the concrete chunk of wall in place...

No one, not even a hide-out specialist which the Germans had brought would be able to find it.

As always, Johanna went to the door while Kees picked up his son and waited for the avalanche of soldiers to roll in. They were thorough, Kees had to admit, but God was on his side and Kees prayed, "Lord, let this ordeal pass by for the sake of your people."

There must have been thirty soldiers in their house. They were all over, in every room and closet. Kees had put Cornelius down because the boy wanted to guard his vegetable garden. Kees could hear the little boy talk to the soldiers. "No, no sir, please don't walk on my plants. This is my garden and when you come back I will give you some cabbage."

The soldier looked at the little boy and at his buddy next to him and laughed, saying, "Lueken Sie mal, einem kleine Gartner, ha, ha, (Look at this little gardener.)" It was an Austrian who spoke and the soldier walked towards Cornelius, took him by the hand and began to ask him questions in Austrian, a language which Cornelius did not understand a syllable of. Just then at that moment the soldier released his hand, the pig in Mr. Groenendijk's toilet next door began to squeal. The soldiers both looked around to see where the sound came from. "Wo kommt das her und wass ist das?" they asked.

Cornelius had jumped between the toilet and the soldiers who were looking the opposite way, Cornelius began to imitate the pig, and several times he made the exact same squeal. One of the soldiers turned around and caught Cornelius in the act. The friendly Austrian laughed but the other soldier took Cornelius by the shoulder and slapped him across his face saying, "Du habest mir beleidigt, du slechter Junge!" he slapped him again, but Cornelius kept squealing.

They all went back inside and the whole company of soldiers with them. They had inspected Kees's Ausweiss and the fact that he was home at the right time outside his working schedule pleased the Commandant. "Endlich einem Hollaender who is obedient to the Reich."

Cornelius was still standing in the backyard, two big tears rolled down his cheek. He did not have any words to say, he just stood there and thought, "It did not hurt and I saved the pig, my plants are still alive." What would daddy say about him? Would he be mad? He did not intend to insult the soldiers, he just wanted to save Groenendijk's little piglet.

Finally he began to cry. The tension he experienced this time had become too much. Besides he was very hungry and thirsty and wondered when his dad would go on a farm trip again.

Johanna had seen the little boy standing there in the backyard and began to cry too. What a brave little guy he was, what could she do to make him happy? Or was he?

She walked into the kitchen when he came in from the backyard. "They were not all mean Mom," he said sobbing. "And one of the two was real nice! Do you have some milk for me, please?"

She did not. She had not had any milk for weeks. The one liter she was entitled to had been sold to someone else or given to a NSB-er. But she had found an alternative which she would not tell Cornelius about. She had to lie to her son so much against her will when she said, "Yes my son, I have some milk. Here, I kept it behind the Curtain to keep it safe from the intruders." She produced a bottle from behind the curtain where she kept her pots and pans. She thought, "I hope he does not notice, he is such a faithful little guy and now even I am cheating him."

Out of sight Johanna had mixed white-wash powder with water. At least it looked like milk, but it did not taste like it. The water in it was clean and it would not harm her little boy, but would the chalkpowder? Or would it help him take in some calcium? Johanna did not really know the consequences; all she wanted to do was to satisfy her boy. When Cornelius drank it he pulled a funny face and said, "This does not taste like milk, what have you done with this milk Mom?"

Johanna could not stand it, what was she to tell the little boy, that he was drinking white wash? She decided to tell him a half truth. "No Corrie, I have added some calcium vitamins. Can you get used to it? It is good for your bones so you better drink it."

She could not keep her composure any longer. She quickly turned around to hide her tears.

The Razzia was huge, with dozens of trucks and hundreds of soldiers, Gestapo personnel and Dutch police. The Dutch police were of course the worst of all. They were hated by Dutch citizens because they displayed their former police authority, but they were really peons of the Germans.

In total two thousand men had sealed off a part of The Hague, a part where the Nazis suspected to find any Jews in hiding. No one could escape; soldiers were on the roof tops shooting at anyone who was running. From door to door the Jew hunters looked for their prey.

When one or more Jews were found, the Nazis would kick them to the street where the others would take over their nasty treatment and chase them into the waiting trucks. Anyone found in the house where Jews were found, the hiders would be beaten and chased into the trucks as well. No one caught could escape. If they tried to run they were shot. Even children were loaded up. One six year old boy was screaming after his parent. He was kicked and then shot and left for dead in the gutter.

That morning twenty two hundredand thirty people were taken

The team taking a break

from that section of The Hague. They had a one-way ticket to the Dutch camp in Westerbork where they received a day's worth of hope. The guards told them when they showed them their barracks, "Tomorrow you will be screened." Screened for what? They did not tell. They were all separated from their loved ones. The men from their wives and the children from their parents. Like sheep they were driven to the barracks, no food was issued that first day, no drinks were to be found and just a bucket of dirty water was waiting at the door of the barracks. Misery was complete, particularly the next morning when they were driven to a waiting train inside the camp.

Everyone was looking for their loved ones, children were screaming to their parents when they saw them at a distance.

They were all pushed into the waiting train like cattle, pushed and whipped into the cattle or freight wagons, standing room only. They were on their way on a seven hour ride to Auschwitz. Often if Auschwitz was full and the gas chambers had too much work, the arriving train had to wait for hours. Sometimes it went back the same way it came for just a few miles. It was detoured to another death camp in Poland called Sobidor, which was another six hours further. No one could move, no one could go the the toilet, people dropped and were trampled. An average of eight percent arrived dead.

They were the fortunate ones. They did not have to suffer any longer...

The roadblocks were removed after three hours of human mis-

Loading the cattle train

ery. The barbed wire was rolled-up, the trucks with victims had pulled out of the streets and the last soldiers had gone back to inflict their misery to other places in the city.

Kees was able to go on the street again and so did many others.

There were two kinds of people now who took to the streets.

The two kinds definitively did not like each other. The NSB-ers became the looters. They had been able to see out of which houses victims had been taken. The scavengers began their clean-up by taking anything of value – stealing art, furniture, anything left behind. They knew they did not have much time to conduct their filthy mission. They knew other, bigger scavengers would soon come and do an even more thorough job. The German scavengers would come back with trucks and load up everything which was left. It happened every time.

The NSB-ers would often get in fights with the Nazis about things they had stolen. They would be the losers all the time. They did not carry the weapons. They were treated like hyenas when the lions appeared.

The other kinds of people who went to the streets where the Razzia had played its havoc were the Resistance people, often with their families, looking for survivors. Many times they found wounded people who had hidden themselves after the cruel beating, whom the Nazis thought they had left for dead. Often they found children who had been left behind by the oppressor simply because they felt they were useless for the Reich. Or, they would find children who hid themselves in closets or attics and had been overlooked too. A group of twenty men and women had gathered at the front door of the van Rijn Residence. They were all in a hurry to begin their risky research job.

Kees spoke to the gathering of Resistance fighters. "Before you all leave, I want to ask you to come to the Groenendijk warehouse tonight. Leave whomever you found at home. Let's coordinate what we have found, how many people we're talking about and what we need to do with them. I have two ambulances on stand-by at Ypenburg, they can take as many as sixteen people to a farm in Woubrugge. I arranged all that weeks ago but I need to have someone go to Ypenburg right now and tell them to come tonight. Also I need to have someone, preferably a girl, to ride her bike to Woubrugge to tell the farmers that people will be coming tonight. Who can do those two missions?" Two hands were raised instantly. All plans fell into place thus far.

They had split up the area where they would do their job. "One warning: stay away from the NSB-ers," Kees said. "At this time they are harmless because the scavengers want to steal as much as they can. Don't interrupt them doing their dirty work. Don't stand in their way. More importantly, if you find a child, particularly if it is Jewish, don't come back here. Take it to your own home and go there in an unsuspecting way. If any one of the NSB-ers sees you, act normal and make yourself disappear. I know this is a difficult task. Make the best of it and don't betray who you are to anyone."

With those warnings in mind, they all went their separate ways trying to save people, more often children. Kees and Cornelius went together. Within ten minutes they found the first child, a five-year old who was hiding in a hall closet. Kees asked the boy's name, but the boy was so scared he could not even remember his own name. Cornelius put his arm around the boy and realized this boy was almost his age. He realized that he could be his friend. He had never seen the boy in the neighborhood, so the boy must be in hiding here, he thought. Finally the boy spoke. "My name is Aaron. I just came here two days ago with both my parents and my sister. They took them all away. I just slid under the bed here and then I ran to the closet when the soldiers had left."

Cornelius knew what to do. He had done it before. "Come, lets go play outside," Cornelius said to the boy. "I know some place where we can play safely." They walked outside and Cornelius looked right to left and left to right. Only one person he saw out of the corner of his eye. He did not recognize the person as one of the Resistance; he could not take the risk of bringing a Jewish boy to his house in broad daylight.

He pulled Aaron back into his house and said, "We need to take your yellow star off if we go play outside. We don't want to be seen together with your star on your shirt. Is there anything we can cut it off with?" He found a knife in the kitchen where Cornelius quickly removed the Yellow Star of David from his shirt.

"Now we can go outside and play," Cornelius said. They went as normal boys do, walking on the streets, kicking something here and there. Cornelius coached the boy gradually as they got closer to his home. He had no idea how he was going to get inside without being seen. He was trying to think, what could he do to distract any person looking through their windows at him?

Cornelius' mind was racing. How could he bring the Jewish boy into his house without being seen? In his thoughts he went over the area where he lived. The barber was not an option...who else? Where could he go with this child? Then it dawned on him: the greengrocer around the corner!

His backyard bordered on Groenendijk's backyard. Harry was in the Resistance too, or was he really? Was he questionable, like his father used to say? He heard his dad's voice in his mind saying, "If someone is questionable you can't take the risk to trust him." Cornelius decided not to trust the greengrocer, but who then?

The answer just rang its box tricycle bell. The baker who rented the closed box bike rode by and signaled to Cornelius, "You boys want a ride?" he called.

They were two streets away from home. Two boys taking a ride from a friend was not suspicious but two boys getting out of a baker's box trike was. But they would not be seen once inside Groenendijk's warehouse. That was it!

When it had become dark and quiet in the Deiman Straat, life became somewhat active. One by one the Resistance workers arrived through the warehouse next door. They came in rented box tricycles with three, sometimes four at a time. The atmosphere was grim but in a way celebratory. More than twenty people had been found. Two of them had been brought to a hospital and the other nineteen were at different homes around the neighborhood.

Soon a discussion began about what needed to be done. "We can still bring fourteen Jewish people to the farm in Woubrugge. How many children do we have?" Someone had made a list. There were eight Jewish children, four Jewish adults and seven onderduikers who had been hiding to escape Arbeits Einsatz. Those people need to find their own hide-out, Kees decided, and the others agreed. If they were not in the Resistance they could find a place. Besides, they should not be exposed to the Deiman Straat headquarters. They all agreed again.

"So let's make a plan," said Kees, taking the leading role as usual. "We are getting two ambulances. They will not come together and they'll be one hour apart to avoid raising eyebrows. We will send them all to Woubrugge. We take the children first because they can all get into one ambulance. An hour later we'll send the Jewish adults. We need you to get all the Jewish people here at nine o'clock tonight. Please bring them in box tricycles four at a time. Then we have to open the warehouse only three times. When you leave here do the same and leave at different times. Some bakers take their trike home in order to start early."

The plan was clear to everyone and soon the unfortunate people who had lost their loved ones would be free, they hoped.

"Whatever we do with this transport, we have to stay in Groenendijk's warehouse tonight." Kees was talking to three men who had remained behind with him in order to help the transportation run smoothly. "If anyone gets to know our secret and gets picked up, they will not have the endurance when tortured to keep this a secret. I have worked too many hours on this hiding place to lose it."

They all understood. They did not even know how Kees did it. To them, Kees lived next-door to the warehouse. They did not know about the secret door underneath the work bench.

Cornelius had brought his friend inside before they all arrived. He had begged his Mom to keep Aaron. "You'll have to ask Dad when he comes in," she said. "He is like my brother," Cornelius pleaded. "If he stays here we can play together." Johanna would not say yes and she did not want to keep her son's hopes up either. "I don' think your Dad will agree with you for the simple reason that the NSB-ers know that we have another boy. They will put two and two together and call the Gestapo. We need to keep a very low profile because of all the things we do."

Cornelius sighed and left the matter alone until his Dad came inside.

Kees never went through the front door when he had his meetings in the warehouse. He too climbed over the back fence into his own backyard, just like Cornelius did.

He came home half an hour later. He looked exhausted when he came in and he kissed Johanna.

"Too many orphans again," he sighed. "Their parents will never come back."

Chapter Thirty Nine

ISRAEL IS CALLING

—ɱ—

I n a Hospital near Schaffhausen, Switzerland, a man was
brought in by ambulance.

The emergency room doctors had examined him but could not
find the reason why he was unconscious. His vitals were all in
order, so the doctors were at a loss.

The woman who had come with him only told them that he had
fallen in the grass and that he had gone unconscious after a few
minutes.

She was asked for his name but she did not know. They
searched for papers on him which could reveal his identity but
there had been nothing. When asked for the woman's identity, she
did not have any either. The only clue the doctors could find was
that both people had a number tattooed on their arms.

The doctors had never seen the tattoos and were wondering
what they meant.

The woman would not tell, she either refused to tell or did
not know. Her remark was, "He will tell you all about it when he
wakes up."

Days became weeks and weeks became months. The mysteri-
ous man was attracting Swiss reporters who wrote headlines like:

"Mystery Man from Nowhere Still Sleeping."

He woke up after seven weeks. He felt very groggy and disoriented. When asked for his name he answered, "Later please," and fell asleep again. The woman had finally told them that her name was Hannah. When he woke up again he seemed more apprehensive and he began to tell an unbelievable story.

"My name is Doctor Henk Ypma. I have come from a German concentration camp located in Auschwitz.

I have escaped with seventeen young Jewish ladies and I have also arranged for twelve more young Jewish men to escape from the same camp. The reason why I was able to organize these escapes is because I was in charge of a research program involving these escaped people. The reports I had made to the German High Command in Berlin caused me to get a great deal of freedom.

I had suggested bringing my research project over to a very secret human research facility located here, close to the Swiss border in the Swartzwalt. The young lady I have brought with me, or rather who has brought me here to this hospital, can testify to my story. I would like to ask you to set up a press conference with the international press because I have much more to say. In particular, I would like to announce what the Nazis are doing in all those so-called 'concentration camps.'"

The two doctors and three nurses who had heard his words were astonished and promised to call a news conference as soon as possible."Now, gentlemen. On a more private note, what are your findings in my personal case? It seems very odd that I have been unconscious for so long from exhaustion. Have you found out what has caused my illness?" The doctors shook their heads and one of them replied, "We are at a complete dead-end of our tests. We cannot find out what caused you to remain in a coma that long."

"Could I see your charts please? After all, even though I am a patient I am a doctor myself," Henk remarked with a smile. It was his first smile in seven weeks and when Hannah saw it her heart leaped for joy.

When the doctors left they said to each other, "You think this man is sane? His story seems quite impossible."

"Well," said the one to the other. "Let's see what he makes of his own charts. If that makes sense we can always call a press conference."

Hannah had stayed with Henk all those weeks. She had slept on a sofa in his room and nurtured him as much as she could. Henk was looking at her, his eyes with tears of love. "Hannah, my dearest Hannah, how much I love you time will tell. For now just believe me when I tell you that soon I will marry you and we will do that in Israel."

The doctors walked in with the charts. Their faces showed total disbelief in their patient's claims. How could he know more then they? After all, they were Swiss doctors. They felt they were made like Swiss watches and this orphan Dutchman thought he knew better?

When they handed Henk his charts and he looked at them they did not expect anything. Henk looked at the charts, not looking for the ordinary but for the obvious because he knew his German colleagues. He knew how devious they could be and he thought of the tons and tons of cyanide which came in by the truckload in the death camps.

Could it be that he had been infected by the cyanide in some way? Could they have administered some of the cyanide in his food? But why would they do such a thing? Perhaps they might have thought that he would tell what was happening in Auschwitz? Perhaps they had believed in his cure so much that they would take the credit for themselves? After all, he was their enemy and he was doing forced labor.

With those thoughts in the back of his mind he began to compare his blood tests from the first day he arrived at the hospital until the day he woke up. There it was. He saw a clear indication of higher irons in the first one and it had been gradually diminishing during his stay at the hospital.

Immediately he knew what the Auschwitz doctors had done, they had tried to kill him by gradually and slowly adding cyanide to his food. It was the only explanation!

"Gentlemen," he began. "Do you still have the blood test results from the first day I came here? If so, please retest or look at the test results, you will find remnants of cyanide in it. You will also see that the percentages will decrease during my stay here. I know for a fact now, that they had tried to kill me. One of the effects of cyanide is that it remains in the blood for a long time if it is administered in a low dosage. When it is being administered continuously, it will gradually build up to a deathly chemical.

I can see what has happened to me was in the beginning stages. I will experience some more effects during the next years to come, but with what I know about cyanide, I can nullify its effects by taking high doses of calcium for a long time.

This also proves that the Nazis are out to kill people and on a large scale in the concentration camps. Please arrange the press conference I asked for earlier. The world needs to know what is happening in the German concentration camps. I myself am proof of their murderous plots."

The two doctors were flabbergasted by Henk's authoratative explanation. They were impressed and he could see that on their faces. They did not even have to go back to his blood tests; Henk had made his own diagnosis perfectly clear.

"You can count on the press conference either this evening or tomorrow morning," the older doctor told him as they left the room.

Hannah had been with him during the entire conversation. "What mean Jerks, those Auschwitz doctors, to take the glory for themselves on the cure for syphilis," she said. "Thank God you cheated them in their own surmise. What are we going to do at the press conference though? You know that the Germans have very long arms and they could come and assassinate us here, even in neutral Switzerland."

"I agree, honey. We will have to use different names and arrange to get alternate ID's quickly. When I was in Holland the first time visiting your brother I met with the Resistance. They not only gave us our escape route, they also gave me all kinds of addresses here in Switzerland. They were the ones who arranged the attack at the trucks when we came out of Germany. I can visit them today here in Schaffhausen and find out how they can get us new ID's."

Chapter Forty

THE ISRAEL CONNECTION

—ɯ—

I n the Neutral country of Switzerland, the Swiss government
allowed any nationality to enter its borders. From every nationality people had come to take advantage of the neutrality. Among
the many visitors were Jews from every country in Europe.

Because Switzerland had announced neutrality, many Germans
had also come into its borders. The difficulty was that many of the
German visitors were Jews and people who were persecuted by the
Nazis. No one could distinguish who were good visitors and who
were bad visitors. That was how so many German Secret Service
and Gestapo personnel had also moved to Switzerland. They were
there to do their nasty job once more. They were there in civilian
clothes and blended in with all the fugitives and Swiss citizens.
Their task was to root-out those who had anything against The
Reich, or those who had told on activities in Germany, such as
their concentration camps.

Among the visitors were a great many Zionists. They were the
activists to help bring as many Jews to Palestine to populate the future country of Israel. The Zionists were mostly secret agents who
had formed a Jewish Council, not like the Jewish Council Hitler
had created in the occupied countries. This council had only one
goal, which was to help people out of the war zones and transport
them to Israel.

Two men entered Henk's room that morning. They did not say much, other than, "Mr Ypma and Hannah, you are in grave danger here. We have come to bring you to a safe place. Please get your things; we'll be leaving in five minutes. Don't talk to anyone. You will not see the doctors or nurses anymore. We have warned them to stay away from you. Hurry please, we will tell you all about us once we are on our way."

Henk looked at Hannah and said, "Can you believe this? Out of the frying pan into the fire, it sounds like to me." He turned to the stranger who had spoken and demanded more of an explanation. The man just raised his hands and said, "You were helped by a group of people at the border weren't you?"

" Yes," Henk replied. "What is that to you? They were our people. We are Zionists and we help Jews get to anywhere in the world from here, preferably to Palestine though," he answered with a smile. "Hurry now, your lives are in grave danger."

No one was in sight when they left the hospital."Thank you for your hospitality," Henk whispered when he closed the hospital door behind him. The car which was waiting was a French Citroen.

The driver was dressed like the men who had helped them get out of Germany, the same kind of battle dress he wore and the same kind of silence he kept. Those are the real fighters, Henk thought; they must have quite a lot of them here in this country. He looked around and noticed that a similar car was following. "Are we in that much danger?" he was thinking as he put his arm around Hannah in a gesture of protection. The two cars sped toward the roads which led to Zurich. No one spoke a word until they drove into a garage, the door of which opened automatically. He saw that when both cars had entered the garage, the doors quickly closed again.

Finally someone spoke. "You are here in the official Palestine Council Building, we call it the Israelian Embassy, even though there is no Israelian country yet. The government of Switzerland is helping and protecting us here. This is where we do all the work to get our people to their destinations. We even have our own planes which are stationed at the Zürich airport to bring people through the Neutral Corridor over the Pyrenees and crossing the Mediterranean to Palestine. So far the German fighters have left us alone but we are not sure it will stay that way. That is why we try to get as many people out of here as quickly as possible. Please come with us to the conference room where you will meet some of our board members who will explain what we would like you to do."

They went up in an old-fashioned elevator, one with sliding steel gates and double doors. The rattling reminded him of the sounds he had always heard in Auschwitz, sounds that made him shiver. They went to the third floor and when the elevator door opened they walked right into a large, brightly-lit room. There were no windows that he could see, but they might have been covered with a fake wall. In the middle of the room was a large conference table and six people were sitting around it at the far end. There was no doubt that these men were Jews. Some were wearing a Yamikah. Some had the long hair with ringlets and most of them had a beard.

The first person who spoke sounded very educated and Henk was immediately impressed by the man.

"Doctor Ypma and Miss Hannah, you are most welcome in this country and at this council. We are very proud of you for taking the tremendous risks you have in bringing twenty nine Jews to us in this country. We cannot thank you enough for the courageous act you have been conducting since you went to Holland. Our people in Holland have kept us informed of all you were doing and that was why we were able to help you at the border some six weeks ago. We are very sorry for the illness which you have suffered since that memorable escape.

We would appreciate it very much if you could tell us all about the things which are happening in Auschwitz. We will listen to any advice of what we could do to end the atrocities which are going on in these camps.

Considering the importance of your escape from Germany, I hope you will understand that your request to have a press conference is denied for reasons of security for you and all of us, meaning the entire Jewish population on this continent." When he had

225

stopped talking the room fell into an eerie silence. No one spoke a word. All eyes were directed at Henk who did not know where to start, until one of the councilmen encouraged him. "My dear Doctor Ypma, how can I help you to begin your disquisition? I believe you could begin to tell us why you got the job in a concentration camp and how you received the opportunity to get to work there in a clinic."

It did the trick for Henk to get started. "I was picked up by the Nazis in Holland, literally picked up out of my bed and put on a transport to Westerbork. As you know that was still in Holland. In that camp people were selected for the kind of slave labor they were going to be used for.

When they found out that I was a doctor they wanted to know what kind of specialty I had studied. I told them I was a specialist in Venereal Diseases. They asked me if I would work in a concentration camp, particularly in Auschwitz. They told me that in that camp mainly Jewish people were housed and that there would be a great opportunity there for my research. I took the bait and was sent to Auschwitz that same day. What I did not know was that it would be a one-way trip, because no one would ever leaves Auschwitz again. I found that out during the first week of my stay. Apart from beginning my research I began to search for a way to be able to leave the camp alive.

In my ignorance I still believed that the concentration camp Auschwitz was what its name suggests – a camp where a certain type of people are to be concentrated, gathered by ethnicity.

When I asked questions from my fellow doctors I sealed my own future. The more I found out what was going on there, the more I knew that I would never be allowed to leave knowing what I had learned.

My fellow doctors were very suspicious of me and of my questions. After a few weeks I had found out the real truth about the camp. I stumbled into an area I was not allowed to be in. Young Jewish men were digging large pits and in one of those pits I saw thousands of bodies."

Henk swallowed hard and his voice began to tremble. "When I

talked to one of the workers, a slave laborer, his eyes were totally hollow. The man did not even have tears left. He told me that most people were incinerated and that the ones buried here were the ones who had dropped dead on their work.

I began to look a little further after that encounter and I volunteered to help in the selection of people as they arrived on the train into Auschwitz. In the back of my mind a plan, though vague, began to form.

We doctors, perhaps five of us forced workers, were sorting the arrivals into five groups. Please Gentlemen brace yourselves for what is following. The five groups consisted of the elderly, invalids, children, workable men and workable women."

Henk paused for what seemed an eternity and when he continued he had tears rolling down his cheeks. "The first three groups were separated and had to wait their turn to strip naked and place their clothes and belongings in front of them. The elderly were then told they were to go into the showers. A huge hall had been converted into what seemed to look like showers. The naked people were driven into the showers, pushed and hit if they did not go fast enough. There was standing room only and when the doors closed, the showers were supposed to begin to spray water. Instead, cyan gas came out of the shower heads and within minutes they were all dead...please, gentlemen, I cannot go any further at this moment. The thought of what I saw when the doors opened is too much to remember."

Henk cried and so did Hannah. They cried uncontrollably for at least half an hour. The men of the council did too, more from the shock of what they had heard. A shock of disbelief and horror filled the room.

The silence was only broken by incomprehensible awe.

When half an hour had passed the men began to straighten themselves, wiping their faces until the chairman said, "My esteemed fellow members, today we have finally heard a reliable confirmation of what we have feared for so long. The numbers did not tally until now. We always wondered how the Nazi killers could house hundreds of thousands in one camp It seemed impossible. Now we know it was impossible. May God bless the souls which have gone before us in such a horrible way." There was dead silence again for a long time until Henk tried to speak. "Please do not hold the work I did against me, all the time I was in great turmoil about this and I thank God I did not lose my sanity there.

All I was thinking of was how I could get as many people out of there without raising suspicion. Then one day, Hannah arrived. She was the one who gave me the idea to save those whom I had brought to Switzerland six weeks ago."

"Tell us about that," the Chairman urged. "Because that, to us, is the greatest miracle of this ugly holocaust." It was the first time that word was mentioned. Until then the word "holocaust" had been a historic word which had never been used in this war.

Henk told them how he had selected Hannah because she had said that she had syphilis, how he had taken her into his clinic and how his plan had come together.

He told them how he had earned his way by reporting the cure for the disease and that he had received praise and privileges from the High Command in Berlin. That those privileges had led to his trip to Holland and there he had made contact with the Resistance who had helped him and who had suggested to get the seventeen girls and twelve men out of Auschwitz.

"We commend you for your courage and praise you for your action. There is nothing we would ever hold against you," the chairman commented. "You have done more than you had to do by saving the lives of twenty nine people, all Jews, by the way. Your greatest achievement has been that you were able to bring us the truth of what is going on in the concentration camps. From now on we will call those camps 'death camps' and the German genocide we will call "the Holocaust."

In front of the Zionist headquarters a car was parked. There were two men in the car. They were looking at the entrance of the building as if they were waiting for someone to exit. They did not know that at that very moment two cars drove out of the garage on the other side of the building on their way to the airport.

Six hours later Henk and Hannah set foot on their new land in Palestine, the soon-to-be country of Israel, a place of final peace for all the Jews in the world.

Chapter Forty One
ALWAYS A STEP AHEAD
OF THE NAZIS

—ɱ—

A Dutch policeman rang the doorbell at the van Rijn residence.
The man in the black uniform with an armband clearly showing his swastika was seen by several NSB-ers on the block. Each
one had thought there would be no reason for alarm. The police
were doing their job and if the van Rijns were doing something
illegal they would be found out and arrested with or without their
help.

The traitors only acted when they would see an opportunity to
get a reward. This time no such reward was in the picture, so they
went on with what they were doing, waiting for a real chance to
come around. The policeman did not bang on the door or yell and
when Kees opened the door he went inside without the threat of a
gun.

The policeman was Jan de Raad, a double agent, and he had a
message for Kees. He worked with the police before the Nazis took
over. He had always despised his fellow policemen who so quickly
had accepted their new German commander. To Jan it was sheer
treason to work with the enemy. How could one be a citizen of a
free Holland reigned by the Queen of the House of Orange and the
next day work for an occupying, lying and killing intruder? Jan de
Raad had decided to use the enemy for the benefit of the Dutch, for
the Netherlands, not against them.

That evening he had brought Kees information which the Resistance had to act on immediately. It was inside information which Jan had picked up from the Gestapo leadership hours before. Tomorrow morning at seven o'clock, the Nazis were going to empty the Jewish Orphanage at the Heren Straat in Rijswijk, just one kilometer from the Deiman Straat. Two truckloads of children would be picked up and delivered directly to Birkenau, a concentration camp for children, a place where thousands of Jewish children had been brought and were never heard from again.

Kees asked for more details but the policeman had to go quickly lest he would be seen visiting a civilian home during his shift.

When Jan de Raad left, he acted as if he was mad at Kees. He yelled a little to make his visit seem like real police business. Kees acted without consulting Johanna. He knew she would agree. There was no reason to make her worried about the pending activities of the Underground.

Kees had a certain method of contacting a group of co-workers in the Resistance. He went to one address and gave the message, the person he gave his message to contacted two others who in turn contacted two others, and so forth. In a matter of half an hour all fifteen bicyclists gathered at the Groenendijk warehouse to hear what kind of plan their leader had made to rescue thirty Jewish children.

Each was to take one child to his own house, return immediately to the Orphanage and pick up a second child.

The whole operation took thirty minutes. The entire orphanage was emptied and the leaders had gone into hiding too.

The next morning the Nazis came in full force, determined to do their destructive work. The house was empty, and no one knew where the children had gone.

Two days later a German ambulance came to the Deiman Straat and entered the warehouse of Groenendijk. The NSB-ers were looking and began to wonder why these ambulances came to the warehouse that often. The Kapper on the corner had taken the initiative to investigate why these ambulances came there that often. He walked over to the warehouse and saw a mechanic beneath the ambulance. The Kapper said, "Hello my friend, what are you doing this fine morning?"

The mechanic knew what the Kapper stood for and together with the driver clad in German uniform they had staged this incident.

"There is something wrong with the driving axel of these trucks and the Germans cannot find anyone to repair them except me. It is my specialty. So you will be seeing a lot of them here in the future, they are bringing us their business now, is that not great?"

The Kapper was a little disappointed that his neighbor was benefitting from the Germans, there was no gain in it for the Kapper. From that day on the ambulances could freely enter the Groenendijk warehouse. Kees had found the perfect reason. He could make use of them as often as he wanted.

Later that evening eight children were loaded into the ambulance and they went on their way to several farms in the Province of Drenthe, just ten kilometers from the German border.

Three days later the second group left for a farm elsewhere. In one more week all the children were safe. They survived. Their sentence was overthrown by the Dutch Resistance.

Cornelius had a job to do. It was getting to be spring early in 1944. The winter was making room for the spring. The plants in the backyard at the Deiman Straat did not know that a war was still going on. The plants grew better than ever, thanks to the fertilizer Cornelius had scooped out of the toilet in Groenedijk's warehouse. The pig had been happy to see a human being clean the toilet which had become his home until the pig had to make its final and total sacrifice and yield its life in exchange for the lives of human beings. The plants had been grateful and grew faster than they had originally planned to grow. The green cabbage was almost as big as Cornelius 'head. The red cabbage was somewhat slower. Marie Brandwijk had taught him all the tricks to grow the vegetables. He had already harvested several heads of lettuce from his garden , much to the delight of Johanna

Tomorrow his dad and Cornelius were going on an important

trip, his dad had told him. They were going to leave the house at six O'clock in the crisp spring morning for a very long trip to the city of Alkmaar in North Holland. There were some forty people waiting for a new Ausweiss and Kees had received them that day for delivery as soon as possible.

Cornelius could not sleep from excitement that night. A long trip was his favorite past time. And he loved to meet all the people underway. He did not fear the German roadblocks. In fact he enjoyed the possible play he had to act, if needed.

It was early in the morning, 5 a.m. Cornelius was wide-awake an exciting day had begun. He did not think of the possible dangers which could grasp them. He was just excited to get on the road and see the countryside between The Hague and Alkmaar. This famous city used to be the center of the cheese industry. Now the cheeses were gone, having been stolen by the Germans. The cheese market was empty and the costumed men with their white hats had been forced to go work for the Nazis. The tower of the city hall still overlooked the scene where the wooden cheese carriers used to be filled with loads of cheese, five-pounders, round and stacked up seven layers high. The clock in the tower was still on-time, although the carillon had been abruptly stopped one day when an NSB-er remarked that it was playing Dutch patriotic tunes, including the Dutch national anthem. The German commander had been outraged and he demanded to see the tower attendant, who had the gall to keep those tunes playing. Every hour after the hour the clock played its tunes, but no more. The tower attendant had been scolded and commanded to change the tunes into German patriotic ones.

The man had acted stupid and said he did not know how to change the tunes and the person who did was dead. The commandant had sent a detachment of soldiers to fix the matter. Half-an-hour later shots had sounded from the top of the City Hall tower. The carillon had stopped. No tunes at all were playing from the top of the City Hall tower, much to the outrage of the population. It had almost come to a riot in Alkmaar. The wise but collaborating Chief of Police had intervened with the citizens. He had told them that the silence of the carillon was not worth the lives of anyone, let alone any of the Alkmaarders.

Cornelius was dressed as usual, or rather, he was packed as usual. This time he had two contraband items on his tiny body. A thousand well-counted food stamps and fifty fake ID cards. The latter were packed on his back while the food stamps were on his chest and hungered belly. This time Johanna had sewed each layer of paper in between thin sheets so they would not crinkle or make a crackling sound when Cornelius would be touched. Kees and Johanna had become artists in hiding the contraband paperwork. There would be no chance of losing this cargo.

Cornelius had his instructions. He was told to lie about everything the patrols would ask him, like, "Do you live in The Hague?" He would answer a different city name. "Any answer would have to be other than the truth," Kees instructed him. "And remember to cry when I tell you." To Cornelius it was all a game and he enjoyed it. "Don't say anything by yourself and don't speak if you are not asked anything," was another instruction he never forgot.

When they mounted the bicycle little Cornelius was not so little anymore. Under his seat were the sandwiches Johanna had made. He would not risk those being taken either. He was determined to make this trip a pleasant and winning trip. Cornelius felt like a Resistance fighter who could handle the enemy like no one else.

When they left The Hague Kees took the narrow roads trying to avoid as many villages and barricades as he could. He knew he could not avoid them all and he remembered the places where the German concentrations were. Once he had passed the city of Leiden he was in the clear for the rest of the day. His goal was to get past Haarlem. After passing that city the next was Beverwijk. Just before that he had to cross the Noordzee Kanaal, the channel which connected Amsterdam with the North Sea.

There he was expecting heavy barricades and lots of roadblock.

Kees was right, the first roadblock appeared after seven hours of easy bicycling and just one kilometer before he reached the ferry.

When the infamous words "Halt Ausweiss" sounded they were

both prepared for the worst.

The soldiers apparently were stimulated by a sense of urgency, but also, it seemed that there was pressure from higher up not to let anybody cross the canal.

Kees had a specially-forged pass which told the reader that he was going to the city of Alkmaar for the factory. He was going to instruct people how to assemble a new device which had just arrived from Germany. Kees even had an example of the device. He tried to carefully tell the soldiers that he could only talk about it to a commander because the device was still a secret to the regular soldiers.

That caused a little turmoil in the ranks at the barricade and soon a Captain was called at the scene. Kees, still holding the bicycle with Cornelius sitting on his seat, told the captain, "Can we have some privacy here for just a minute? I am on an errand for the factory to explain and instruct some of your officers in the city of Alkmaar. I am not to show what I have to anyone but a captain or higher." The captain looked at him in disbelief – a Dutchman on a mission for us, the Germans? He demanded the papers Kees had handed previously to the soldiers.

"Sir eh...Herr von Rein," he began, almost tripping over his own words."Do you mean to say that you know more than us about this secret thing you have with you? I am sorry but I will have to see what you have and what it can do before I believe a word of what you are saying. By the same token you might be smuggling some secret weapon to the Resistance in Haarlem. Place your bike against that wall over there and come with me, you can leave your child there on the bike, he will be safe as long as you are telling the truth.

Kees knew what was going to happen, the Resistance leaders had sent a telex message just hours before, signed by the Captain in charge of the factory where Kees was doing his slave labor. The entire message was a fake and so was the signature of the Captain.

The Telex read: *"If a person arrives at your barricade and his name is Kees van Rijn please make sure he is the real Kees van Rijn. You can recognize him easily because he always travels*

with a young boy on the back of his bicycle. The boy's name is
Cornelius. Mr. van Rijn is a specialist in trigger devices and very
valuable to the Reich. Please give him all the assistance you can.
Signed, Herr. Oberst Captain Heimil"*

The captain looked at Kees and then asked, "Wie Heist der
Jungen?" Kees was familiar with the trick, he would first ask him
and then he would ask Cornelius, but he was not told what to
answer and remembering his instructions he would lie. A sense of
panic began to well up in Kees. Then he decided to give Cornelius
the sign to cry. It always worked the minute Kees gave the sign,
Cornelius began to cry.

Several soldiers walked over to Cornelius and tried to comfort
the little boy. It did not help. On the contrary, Cornelius began to
cry louder. The captain saw the scene and decided to give up his
suspicions "Gehen Sie mal, Gute Reise Herr von Rein," he said.

When Kees rode away from the barricade he said quietly,
"Good job, you did it again my son."

The Resistance in The Hague was often a step ahead of the
enemy. This time they had taken a major risk but it had paid off.
Kees' trip was very important to the country. Several important
people were waiting for their new ID's in Alkmaar, but Kees was
not out of trouble yet.

In a Reformed Church in Alkmaar a group of more than twenty
people were praying for a miracle. Several of their friends had
been arrested that day and no one knew why. They were not Jewish and they were not NSB-ers, who sometimes would get arrested
because they had acted too fanatical. They were not Resistance
fighters. They were all in the medical field doing their every day
jobs in hospitals and clinics. Why had they been arrested and what
was going to happen to them? That was the big question on the
minds of everyone present. If it was because of their profession,
who was going to be next?

No one dared to go and ask in fear of having to undergo the
same lot. Pray at that time was the only thing one could do.

Kees was directed to that church. It was to be his contact address and it would be there where he knew people were desperately

waiting for the ID's he and Cornelius were bringing. Why they would need new ID's Kees would never know nor ask. Everyone had different reasons. Kees was just the messenger, the courier for the Resistance.

It was not until the next day at 1:00 p.m. when Kees arrived at the Christian Reformed Church in Alkmaar. They had stopped at a farm Kees knew the people from on a previous visit. They had been welcomed like royalties, had a great meal and slept as if there was no war going on around them.

Their final distance was about four to six hours to ride, provided there were no further road blocks. Of course they had been stopped three more times but they had been simply routine stops and Kees' papers had been readily accepted.

Kees did not expect so many people at the church. Normally his contacts were two or three people at the most. He was surprised and his natural instinct told him that there was something wrong with this picture, something which was too unusual in the circles of the Resistance.

He looked inquisitively at the small crowd and wondered who his contact would be, when a heavy-set man came walking towards him. Jovially, he spread his arms in a gesture to give Kees a big hug. What bothered Kees at that point in time was that the man had mentioned his name loudly and for everyone to hear. What was going on with these people? Did they trust each other that much?

The heavy man spoke, "Mijnheer van Rijn, we have been expecting you anxiously. We have a great number of people here who need what you are bringing. Can we have it please?"

This was too crazy and Kees had to take action immediately.

"Sir, what is your name?" Kees asked.

"Jaap van der Gast," the man answered.

"Before we can produce what you need, can we go somewhere in private please?" Kees demanded.

"Sure" was his reply, "but I don't know why that would be necessary."

"It is the way we work in the South, we call it 'secrecy and safety,'" Kees replied. "Please, this way," the heavy man said, pointing towards the door which obviously led to the vicarage. When they entered the hallway Kees saw dozens of suitcases and wondered if they belonged to the men inside the church. They sat down on a couch and Kees had to relieve his mind. "Jaap, please don't get me wrong on this, but do you personally vouch for all those people in the church? Are you sure there are no traitors among them? If you are not sure you could have blown my cover once and for all times. I am very much disturbed to be confronted by so many people, so many strangers at one time."

"Jaap, who are all these people in the church? I need to know in order to help them with their Ausweiss I have the ID's here with me but I cannot just hand them out to the people. Do you have a list of names and what they do?" Kees had perhaps become a little over-cautious but Jaap reassured him that they were all approved Hollanders. None of them could possibly be NSB-ers.

"Let me look at that list please," Kees said. Jaap produced the list from a drawer and handed it to him.

"Wait a minute!" Kees exclaimed. "Are they all doctors?" Jaap nodded his head."Yes, in fact we have practically all the doctors who live in this city here except for three of them who have been arrested this morning."

"Really?" Kees interjected. "Why would the Nazis all of a sudden start chasing doctors?"

"We think," answered Jaap, "that the Germans want to use the doctors in the Arbeits Einsatz and they will take them all away to the front-lines. That is a rumor we heard a few days ago. The question is why they only picked up the three and not the rest of them. We need to find out about that quickly. Meanwhile, the doctors in the church need to go in hiding and receive a fake ID card."

Kees agreed with the last statement, but he wanted to know more. "Do you have a policeman inside whom we can trust?"

Jaap shook his head. "Not that I know of. We were thinking if you had any connections higher up who could find out about the situation." Kees thought long and hard and when he finally spoke he had made a decision. "First of all, we need to bring these people here into a safe place. This church is too obvious for the Germans.

They could come at any moment and scoop them all up into their trucks. Secondly, do you have a telex available which is safe?" Jaap acknowledged both questions.

"We have about four hours until night falls...how is the curfew in this city?"

"Not too bad, they don't have that many soldiers and police here. Besides, we have lots of alleys and backyards we can move through. What do you have in mind?"

Kees was thinking again for a while and said, "I know of three farmers fairly close together where we can bring them. I will have to go there now quickly and prepare the farmers for a large arrival. When I come back they all need to be ready. Make sure no one leaves in the meantime or they will jeopardize the entire operation and in particular their safety. Don't tell anyone where they will be going. I will also need at least four more of your local Resistance people to help us tonight."

Kees called Cornelius. "Son, let us take off your clothes and relieve you from all the papers you are carrying. We can hide them here in this room and no one will find them. Jaap, where can we put this stuff? It took them less than two minutes to remove all the sewed up packets from Cornelius and when he was dressed again he was a lot skinnier. He made a sigh of relief and shook himself like a bird which had just taken a bath.

Kees took immediate action, and said, "Please bring me to the Telex machine we talked about, can we do that pretty inconspicuously?"

Kees would not go any place without Cornelius. They put him in the seat and walked with bike on his side toward an office just half a mile away.

Kees went to work on the telex and typed:

"<*Daniel 2:2: Why were they called in? The king wants answers now.* >Corrie>."

When he had sent the message he told Jaap that there would be an answer within ten minutes and they would have to wait for that. Even though there was no time to lose, it would be important to find out what was behind the arrests. How could the Germans leave the entire population of a city without doctors? Was that another way to eliminate their opponents and win the war?

The answer came sooner than they had anticipated:

"<Daniel 2:10, 11 and 12.>HQ>."

Kees had to let it sink in for a minute and then he said, "I need a Bible, let's go back to the church and decipher the answer. We need to know right now. Apparently it is a situation which is familiar to everyone at headquarters in The Hague."

Kees knew his Bible very well. This text was about the King and his "doctors" but he really wanted to know the exact wording. When they had returned to the church and opened the Bible, Kees read aloud, "There is not a man on the earth who could declare the matter...and it is a rare thing that the King requireth...and commanded to destroy all the wise men..."

"There it is," Kees proclaimed. "The Nazis are going to destroy all the 'wise men' The German Command have made a decision to begin Razzias to catch all the doctors in the country.

A warning has gone out through the whole country. I am surprised you have not picked up on it here in Alkmaar. We need to do as I told you earlier, get these doctors to hiding places, give them fake ID's and try to keep them safe. We need a photographer to get their pictures. Even before tonight when we take them to the farms they should at least have different ID's."

"I have a Photographer on stand-by, he knew of your arrival and of the number of ID's which you were bringing. Let me take care of that detail while you go visit those farms and prepare them for the arrivals tonight."

Kees mounted up with Cornelius on the backseat and rode his bicycle out of the city. It was only three kilometers away when he reached the first farm. The farmer and his wife had been very helpful on many occasions and when they saw Kees driving up on his bicycle they were pleasantly surprised.

"Look who is here, Kees and Cornelius, all the way from The Hague! What brings you to our humble farm-house today?" the farmer announced. "The usual," Kees answered. "We have about six people who need to go into hiding here tonight. It is a matter of great urgency, can you help us?"

"There is more," Kees continued. "We have need of three other farms to hide these people. Can you help me with that as well?" The farmer nodded and said, "Of course I can, anything for our country and for our people. May I ask who these people are we will be hiding? Are they known Jews?"

"This time they are no Jews my friend," answered Kees. "There is a new offensive by the Nazis. This time they are going after the professionals – the doctors and even the lawyers. They want to remove them from our society so life can become more difficult for us. Can you imagine if all our doctors are gone? What will happen to the sick"?

"Yes I can," replied the farmer. "People will die like flies and resistance will come to a minimum. We will have to do everything we can to avoid that."

"We, the Resistance that is, are providing them with new ID's and gradually they will be able to help patients again by visiting them at their homes," Kees said. "They can also go into the hospitals as visitors and assist the nurses with their advice. I know it is going to be hard but with God's help we can do it. The Nazi dragnet has many holes in it. We Dutch are good fishermen and we find any gap to swim through."

With that Kees ended, saying, "I have to go now, can I count on you to notify the other farms? They will be coming around eleven o'clock tonight if all goes according to our plan."

At the church there was a lot of activity going on when Kees returned. A photographer had taken pictures of people whose ID's were going to be changed. The ID's had pre-printed names on them and some of the doctors had become picky about their new name. When Kees walked in there was a noisy crowd discussing and arguing.

The noise was too much, it could attract the attention of a by-passing NSB-er and that would be the end of all of them. So Kees, raising his voice as little as possible, called out, "Gentlemen, gentlemen, may I please have your attention? I have come all the way from The Hague to help you in your predicament. With the noise you are making here the Germans could march in at any moment and arrest you all. Please understand the gravity of your situation and be very quiet. Jaap, did you get other Resistance people to come yet?"

"They should be here any moment. They are coming in two's and will enter the church as if a service will begin."

"Is there anyone here who can play the organ?" Kees called out softly. "My wife can," one of the doctors answered. "Shall I go get her?"

"No sir you should not go outside at this moment, it is too dangerous and it could jeopardize the safety of us all."

Chapter Forty Two

THE NSB-ER

—∽—

"Jaap, can you send someone to go get her? We need to re-enact a church service and everyone needs to sit down as if it is a service. Minister, can you arrange that? I don't care what you preach as long as it is not against the Nazis. Then when an NSB-er walks in, he'll see what they are used to seeing: a church service in progress. Jaap, when your people arrive I need you to have them create a ring of two hundred meters around this church. Set up a warning system so we will not run into any surprise visits."

Cornelius was sitting down in one of the isles and heard his dad in action. He was so proud of him. His dad was such a great organizer! Within ten minutes the church had become a *real* church with the organ playing and a preacher preaching. Anyone could come in and accept the normality of a church service.

Peter van Welzen had been in the NSB since the first day the Dutch had surrendered. He thought that if you could not win then you should join the winners and in the end, you will win. He had never thought he was a traitor and when the German seminars and up-sweeping meetings had begun he had gradually become what he was now: a peon of the Nazis. He was one they could use anywhere at their discretion. They could make him do what they wanted, because any wrong move of a NSB-er meant the firing squad.

What made the NSB so attractive in the first place and what could bring normal Dutch citizens to become traitors?

The organization named NSB was founded by the Nazis long before the war had begun. As early as 1933, the Movement had been set up in Germany with the ultimate goal to spread across Europe. The letters stood for *d* (National socialistic Movement). When the NSB began, the promoters appealed to the masses with all kinds of humanitarian slogans. The weakest and most idealistic of the Dutch people joined the German originating party and thus signed away their rights to be true Dutchmen.

Peter van Welzen was such a person, but sometimes he felt uneasy about his role. All the people he had betrayed were gone and they seemed never to come back. What had happened to them? At the end of the war many of the NSB-ers committed suicide because of their gnawing conscience. Peter was having those known feelings when he walked by the Christian Reformed Church in Alkmaar. He thought that if he went into the church and listened to what God had to say to him it might take away the awkward feelings he was fighting with. He took a bold step and went inside the service that was going on as usual. It was like he had been used to before the war, and something inside him stirred up the memories of being able to look straight into people's eyes without feeling remorse. What was happening to him?

The feeling did not last very long, when he felt a hand on his shoulder from behind him. He turned around and saw one of his former good friends with tears in his eyes, shaking his head.

"Peter, so good to see you here, I have not seen you for so long, what have you been up to?"

Peter did not know what to say, he was at a loss for words and his mind was at a crossroads of remorse and fear. The man who had put his hand on his shoulder changed his gentle touch into a grip, pulling him out of the isle by his arm and towards the front of the church. Peter panicked, did they know what he was, what he had become, and did they know his intentions to betray people? His own fellow citizens and brothers? The man pulled him inside a room to the side of the pulpit. From the corner of his eye he could see how the entire congregation was following them until they were out of sight.

Suddenly and without any warning, the man turned him around. Before he knew it he was handcuffed and pushed against the wall.

"This day, my friend Peter van Welzen, you have been weighed and found to be too light. It is too late my friend, this was the last time you were planning your evil against your fellow men." He was roughly pushed into a closet and heard the door locked behind him. Peter's mind was racing, what had he done wrong today? Why now? How could he talk himself out of this situation? He began to scream and bang on the door. It was not a heavy, solid door, and he knew that he could break it down eventually. He heard the lock open again. The friend who had brought him there had a roll of duct tape in his hand. Peter began to scream louder but the man pushed a rag into his mouth. He was thrown backwards and fell on the floor. The tape began to circle his face until only is nose was left un taped, at least he could breathe. Then he felt the tape going down his body encircling his feet and his legs. He could not scream and he could not move. Finally the man spoke, "You filthy betrayer. Don't worry. We will help you out of your misery soon."

Was that a promise or was it a threat? He had to wait and find out. Perhaps the preacher would try to convert him after the service, or perhaps they would bring him out of town and drop him off somewhere in the meadows and he would have to walk back home. Perhaps he should quit the NSB, he was having too much remorse anyway. Perhaps he could get out of the country like so many Jews had done, through Switzerland or the mountains of Spain.

The little incident had brought fear into the men in the church.

Were they that close to being betrayed and arrested?

The photographer had developed the pictures for the ID's. He had made great efforts to have each person look different than he looked before. He had used some wigs and moustaches and even some noses and eyelashes. The men were invited to come to Kees one by one and receive their new ID card. Some were embarrassed by what they saw on their ID. They would have to keep their disguise attributes. Kees was telling them to use them whenever they would go outside until further notice.

"This, Gentlemen," Kees had announced, "is serious business. Don't under-estimate the enemy. They are determined to get you and you will have to be the one to defeat them in their pursuit. We cannot help you once you go onto the streets." The atmosphere of disbelief which had been in the church when Kees had arrived had made place for anxiety. These people were doctors who had studied for years. They knew a lot, but warfare was beyond their comprehension.

The men were almost ready for their move to their temporary hiding place when one of them posed a valid question. "What about our wives and children, Kees?"

"For the time being they will be safe. The HQ in the Hague has sent extra Resistance personnel here to help protect them. They are used for surveillance and they will report immediately about any activity. They will warn your wives and children and protect them or take them into hiding if need be." It was a legitimate concern and even Kees had his doubts about what the Germans would do if they did not find any of the doctors at home.

Kees would see if he could get the local churches to issue a letter to the commanders in the city of Alkmaar, requesting them to keep their hands off of innocent women and children.

Often such letters had been issued. Sometimes they had had the opposite effect, but in the case of women and children who would be helpless against the soldiers, church letters had worked.

The doctors left in little groups of four under the guidance of a local Underground worker. They knew the back-roads and the alleys. Through fields and orchards they walked their way into one of the four dedicated farms. Peace had come to the church, where Cornelius had been sitting and looking in wonderment at the hustle and bustle of the Resistance in action.

He had found a notebook in one of the pews with some pages of writing in it, perhaps from someone who had been making notes of a sermon and had forgotten the notebook. Cornelius had made drawings of the windmills he had seen on the way to Alkmaar. He was drawing the different kinds of windmills, those which were used for pumping water out of the Polders, and the one which was used to grind grain and wheat. Then there were those windmills which were surrounded by logs which were floating in the water. He once saw them pulling logs out of the water and sawing planks out of the logs, while the Germans loaded the planks onto trucks. Had they bought them? Perhaps, but the Germans never paid for anything.

Around the church the cordon of Resistance men was gradually breaking up. The church, which had been the center of activity, would no longer be suspect to anyone. Soldiers would not be interested in a church at night and NSB-ers would not dare to go into a church at night by themselves.

The men were gathering in the church to discuss what further action was needed to resolve the doctor crisis. The person who had taken Peter van Welzen out of the church sanctuary into the separate room spoke. "What shall we do with Peter Van Welzen? You all know how many people he has betrayed. He could have blown our cover here tonight as well if I had not spotted him and disabled him. I have him gagged in the closet over there" The question hung in the air for a long five minutes. None of them were killers. None of them had ever killed a person. They were not about to even think that way. "Peter has to be taken out of his activities. He has cost us too much trouble and he will continue if we let him go."

"Yes I agree," said Kees. "What do you have in mind with him?"

"Can we make peter Jewish? Give him a Jewish name and an ID with a 'J' on it?"

"Go on," Kees encouraged.

"If we change his identity into Jewish and drop him off at the police office in Haarlem they will take him to Westerbork without questions asked. If he says he is not who is on his ID they will laugh at him. That will get him where he has sent so many people, possibly to Auschwitz. He will be able to experience what he has done to the people he had betrayed and in the meantime, he will be out of circulation here."

It was a bold plan. The person who had spoken had no idea that he had sentenced Peter van Welzen with the death sentence. It was a solution Peter deserved but who were they to be the judge and jury, even the hangman?

Kees had his doubts about the plan and made them known. "Is it right for us to sentence a person? Can we not just hold him captive and talk to the man? I don't think we should stoop to the level of the enemy. Do you? Is there a volunteer here who will take this man into temporary custody and try to persuade him to change?"

It was a dilemma for most of the people present. They were all thinking of a plausible solution when the pastor of the Church spoke. "Gentlemen, as you know I am not part of the Resistance but being a man of God I strongly sympathize with Kees here. We are different than our enemy. And we have to give our fellow men a second chance. That does not mean we can let Peter just go his merry way. It means we need to try to save him from his iniquity and see if he will repent."

Several "Amen's" could be heard. When he continued you could feel the relief which was building in the room.

The pastor continued. "It would be different when we would have been attacked by someone and during a fight someone can get killed. Then we are talking about defending ourselves. In this case we have a repeat offender who, during peace time, would be sentenced to jail time during which he can think about his mischief done to others. Since we don't have a jail and the jails we have in the city are manned by the enemy, we will have to create a jail. I don't think the church would be the right place for that purpose but gentlemen, I do have a proposal. I have a cellar in the vicarage. As you all know I am not married and I have a housekeeper who is a dedicated Christian and an upstanding citizen. I propose that I will talk to her right now and if she agrees. I will take the task upon me to keep Peter in my cellar. I will talk with him daily and I will try my best to teach him that he can turn from his wicked ways, repent and he will be saved. If I can have a moment I will go and talk to my house keeper."

He left; the men in the sanctuary were in awe about the sim-
plicity of the pastor's proposal.

Kees, who had felt very uneasy about the situation, took a deep
breath before he spoke again. "Gentlemen, I am pleased about
what you have accomplished tonight. I am urging you to stay the
course. It is good to see that none of you are cold-blooded killers.
We cannot be that way and ever win his war. Our mentality and
our conscience will bring the victory, with the help of God. Now
that it has become too late for me to begin my travel back to The
Hague I must ask if someone here can provide me with a bed for
the night where my son and I can sleep for some hours before we
begin our journey back. Many hands were raised at the same time.
Kees was pleased to see that almost everyone was like-minded and
that their doors were open to help their fellow citizens. When the
pastor returned, the display of bravery continued.

My house keeper agreed to take this man into our custody but
we both feel that we will need help for the next couple of days to
ensure that we will be able to keep this man captive without any
trouble." Again, many hands were raised. Peter van Welzen was
safe for the time being and by the grace of God he had received a
second chance – something the Nazis would have never done.

They brought Peter to the cellar of the vicarage where the
Pastor's housekeeper had already prepared a bed for the prisoner.
Two men had taken up the task of bringing him, still gagged and
tied up, to the cellar. When he was sat down in a chair they told
him that if he would behave and not scream they would untie him,
take the tape from his face and feet and talk to him like reasonable
men. Peter nodded his head.

The tedious and painful job to pull the tape from his face began. With a face full of fear and pain Peter was finally able to talk
again.

He did not talk, instead he fainted, the tension and the fear of
what might come had taken its toll and he passed out. For a brief
moment he did not have to deal with his gnawing remorse.

Chapter Forty Three

JUMPING FROM A TRAIN

—⚏—

T he train had been loaded. All the wagons had been locked
behind the Jews who had waited for five hours at the main
station in The Hague. The soldiers had kept the captives in check
with their guns. An occasional shot was heard when someone made
a move which the soldiers did not agree with. The people had been
waiting patiently, often times sitting on the only suitcase they had
brought.

They were all like lambs going to the slaughter house. How
true this was no one really could comprehend. That the Nazis
would kill them all, right after their arrival in Birkenau, no one
could ever believe. There were two Jewish brothers, David and
Ishmael Schmall, among the crowd. David was the youngest at
only seventeen and his brother was twenty. Their parents had been
taken while they were in the woods having a good time watching
birds on an early morning in March of 1943. The two of them had
been determined to find out where their parents had gone to that
morning. No letter was left and the house was almost emptied.
Even the bed sheets and blankets had been taken.

Later that day they had a visitor from the Resistance. He had
told them that they were looking for young children. The man had
warned them to get out of town and go to the north country. "There
the Germans don't have a stronghold on the people like here. It is

your only chance to survive this war," he said as he left.

They had not accepted their fate; to lose their parents without knoing where they had been taken was not an option. They had begun to inquire. They had gone to the Jewish Council in The Hague and asked many questions without getting a satisfactory answer. After days of roaming the streets, avoiding any contact with the German soldiers they had decided to go to their uncle Kees in the Deiman Straat. They knew he worked for the Germans, perhaps he could find out what had happened to their parents.

It took a long time before the door opened and Aunt Johanna greeted them. She pulled them quickly inside and closed the door before she said a word. "What brings you boys here? David, I have not seen you for a year and Ish, boy you have grown up. Look at that black beard, you really look like you father," she had said.

"Come on into the living room and tell me what your visit is all about." They could not fathom how ignorant their aunt seemed; didn't she know what was happening to the Jews in the city? Ishmael being the oldest took the lead and said, "Aunt Jo, haven't you heard about the massive disappearances of people? We went to the Jewish Council and they said that all Jews are being sent to a concentration camp in Germany. The council told us that we have to obey the German commands and have them take us there too. They are going to build special Jewish towns somewhere where all the Jews will be able to live together. Isn't it odd that people are arrested to go there?

"Aunt Jo, you are Jewish. Why haven't you gone yet?" David asked. "Where is Uncle Kees, can we talk to him? Perhaps he knows something you don't and maybe he can give us an advice what we should do. We certainly don't feel like going somewhere we don't know anything about." Johanna had shaken her head. "No, uncle Kees is not here right now, I hope he will be back tonight. He went on a trip with Cornelius on his bicycle. Boys, I know he will tell you things you cannot believe and I want to urge you to stay here until he comes."

"Oh no, Aunt Jo we cannot stay. We have research to do and we don't want to waste our time just waiting here," Ishmael told her.

"Now listen to me, I will tell you one thing which should persuade you to stay. Your uncle is in the Resistance and he does a lot of work to protect Jews all over the country. If there is anyone who can give you answers it is your uncle. Besides it will be very dangerous for you two out there. If you get caught you will be shipped off or go to jail until you can be shipped off. The Jewish Council is completely governed by the Nazis. They will only tell you to obey the German commands to save their own hide. Believe me there is a war going on out there. That war is more against Jews than against the Dutch and since you are both Jews and even look like Jews your freedom is hanging on by a thread and you won't last much longer if you go outside."

It finally sank into their heads that something strange was going on and that they better wait for their uncle. Aunt Johanna spoke again, her tone was now sounding like she was afraid. "Did you see if anyone followed you or saw you when you rang our doorbell?"

They both shook their heads. "We cannot take any risk, we are surrounded by NSB-ers here in this street and they report any one coming or going. Here is what you both need to do, and please take this seriously. It is almost dark outside; in ten minutes it should be dark enough not to be recognized from across the street. I am going to let you out as if you are leaving. We are going to be loud, when we say goodbyes, just to create attention. Then you will leave and walk to the left for only twenty meters and you turn left. Right around the corner is a portico; you go into that and up the stairs as quickly as possible. You need to ring the doorbell on the left door as well and an old lady will open the door. The minute she opens you have to say the word 'Graag' and she will let you inside quickly. Is that all clear so far?"

They both nodded but did not understand what the charade was all about.

"Once you are inside the house, the lady, you may call her Aunty Beth, will show you what to do." The clock seemed to be ticking slower at that moment and the darkness seemed to want to wait a little longer to provide the cover they so desperately needed. At last Aunt Johanna said, "Okay, let's do it now." She led them to the front door, opened it, and walked them out the door. She gave each of them an elaborate hug and loudly proclaimed, "So good to see you boys, come and see me again soon," and she pushed them in the direction they should go.

Both of them were flabbergasted at the hullabaloo they had been through. They did what their aunt had told them.

The old Lady opened the door; they both said the word and were led inside without any further ado.

Her first words were, "You boys in trouble?" They shook their heads simultaneously. "So why did you come here using the code and all?"

They had never heard the word "code" from Aunt Johanna and they told the lady that they were her nephews and that they were to wait for their uncle to come home. "Oh," the lady answered. "I know what you need to do, sit down for a minute and I will tell you. We will have to wait half an hour. That is the agreement I made with your aunt and uncle. Then I will bring you to our balcony in the back and you need to climb down from it to the backyard and parking place of Mr. Groenedijk's warehouse. There will be a door to the right which is open. Go through that door and Johanna will meet you there."

They did not understand why this was all necessary, but since the two ladies had prepared it in such a manner they went with the flow and did as they were told. Once inside the warehouse, they were surrounded by box tricycles and bikes.

On the right hand side against the wall they saw a large worktable which slowly began to move forward.

They could not see a person moving it and went to look at it from close by. Then they saw two hands pushing the table away from the wall. It was obviously rolling on wheels and it did not seem too heavy to move. They helped push it further and then they saw Johanna, who had opened a hatch through which her hands had been pushing the table away. "Surprise," she said quietly. "This is our hidden entrance and nobody knows about it. No one can see us coming or going and it has to stay that way. Come on down boys and I will show you something."

The doorbell rang and loud knocking could be heard on the door of Johanna's house. Those NSB-ers have done it again she thought and quickly ran across the sandy floor underneath her home, up the ladder through the closet and into the hallway to open the front door.

The two boys saw some mattresses and nothing else which would betray that there were fifteen people living here.

When Johanna opened the door she was pushed aside roughly and half a dozen soldiers began to search the home. They could not find anything even in the backyard there was no sign of any others.

The lady which they had intruded upon so cruelly was sitting on a bed and apparently crying. The leader of the soldiers remarked to the others, "NSB-ers, we should hang them and send them off to a concentration camp too. They give us more trouble than we can use. Gehen Wir mahl!"

Johanna stepped on the crackboard twice. The boys heard the sound and wondered what it meant. Suddenly the wall on the opposite side of the sandy area under the floor began to move. To their great surprise the two young men saw the wall move all the way open and it seemed like dozens of people came walking out. What was this all about and who were these people? They did not have to wonder for very long when one of them introduced himself. "I am Joseph Rosenberg, and who are you?"

"We are the Schmall boys, David and Ishmael." He held his hand out to shake Joseph's. "We just arrived here and did not know there were so many people here. Are you in hiding?"

Joseph nodded and said, "Yes we are, all fifteen of us. But five of us will be moving tonight when Kees comes back home." The introductions went on for a little while as each person shook their hands until Johanna came back down.

She addressed the young men, saying, "You see what happened?"

They did not and shook their heads.

"Your coming here at our front door caused the NSB-ers in the neighborhood to call the Gestapo and they immediately came to investigate. That is why we don't want anyone to come to our front door. The Germans keep a close check on our house and have the NSB-ers warn them if we get a visit. I am glad I ushered you guys out the door and in through the warehouse, nobody knows that you are here now. You will have to remain here for a while until your uncle can find you a more permanent hiding place on one of the farms and if you are lucky you might even get on your way to Palestine."

Johanna went back upstairs through the secret passage, up the small ladder, through the wall in the closet. It was a routine she did many times a day, bringing food and tea and water for washing and all kinds of messages to keep the Guests down below more or less alive.

When Cornelius was lifted off the bicycle after a trip of 15 hours, he was so stiff he could hardly stand on his feet. Kees was the only person who could enter the house without getting suspicion from the NSB-ers. They knew him but they were very curious what he was up to all the time riding his bicycle. Kees was exhausted when he came home. When he had stored his bicycle in the vestibule of the house he blobbed down in a chair and let out a deep sigh.

"Johanna my dear, there was so much going on in Alkmaar that I cannot even begin to tell you what happened there. How have you fared these three days while we were gone?"

She told him about the food shortage and how hard it was to gather enough drinking water. "The city water system has come to a thin trickle and I have been gathering water from the rainfall. I have practically every pot, pan and container outside when it rains. With so many people down stairs I don't have enough water. I have cut down washing water to twice a week .It is beginning to smell down there. And…oh, Kees," she said as she began to cry. The shortages were taking a toll on the stout and hard-working woman. When she re-gained herself she said, "We have two of my nephews below. They came here late this afternoon, rang the doorbell, of course, which triggered a visit by the Gestapo. But I was able to play it safe because I had the boys leave in an obvious way and come back in through the warehouse.

"Let's get them up here and I'll see what's going on with them. Perhaps we can help them get out of the country. Have they heard anything from their parents?"

Johanna did not know. "All I could do is get them safely out of here and guide them the way down." Johanna took the initiative and went to get the two nephews. She never raised her voice or called someone from below, she took the time to go down the ladder and walk over to the persons she needed to talk to and softly invited them to follow her upstairs. She never took a risk to expose the hiding place with loud noises or yelling.

When she came upstairs, Cornelius had fallen asleep on his Dad's lap. She picked him up gently and brought him to his bed. He'll sleep for a long time, she thought. Tomorrow he'll go after the pigeon eggs as usual. There should be quite a few of them after three days.

Kees had skipped the welcoming act with the two young men and went straight into the situation they had found themselves in. "Do you realize how dangerous it is for you two to be on the streets right now? You are not wearing the Star of David either. Do you have your ID's with a 'J' on them?" They both nodded and said "yes we do and we are mighty proud of it."

Kees continued, "But are you aware what is happening to all the Jews in this country? I take it you had a little chat with the people downstairs. Have they enlighthened you about the goal the Nazis have in regards to the Jewish people?" Kees blew out question after question the boys could not answer. When he had finally ended his rhetoric, they both asked him to tell them the entire truth without any further questions. Kees warned them. "You better brace yourselves because this is going to be very ugly, you better be prepared."

"Try us," Ish invited. "We can handle anything after what we experienced in the past few days."

"I really don't think so," Kees said. "First of all, the Nazis are out to destroy the Jewish people, to annihilate them from the whole earth.

Systematically they have administrated who the Jews are and where they live. Now, methodically they have first invited everyone to pack up their belongings, limited to one suitcase mind you, and come to the train station at a certain time. The Jewish Council has advised them to do what the Nazis tell them.

Thousands, no, hundreds of thousands did what they were told. They were transported in cattle trains to three major concentration camps. Do you get the irony of that?

'Concentrate' is the word it comes from! Lately we have found out that those camps are not to concentrate the Jews. They are to kill them. A doctor came back from there and told us that the people are gassed to death the minute they arrive and then afterwards they are incinerated in giant ovens. If the ovens cannot handle the numbers the bodies are dumped in large pits, sort of mass graves as they called them."

The two young men were spell-bound and aghast and with a hoarse voice David asked, "Have our parents gone there?" Kees merely nodded his head. "I am sure of that. Boys believe me when I tell you that if you are not very careful you will be next."

"So what can we do to avoid that?" Ishmael asked, still in shock over the horrible news.

"By going underground and staying underground either until this war is over or flee to Spain or Switzerland. We actually have channels by which you can get out of this country and through Belgium and France to those two countries. The very first thing you must accept right now is that you can no longer be or look Jewish," Kees said. "You cannot go outside without a different ID card than the one you have with the big 'J' on it. Are you willing to change your identity?"

It had become very quiet in the room; the two young men were letting what they had heard sink in. It was David who spoke first.

"Is there anything we can do to help, just like you are doing Uncle Kees?"

"There is and there is not," Kees answered. "With that I mean for Jews it is too dangerous to be involved with the Resistance but on the other hand we need anyone to help, even if it is only to help make counterfeit paperwork. It is all literally underground work. Sometimes you will have to go outside. It is then when the greatest danger lures everywhere."

The two young men had kept their composure all through the nasty instructions they heard. Kees could see that they had to swallow a bitter pill. Would they be strong enough for the Resistance? Kees decided not to take a risk; at least he would first give them a chance to prove themselves. Perhaps later they could move into more risky jobs. "For now, I need you to stay here until I can get you a new ID. Then you will have to change your appearance, shave off the beard and make your hair blond. We have stuff you can do that with. Aunt Johanna will help you with that. Then we will take your pictures, only when that is accomplished you will be able to do something for the Resistance. I hope I made myself clear about all this?" They both agreed, and told Kees they would do whatever it required if it was only in honor of their parents.

Two days later the two young men made their first mistake. They had been restless down under the floor and one morning they thought if Johanna could go into the Groenendijk warehouse they could too. Ignoring the warnings from the other guests they went up the ladder on the side of the warehouse and moved the workbench. They walked around the box-tricycles and went into the back, to catch some fresh air. The Kapper on the corner saw the two and called the Gestapo. Within minutes they came and arrested the two. They still had their old ID's with the "J" stamped on it. That fatal day, Kees had to see his two protégés being arrested and taken away. He never heard from them until they jumped from the train.

Chapter Forty Four

NSB-ER REDEEMED

—⟡—

I n the vicarage of the Christian Reformed Church in Alkmaar a miracle was occurring. For days the pastor had gone down into the well-guarded cellar and talked to Peter van Welzen. He had confessed of all the traitorous things he had committed. It was not really what the pastor had wanted to hear.

After the first two sessions the pastor had noticed that Peter was changing.

He had become milder and friendlier. Was it fake or was it real? The pastor could not tell yet.

He kept listening and when Peter had told all his stories of treason and collaboration with the enemy he began to talk about his personal faith. It was at that point that the pastor had felt Peter was changing.

After two weeks there was a noticeable change in Peter. He had asked for a Bible and was reading it constantly. The pastor asked him if he wanted to accept Jesus as his savior. Peter had earnestly agreed. "Now you are a new creature," the pastor had told him. "What are you going to do with your life Peter?" He did not know. His wife did not know where he was or if he would even come back home. "One thing you will have to do, once you are right with God you will have to get right with men as well. God has forgiven your sins, but men, particularly those who have lost a loved one because of your treason…Peter, how are you going to face them? Do you think they will forgive you?"

Peter had his doubts about that. When the pastor spoke he made an announcement Peter would never forget. "First of all, you are going to have to face your wife and your children and ask them for forgiveness. Are you ready to do that whole-heartedly?"

Peter said he was, but the pastor gave him an assignment before he would do what he had to do. "Peter you need to pray about this tonight and ask God to lead you in this. If God is for you, who will be against you?" He agreed to do that. When the pastor left the cellar he left a broken man behind him, but he knew that he would be strong in the morning and ready to face his family.

The pastor took the bold step to visit Peter's family that evening. When he rang the doorbell and the door opened he was greeted by a woman who had obviously been crying. She knew the pastor and her first reaction was to ask, "Have you heard from Peter? He has been gone for more than three weeks and I never heard a word or sign of what he has been up to. I have done a lot of praying these last few weeks, I knew he was on the wrong path, being an NSB-er and the things he did with the Nazis. I never agreed with him and I hope it is not too late or that he has done something the Germans might punish him for."

"No, Jennie. None of those things you said have happened. Something else has though, and I think your prayers have been answered. Your husband was caught by the Resistance three weeks ago. They suspected him of spying on a situation with the doctors of this city. Peter was arrested by the Underground and has been incarcerated in my cellar all this time. The good news is that he is completely turned around. He has confessed his sins and received Jesus as his savior. Your prayers have been answered Jennie. He will be ready to face you and the children tomorrow at my vicarage, say at ten?"

Jennie was elated, her husband a Christian and not a NSB-er anymore. Only God could have done that.

The pastor should have consulted the Underground about the situation with Peter but he did not and he would regret it later.

Peter made up with his family that next morning. The pastor announced, "Peter you are free to go, now make your life worthwhile for the good of this country." He solemnly promised he would.

The Nazis did not know that Peter had changed. He received a message to report to the local Gestapo office immediately. With lead in his shoes he went and when he received his assignment he did not say a word. He had to visit three addresses of doctors who had not been on their post for a long time. The German told him that if he found them, he would have to call for backup in order to get them arrested. Instead Peter went to warn their families that they were sought for arrest. When NSB-ers who received a task from the Nazis did not come up with the required result they became a suspect right away. Peter was then put under surveillance and fell into a trap.

Only a month later he was arrested and sent to the Oranje Hotel, the most feared prison in The Hague. He was tortured until he could not stand it any longer and he broke. He was not strong enough and untrained to withstand the horrible abuse the Germans inflicted on turncoats. No one knows how many had been arrested as a result of Peter's arrest.

One of them was the Pastor of the Christian Reformed Church in Alkmaar. Together with Peter they were brought to the Dunes of Waalsdorp and while facing the firing squad they were able to sing a song of praise to their God.

Once the Germans picked up their targeted people they did not waste any time. Within days after their arrest the two Schmall men, David and Ishmael, were trucked to the train station for transport to Westerbork. From there they would be assigned to a particular concentration camp in Germany. The first choice was always Auschwitz, but if that destination was too clogged up with people the second destination would be Birkenau.

The Nazis in Westerbork would select them by strength, age and work ability.

The two young men were strong young men so they would be put to work digging pits and cleaning out the gas chambers. Those jobs would take all their energy until they collapsed. Then and only

265

then, if the Germans could not use them any longer their turn for the gas chambers had arrived.

David and Ish had been waiting at the station for a long time. Everyone had come and stood there for a while until their legs could not handle their weight anymore and they would sit down on the concrete platform.

Sometimes the Nazis would come close by and poke them with their guns, telling them to stand up. Some did, some could not, and the Nazis would walk on.

Ish and David had been watching the loading of the wagons. They had noticed that there was absolutely nothing inside the wagons. They saw that as many as a hundred people were loaded in each train car and then while they were pushed back with gun butts, they closed the sliding doors, locking them from the outside.

The latch which held the door together was pulled down firmly so that it would not be able to pop open by itself. David shook Ishmael's arm and said, "Look how they close and lock the door. If we had a steel rod, which would fit in the crack of the door, we should be able to raise the latch from its cradle. But how do we find a thin rod, or anything we could do that with?"

Both of them began to look around. Was there anything they could pull loose, a bar or a thin peace of pipe? They kept actively searching until finally David found it. It was a crowbar stuck behind a bench. "Someone must have left it there on purpose," Ish remarked. "But now that we have found it how are we going to get it inside?"

David came up with a solution. "Here Ish, I can stick it up my trouser and into my sock at the bottom. My shoe will support it. I only have to limp a little. There are many people here who have stiff legs. I even saw someone on crutches. I wonder if they will allow those on board of the train?"

At that very moment they saw a man being pushed into the wagon while his crutches were taken from him. "Well, there is your answer. So let's try to get this crowbar where no one will be able to see it and when we are pushed towards the loading train, let's try to stay behind so we will be the last ones in."

"That sounds like a good plan," David agreed, and at the same time the crowbar was no longer in his hand. He had slipped it from the top of his trousers into the right trouser leg. "Let's see if you can walk with it without it showing. I think it will work. Here let me walk close to your right side so they will have to see me before they see your limpy leg."

When their section came to be loaded up the two stayed together real close. To the Nazis they were nothing more than cattle to be driven into the wagons.

They were pushed and beaten until all one hundred people were inside and the doors were shut. David stood on one side of the opening and Ishmael on the other side. Both were pulling at the doors without the German soldiers noticing it.

They yelled and cursed because the doors would not readily shut. Finally they had managed to get the two doors together. With great effort they raised the hatch and tried to slam it down in the cradle. The first attempt failed because David and Ishmael were still pulling at the doors. The second attempt worked better even though the latch did not totally close. The soldiers had more to do and left the door lightly latched.

The other captives had been watching the two in their struggle against the locking of the doors. They did not think much of the boy's efforts until two hours later.

It was when the wagon train slowed down because of the barricades which came in sight at the Moerdijk. It was a long railroad bridge over the river the Maas.

The barricade had to be opened for the train to pass and as a result the train slowed down to a speed of eight kilometers per hour. David had already taken out the crowbar and was prying the sharp end through the crack in the door. After five minutes of pushing and sighing he had the end of the crowbar right underneath the latch.

Now he had to raise the crowbar, but it was not going up between the tight cracks. Ishmael took off his heavy boots and began to hit the crowbar on the inside of the door while David held it in place. Slowly but surely the crowbar went upwards.

Slowly the latch began to move up and up and then with a shock the latch tumbled over to the other side leaving its cradle for good.

David said to his brother "Wait, let me see exactly where and when we should open the doors and jump."

Together they had made a plan to jump out of the wagon the moment the train would begin to pick up speed. That, they reasoned would be the moment when they would be out of sight of the soldiers at the barricades, who presumably could not care less what happened with the passing train.

That moment was getting closer and the train was beginning to speed up. Suddenly at the sign of closing their eyes, they both pulled at just one of the two doors. The one door slid open and without any hesitation they both jumped, hoping they would not hit the rails or a signpost.

Their jump cleared all obstacles. They felt as if they were falling for a long time. The bridge at that point was twelve meters high; when they hit the water they went down under, deeper and deeper.

The other involuntary passengers could not believe their eyes, but no one would follow their example. They were all too scared to attempt an escape. Didn't the Jewish Council urge them to obey the enemy? Time after time they had received letters from the Jewish Council that obeying the enemy would be for their own benefit.

David and Ishmael swam back towards the railroad track. They planned to stay underneath it until dark. The water was not too cold. They both wondered how long they could stay in the water. It must have been around five in the afternoon in the month of March when water should be around ten degrees Celsius.

After three difficult days of hiding and crawling through orchards and ditches, the two young men finally reached the city limits of Rijwijk.

They were only one mile from home, their own home, when the two exhausted men realized that going home was definitely not an option.

Would the Germans have known by now that they had escaped? Or did they? The question hung in the air for days.

It was the first question they asked their uncle Kees when they entered the Groenendijk warehouse from behind, the way they had done it before. It was a pleasant surprise for the friends and family in the Deiman Straat.

It was also one of the very few times someone had been able to escape from a one way train to Auschwitz.

Chapter Forty Five

CORNELIUS' LITTLE FARM

—⚏—

In the big city of The Hague the food scarcity became bigger by the day. The Germans were punishing people for hiding the Jews.

The distribution of food was brought back to a minimum. At the headquarters in the Binnenhof, Seys Inquart and his Generals had decided that wherever illegal food was found, the owner had to be deported and the foods seized and sent to Germany to feed the soldiers.

Cornelius had expanded his little farm in the backyard of the Deiman Straat. He was now growing cabbage in different varieties and his cauliflower was ready to be eaten. He had plenty of lettuce, so much that some of it was already going into seed.

He faithfully collected the seeds so he could sow some more. He had found some peas at the Brandwijk farm and had neatly made rows in the back yard where the peas now had begun to germinate.

The last time he was at the farm he had walked into the meadows and on the side of the small river he had found a duck's nest with eight eggs in it.

He had taken the eggs, except for one, because he had learned always to leave one egg in the nest so the duck would continue laying eggs. He had asked Marie Brandwijk how he could find out if

271

he could eat the eggs and she had shown him what to do.

"You take each egg and put it in a bucket of water. If the egg floats you can eat it and if it sinks it has already been brooded and the chick might be coming out soon," she had told him. "So if they are brooded, can I just wait until the chick comes out?"

"No, you have to continue the brooding, normally the duck sits on the eggs for twenty four days and then the chicks begin to come."

Cornelius had thought for a moment and asked, "If I put them back in the nest they will come out, but then I can't catch them anymore and if I keep them I cannot sit on them or they will break. Could I put a woolen sweater over the eggs?"

"No silly, you have to give the eggs warmth. I'll tell you what you should do if you want to brood the chicks. You'll have to take the eggs and make a little nest with pieces of cloth, some leaves or grass, and some feathers if you can find some. Then you get a light bulb and hang it over the nest with eggs. Now depending on how far this duck was along in its brooding you can soon expect the chicks to come out."

Cornelius was fascinated and determined to do what she had told him. He placed the eggs in a box under the seat of his father's bicycle and when he came home he organized the little duck's nest.

He found an old lamp out of which he took the bulb fitting and plugged in the wire. It burned! In the back yard he made a little pen with boards and a long stick from one side to the other and hung the light bulb over the nest.

He could not wait to see the chicks come out. Every morning he got up early and went to his ducks' nest to see if the chicks were appearing yet. Sometimes he took an egg and held it to his ear to see if he could hear something. It took nine long days before the morning came when he saw one of the eggs moving.

He called his mother, "Mom come and see! One egg is moving!" Then he saw a beak come through the shell. The little chick seemed to be fighting for its life when finally, it broke lose. Cornelius carefully removed the broken shell.

That evening five of the eggs had been broken and five tiny

little chicks were huddled together in the nest. He wondered when the rest of the eggs would be finished. Sadly, he found out days later that those eggs had been spoiled. He wondered why, and planned to ask Marie about that.

When his dad came home that night he could not wait to tell him about the birth of his duck chicks. "But dad, when are we going to the Brandwijk farm? I need to ask Marie about some things. I need to know how to feed these chicks or they will die. Can we go tomorrow please?

"I'll tell you what you can do before you go," Johanna budded in. "I can cook some oats, and after is has cooled down you need to make it real fine. They will eat that and stay alive until you can talk to Marie."

Cornelius went back into his little farm in the backyard. He walked through his rows of vegetables and looked to see if the strawberries were beginning to bloom yet. He was startled by the squeals of the pig next door in the toilet of the Groenendijk warehouse.

Then he heard loud German voices, then some more squealing. He climbed on the fence to see what was going on next door. When he looked through the little toilet window he saw what was happening. The Germans had found the pig, which had grown big and were trying to carry it out of the toilet. How had they found out about the pig, he wondered?

An hour before the happenings in the warehouse Mr. Groenendijk had heard a knock on his door at his home two streets further. Two Gestapo men and a police man in his black uniform and the hated band with the black swastika on it had pushed themselves into his home.

They told him that he was under arrest and demanded him to take them to his warehouse. They wanted to do a search of it because they had heard some unusual noises coming from it. Besides, he was under suspicion of hiding Jews there since a few weeks ago two Jews had been arrested in his rear parking lot.

How had these men gotten into this rear parking lot, they wondered and told him that after the search he had to come with them

273

to the local police station for interrogation.

Groenendijk had gone with them hoping they would not find the secret passage-way to the Van Rijn Residence. They would find the pig he knew and thought about his plan to slaughter the pig just days ago.

Chapter Forty Six

BICYCLES SEIZE

—⟋⟍—

I t was late in the evening when Kees came home from a short
trip to a printer in Delft. He had Cornelius in the back seat. The
boy had been packed with pamphlets and food stamps.

Kees had instructed the boy once more, "Make sure to distract
the soldiers when they stop us. Never answer any questions and
if you have to, tell them something different than the truth. Never
say any names, lie about whatever they expect to hear. Above all,
when I give you the wink, you begin to cry and keep crying until
they let us go."

It had become routine for both of them. They were a great team
together. The Germans had never frisked Cornelius. But Kees was
always subjected to thorough searches.

This time the load they carried was very important. The pamphlets were meant for the doctors in The Hague. Their time to be
arrested was coming up, Kees was told by an insider – a double
agent.

The Resistance was prepared for the attack on the doctors of
the city. The warnings had to go out the next day. They needed to
be hand-delivered by dozens of couriers, mostly 12 to 14-year-old
girls, who would walk from street to street and visit several addresses. The recipients would each get ten pamphlets which would
in turn be delivered by them to addresses close by.

It was an amazing network of people and the young girls were never suspected by the Nazis until a new order was announced. The order said, "All bicycles will be seized when used by anyone under the age of twenty-five."

Not everyone was familiar with the new rule; the young girl couriers had been using bicycles all the time to get their messages quickly to their destinations. The number of people who lost their bicycles the first day the new order had come out was astonishing.

So many people got stuck by losing their bicycles that the Germans had to have the riders bring them in large groups to the German-seized warehouses. They were guarded by soldiers with guns at the ready until they reached the storage places.

The people who had to bring their bicycles in, were first searched and then they had to wait until their Ausweiss had been checked. It was at that point that the Nazis found out why so many young girls had been on the streets so often.

They found the pamphlets and some of them had fake ID's together with their old ID's.

The dreadful day of the bicycle seizures.

276

That terrible day was later called "the bicycle disaster" because as many as two hundred young girls had been arrested, some were interrogated, and some were tortured in order to get them to betray their sources. That dreadful day became a big set-back for the Resistance. Only two of the couriers were sent to Auschwitz because the Nazis had found out they were Jewish.

The trip from Delft to The Hague was a pleasant one. Kees enjoyed riding along the river the Vliet with its quaint farm houses and the absence of German patrols. Nature in full spring attire was a delight for father and son but the trouble always began at a bridge called The Hoornbrug.

It was the bridge which had become the main entrance to the city where a large barricade and many soldiers, tanks and machine guns controlled anyone who wanted to enter the city of The Hague.

Kees had entered the barricade on the west side of the bridge; it was the place where only pedestrians could get through. Most of the time he could get away with that, but not this time.

The new ordinance about the bicycles had made passing the barricades much more difficult. Kees was sent to the middle of the bridge.

A group of Gestapo inspectors were checking every passenger with a bicycle. Kees could see the nasty people interrogating young girls and taking their bicycles away. Some of the girls were put on a truck which was already partially-filled with people."

Kees rubbed his forehead and thought "How are we going to get through this one?" When a Gestapo officer came aside of him and demanded that he surrender his bicycle. Kees protested and produced his pass from the factory.

The man looked at it and still demanded Kees to get off his bike. Cornelius felt the pressure mounting and began his crying routine.

For a moment Kees thought that this time his crying son would do him no good, but when the man looked at Cornelius who was really giving a show this time the man said, "Eine Minute," and went to a group of officers who apparently were higher than himself.

After the man spoke, Kees noticed that they were looking his way. When one of them shook his head Kees' blood began to get icy-cold in his veins. Why would he be nodding in his direction? Kees prayed hard, "Lord I need your intervention and your grace."

After what seemed like an eternity, the man came back with a soldier. He issued an order which Kees could not understand. Then he saw the soldier bend over at his bicycle wheels and unscrew the valves. The Gestapo officer told him with a cruel smile, "Gehen Sie mahl spazieren, Guten Tag Herr Van Rijn (Go take a walk.)"

Kees was allowed to go through the barricades and he was grateful, at least he was not far from home. He had saved his precious cargo and kept his bike, even though he could not ride it until he came home.

When he arrived on foot, walking the last kilometer and a half, he told his wife Johanna, "It seems a new tactic to begin pestering the population, just to irritate us until we do something stupid. The Lord clearly protected us today. Let his name be praised."

The real difficult task was ahead of him. That evening under a cover of darkness, Kees would first get his friend Henk involved. Together they would get the courier network going.

It would go slower than before, now that so many bicycles had been seized and a number of girls were still missing. The job had to be done and it needed to be done quickly. The lives of so many would be at stake. A city without doctors would be in serious trouble.

Chapter Forty Seven

A DIFFERENT KIND OF GUEST

—⚊ɯ⚊—

T he early summer drew people from The Hague to the beach
in Scheveningen, despite all the military activities around the
bunkers in the dunes along the Noordzee. The soldiers patrolling
the beach would not do anything to the bathers at the beach. They
would just gasp at the sunbathers.

Kees and Johanna had decided to take Cornelius to the beach
that day. It was nice and warm and the fresh sea breeze would be
good for them. Cornelius could play in the water if it was not too
cold, it being so early in the summer.

The trip to the beach took about two hours. They went through
the center of The Hague passing the Binnenhof which now looked
like a war zone, (which it was) It hurt Kees in his heart and soul
to see the machine guns and tanks in front of his beloved government's ancient Binnenhof.

One day it would be restored into its original glory. Kees knew
it would happen but how and when was still a mystery.

They passed the dunes where all the Van Rijn children used to
jump from the highest dunes and land into the soft sand.

Kees saw the place where so many brave friends had faced the
firing squad. He had to swallow hard to accept the memories of
them but he knew he could not be revengeful. He had to accept and
expect that the end would come some day and then there would not

be firing squads any longer.

When they reached the beach, it was a different sight than they had been used to. The enemy was everywhere. Their vehicles and their cannons were aimed toward the sea. That is from where they were expecting the allied invasion to come.

Kees had to forcefully clear his mind. It was too much to bear to see his beloved country ransacked and robbed.

He decided to take the day off from thinking about it, to give his full attention to Johanna and Cornelius that day. "For today there is no war," he demanded his mind to think. "Just for today," he promised himself.

Cornelius began to run to the water and Kees saw him run smack into a shabby old man who had fallen backwards into the sand. Kees ran over to him to help the old man up. He found the man smiling and apologizing. "No matter," he said with a Friesian accent. "This is the play ground for children. I should not be here and be in their way."

The humbleness of the man hit Kees and he felt that this man had to be well-educated, someone with a past of leadership.

Kees introduced himself; he had a feeling that this man might need help. He asked the man if he was from around the city. He shook his head and said, "Friesland."

"What brings you to the city here all the way on the coast of the Noordzee?"

The man raised his hands and said nothing.

Kees realized that in this time of war he could not be asking strangers questions. Who knows, the man might be in the Resistance and he would not know that Kees was either.

Kees decided to give the password a try, just to see the reaction of the man. "Graag," Kees said, right out of the blue with no meaning other than being the password to recognize a Resistance worker. The man answered with the same word and it brought a light to his eyes saying, "I was hoping you would say that."

"Would you mind to sit down with us, over there? Perhaps we can help each other, particularly since I live here and you have come from so far away from the North?"

The old man readily consented to Kees's request. "I would like to get to know someone in this city, it would make the work I do a lot easier."

They walked to the spot where Johanna was sitting. She looked inquisitively at her husband.

"This is a friend from Friesland," he said, realizing that he had not gotten the man's name. "Eh, this is, eh…" The old man got the hint and took Johanna's out-stretched hand. "Coert van der Laan," he said very softly. "From Dokkum."

Johanna felt good about this man already. His eyes were friendly and his manners very cordial. "Please sit down with us Mr. van der Laan. It is nice to meet you."

He sat down on the large sheet they had brought. The man looked around and checked where the nearest military detachment would be and how close others were to them.

He seemed to be very careful when he spoke. "I work entirely by myself. I spent my life in the Dutch army. I became a sergeant fairly young, I was only twenty one then. They sent me to Indonesia at that time. When I came back home in Friesland ten years later, I was promoted to First Lieutenant and dismissed from the army because I had varicose veins.

They decided I could not stay in the military because of all the walking I would have to do. It never bothered me during the rest of my life, but that is what the doctors decided at the time.

Instead, I worked for a security company and had a great and easy life, never got married, never got in trouble, and then the Germans marched into our country on May 12, 1940. I was sixty-five then and retired from the security company. I was dreaming of joining the army, but they did not want me. I was outraged, at the Germans but also at the Dutch military because I knew I would be an asset to them if they let me.

I used to be the one in Indonesia who was always sent out to spy on the enemy I would find out details no one else could. I knew that that was my specialty, I guess they would call me a spy now."

Kees laughed when he heard the word "spy." This old man, a

spy? That would be the joke of the century. But the man went on. "In those first days of the war I went spying on my own. I gathered information on the movements of the enemy, made maps of where they were heading and put it all together in an envelope and took it to the Commissary of the Queen in the capital of Friesland, the city of Leeuwarden.

It was information our soldiers and their commanders could not get but I knew how to get it and I knew how to make it useful to our people.

"As I said before, now I work on my own, without anyone telling me what to do. I gather information where I think it will be most useful for our government and sent it to them. I do it for my Queen and my country because one day this oppressor will flee."

The tone in which this old spy spoke was gentle but firm. It was coming straight from the heart. It made Kees' heart swell with pride for his country and its citizens.

Coert van der Laan had talked there on the beach of Scheveningen. He had kept on talking for hours while Cornelius played in the sand and Johanna did as if she was sleeping.

His encounter with the Commissary of the Queen in Leeuwarden did not have much impact. His Excellency simply did not know what to do with the information the nervous old man had given him. At least he had commended him on a great job and he had promised to send the information on to the appropriate authorities.

To Coert it did not sound very appropriate, and he had decided then and there that he would have to work by himself and get the information directly to the highest authorities. He knew the way and he would make sure his work would not be in vain. A spy's work was a job from the bottom to the top, he had always understood. This time he worked for his own country by himself and directly for the government which was not present in the country.

He had to find a way to get all his findings to England. It was in 1940 just after the war had begun that he made the decision that most of the information the government needed was the place where a counter attack could begin and that was at The Noordzee coastline. It was the entire coastline of Holland, from the top to the bottom of the country.

He took a train to the city of Harlingen and was determined to walk straight to The Hague and begin his spying where it was most needed. From Harlingen he walked to the Afsluitdijk. He figured he could make it from there across the Afsluitdijk through North Holland to The Hague.

Alas, he did not know that the Germans had already taken possession of the Afsluitdijk.

They were still fighting in those days and the Germans told the old man to go back home, that he had no business in the middle of the on-going battle. It was too dangerous for an old man, they said. Back at home he decided to wait a few weeks. He saw how his country's army was defeated in just over a week and he heard how his Queen had fled to England along with a majority of the government.

The old man did not want to accept defeat. As an ex-military man, he did not accept defeat. He was convinced that the fight would continue and that it was a fight which would eventually be won, but it was a military matter. It was not something for a bunch of Resistance people who did some harm to the enemy without chasing them out of the country. That was not the way a war was won.

He apologized to Kees about his remark on the Resistance. "I don't mean to make you look negative. I mean to say that the actual fighting and regaining of the country is a military job. The Resistance has a different kind of job, I do realize."

Coert van der Laan understood that the government in exile needed information in order to prepare a counter-attack. Who was going to supply that to them?

He felt called to do it. Who else had such a great experience and an analytical mind about military business?

"That is when I made the decision to become a spy, and now I am here to do my job I could sure use a place to sleep though, and if you feel called to help me," he had said boldly, "By all means do what your heart tells you to do." Kees had listened intently all that time and the minutes had become hours.

He was a fascinating person this Coert van der Laan, but could he handle the activities at the Van Rijn residence? Even more importantly, could he withstand an interrogation from the Gestapo if he was ever captured? That was a great possibility in the city of The Hague, with its thousands of Jews in hiding and a very active underground.

Kees decided to talk it over with his friend Frans. He would invite the old man for just one day and ask Frans to come and visit him so he could evaluate the validity of the old man.

The time had come that they would have to go home. They would ride their bicycle but the old man would have to walk and follow them. It would be a slow ride back to the Deiman Straat. Kees had made a decision to help the man, provided he was legitimate.

He was going to find out about that soon. Kees could not jeopardize his own activities, not just yet, just in case. One never knows during war time.

The lonesome, shabby old man's stamina was amazing. He ran the whole way behind their bicycles and did not even show any tiredness when they arrived at home.

He was a loner, that was for sure. He had told Kees about his wife and how she had died from sadness because the Germans had chased her Queen out of the country. They had never had any children. So in his shabby clothes and his greasy old hat, no one would take him very seriously. That was his best defense.

He almost became invisible to the enemy.

When he had decided that the Noordzee coast would be the best area for his research, he had wondered how he was going to stay alive. Kees had given him hope. If it worked out with Kees he would have found his personal headquarters.

To this spy it was a simple fact that a counter-attack had to come from the sea by means of England, the leadership needed to know as much as he could gather for them about what the Germans had in place on the Dutch coast. How strong they were and what kind of weaponry they had to expect. He was the one to supply that information and he did not expect anything in return.

Kees showed the old man where he could sleep. He was grateful and told him that he had not slept in a real bed for the last two weeks. "We will have a little bible study and a friend of ours will be coming to join us. Would you like to participate in it too"? Kees had asked.

"I would be delighted to join you. A Bible study is one of those things I have missed while I was on the road."

Before the Bible study began one of the Schmall boys had asked for permission to come upstairs. They had developed a knocking code on the floor from the bottom. Five short knocks meant that someone needed to talk. Four meant "we are in need of something." Three knocks meant "we need to make use of the toilet." It was a helpful system for both the hidden and the hiders. Coert had wondered what the knocking was all about. He did not ask Kees which made him wonder if Coert was aware of this house's secret hiding place.

They had to be very careful because the enemy came in many devious forms. If someone was not curious about unusual sounds coming from the floor there was cause for concern. They would find out tonight and if this man was a spy, a spy for the enemy, he would not leave the Van Rijn residence in freedom. He could count on that!

Kees had to send a message back that he could not have any visits from below that evening. His mind kept saying, "Keep it safe for now."

The two young men David and Ishmael were terribly bored. Their return to the Deiman Straat had been a miracle. They were more or less restrained to the hiding place and they realized that their little search for air that time a few weeks ago had been the reason for their arrest. They had mourned about the loss of their parents. At last, they had accepted their situation and hoped that they would soon be helped to get out of the country to a free and neutral country like Switzerland or Spain. Or even to Palestine.

Kees had an idea how he could get them to Switzerland. He would have to talk to the people at the airport to see if they could get one of the ambulances. The men in the hidden hanger had become the transport specialists for the Underground. With several ambulances stationed there they were able to transport many people daily without ever raising suspicion.

The real challenge was to create the forged transportation paper-work with which a German officer would be sent back to Germany.

For that, the Resistance had a specialist, a double-agent policeman who worked closely with some doctors in the hospital.

Whenever a severely wounded officer would be brought in to the hospital the doctor would give the information to the policeman who in turn would bring it to the specialized printer.

Whatever forms were needed had already been stolen weeks before-hand, so that when an officer needed to be sent back home in Germany or Austria, a transport would be arranged by the Underground. Often this happened simultaneously with the real transport of the actual patient. A picture of the officer was also stolen from the records in order to make the fake officer look even more like the real one.

If the two Jewish cousins could catch a ride in an ambulance there would hardly be any risk involved. He could possibly send three more people along that way. It was becoming crowded in his hiding place. Kees was sure that there would be more Jews to come soon. He had to make sure they he had a place for them.

The dragnet of the Nazis was becoming more intense by the day. It was harder every time to bring people from one place to the other. Even at the farms the Nazis had become more aware of Jews being hidden. They would find some hiding places only when NSB-ers had become involved in finding them.

Kees made a plan for the next day to begin working on the transport of his cousins which also entailed a visit to the secret Zionist organization in The Hague.

Whenever Jews were sent to Switzerland they would be received by the Zionist Board in Basel. They would be registered by them as Palestine citizens and flown to Jerusalem as quickly as possible. There was a huge underground organization of Jewish Zionists who had abilities beyond measure to help the fugitives who had the desire to go to their promised land.

"Was this something the two Schmall boys were ready for?" Kees was thinking, but then again who would not want to be air-lifted out of the misery of a world war? He would talk with them the next day and explain what they could expect in the near future. Kees was almost jealous of them, because he had to stay and fight the fight, but for how long? Only God knew.

Frans had arrived at the Van Rijn residence and Kees had picked up his Bible to begin their study. Coert had shaken hands with Frans and they had exchanged some conversation. Frans seemed to be impressed by the shabby old man. He had asked how he was getting his spying information and how he would get it to the government in England. The man had laughed at their question.

"I cannot tell you how I do it, I just do. I just go to the places of military concentrations and look. Sometimes I make some notes in my little note book, in code of course, because if I ever would get captured it would have to make no sense to the enemy.

I often write little notes about the weather and write that there were a certain number of clouds in the sky, meaning guns, cannons or machine guns. If anyone catches my notes they will think that I am an old nut who counts clouds.

When I have significant information, I get a milk bottle and write a detailed report, not using any codes then, because the report is going to England and they don't know about my code system. So far, I have probably sent twenty bottles to England. I don't know how many have arrived yet. I make three copies of each report and use three bottles for each message. One of them is bound to arrive.

When I ship them off I go to Hoek of Holland. I walk to the end of the pier and drop them in the water, only after I have cal-culated that the tide and the winds are in favor to bring my bottles across to England.

When they ended the evening, their talks had been much more about the war than about the Bible, Kees depended on Frans's opinion about the old spy. If Frans approved of him he would be ok to help and Kees would gladly give him room and board as far as the food supply would allow it.

It was late in the evening after an exciting day. The three men had something in common which made them want to keep talking. The common denominator was: this is our country and soon we will get it back from the aggressors.

It was late and the curfew was in effect for four hours when Frans left for the short walk to his house. He was always very careful and knew how the Germans operated. Stealthily, he moved from portico to portico and through bushes in front yards until he reached his home. He thought, "This old man...I wish there were a lot of them like that. The war would soon be over..."

For Kees is was late too. He had to go to his slave labor job at 4 a.m. He had only three hours of sleep ahead of him and he had to be there on time. He wanted to maintain his good report because only that way he was able to continue his underground work without raising suspicion.

Cornelius heard his father get up early and he was wide awake when the front door closed behind his Dad. He was startled by an awful thought. "What if dad never came back just like it had happened with so many families?" Even his two nephews who were sleeping beneath the house had experienced that. What would he and his mother do to survive?

The thought kept running through his mind. He could not sleep any longer. The what-if had made him wide awake. He decided to go to his little farm as soon as it became light outside. It looked like it was already getting close to daybreak.

His little farm in the back of the house was thriving. By now he was harvesting something every day. His garden had become a blessing to a lot of people in the residence and those beneath the house. His ducks were growing well. Every day he went to the stream close by with the cross net he had constructed himself out of an old bamboo fishing rod he had split.

He would let the net down into the water and wait for five minutes. Then he would quickly raise it and usually a dozen or so little fish would flounder in the net.

He emptied the cross net into a small bucket and lowered the net again and again until he had a bunch of the tiny fish lively swimming around in his little bucket. Every day he would quickly bring the bucket home and put it in the cage he had made for the ducklings. Three of them had remained alive. They would fight around the bucket to catch the little fish. Within minutes all the fish were gone.

His duck were growing well and one day soon he would have to slaughter them. Having been on the farm had made him understand that the purpose of animals was to be eaten. At his young age he did not have a problem with that.

Cornelius had become quite the farmer. In the early mornings he loved to be outside in between his growing vegetables. His strawberries were bringing him some beauties everyday. He had instructed his mother Johanna to pick the strawberries whenever he was gone on a trip with his dad. "Don't pick them too early and not too late either," he had told her. "They have to be red all around, not just on the top or they will be sour." He had mimicked Marie Brandwijk when she had given him the same instructions.

When the sun came up it was still only 5:30 in the morning. It was crisp and clear outside, no one would expect that a war was raging in the country and all over the world as well. No planes were in the morning sky. The whole world was still at rest.

The sound of many engines broke the silence. The slamming of dozens of truck doors rudely awakened the citizens in the Deiman Straat. Then the German voices sounding commands could be heard all over the streets. The commands were followed by the sounds of doorbells and loud knocking on the doors. The voices which screamed "Aufmachen snell" seemed meaner than ever.

Cornelius heard his mother scream at the top of her voice, "My husband is not at home, he is at work in the factory!"Then a moment of silence and then another command was heard rashly and demanding, saying, "Hause Suchung," which meant "search this house."

At the same time a dozen soldiers poured into the house and began to search the home, looking under beds and opening closets. Even the secret wall was touched.

The table in the front room was moved to the side. Cornelius could hear a voice call out triumphantly, "Aha! Was haben wir hier?" He knew the triumphant finding would turn into anger when they saw the concrete box under the floor below where the table had stood.

He smiled about Frans's idea. This was the hundredth time they thought they had found the entrance to a hiding place. Each time it had turned into a disappointment for the Nazi Jew-hunters.

A group of four soldiers had walked into the boy's little farm and spotted the little boy. He was tiny and thin, his big brown eyes wide open reflecting the bright morning sum.

The soldiers looked around the yard. They went into the small shack and came out still looking around. They saw the little duck pen and the three ducks in it. One of the soldiers tried to catch one of them when a voice from behind him interrupted his action. "Wass machst Du then, Fangest einem Ende? Lass es mal fur den Junge! (What are you doing, catching a duck? Leave it for the little boy!)"

With that command the soldier stood up and walked back into the house.

The man whose voice had commanded him came walking towards Cornelius and asked him in a friendly tone, "Where is your daddy and all the other people who are supposed to be here?"

In an instant Cornelius knew what to say and what not to say. "Please sir, my father is at work. He works for -the factory – Simowitz - in the city - he, he - left two hours ago. No one else -lives here - just me - and my mom - and dad. Please Sir, don't step on my vegetables. This is my - little farm - here would- you like a -strawberry?"

He said it in a stuttering way, which he thought was a good way to catch the man's attention. Cornelius had just found a nice big red one and stretched out his hand toward the sergeant. The man took the strawberry and turned around rather quickly. He would not want to show this little boy the tears he had in his eyes. Here was just a tiny boy protecting his plants and giving his enemy some of its yield.

How much this boy reminded him of his own little son back in Germany, where he too had his little garden and grew strawberries just like this one.

Chapter Forty Eight

PIGEON EGGS

—◊—

"How soon could this nasty war end?" he thought. His attitude changed the minute he walked back into the house. With the authority he had received when he had earned the stripes on his sleeve, he commanded to get out of this house.

All of them left immediately. Cornelius could hear them ringing other doorbells and shouting their commands. Once more, by the grace of God, the Van Rijn family was spared as well as fifteen scared out-of-their-wits Jews underneath the concrete bunker which formed the staircase.

Houses where NSB-ers and the "loose girls" lived, as Johanna called them, were also entered. The Nazis trusted no one, not even the ones who collaborated with them. The soldiers had no harvest in the Deiman Straat that day. The Jews who were in hiding were hidden so well that they would never be found.

Cornelius waited a while before he climbed to his egg farm, as he was calling it, on the roof of the Groenendijk warehouse. He had not been able to take the eggs out of the pigeon nests for a few days. He did not want to miss out on that harvest. He had brought up the rope which was attached to the bucket, which he had waiting to take down the eggs. To his astonishment there was not one egg in any of the nests. He did not know what had happened. Was someone stealing his eggs? Even the marked ones were gone. That was disastrous because the pigeons would quit laying eggs if none were left in their nests. He was shocked. Who on earth would have stolen his eggs?

He decided to keep an eye on the roof and made a plan which he wanted to implement that day. He was going to stretch a fine thread from his mother's sowing box, from one end of the roof to the other. If someone was stealing his eggs he was determined to find out.

His plan became a little more elaborate an hour later when he told his dilemma to the old Mr. van der Laan who did not get up as early as his Dad.

The old man had literally gone underground into hiding downstairs when he had heard the trucks coming. It had been his alarm which had caused the Jews down below to retreat into the staircase bunker.

When Coert came back upstairs he was pushed into a chair by Cornelius, who seemed to be upset about something other that the Razzia they had just experienced.

Cornelius had cornered the old man and began to talk to him. "You are a spy, so you should find out for me who is stealing the pigeon eggs out of the nests on the roof next door." Coert had to laugh at the assertiveness of the little boy.

"I was getting six or seven eggs every day and I left one egg in the nest all the time so the pigeons kept making new ones," Cornelius said. "I just came from the roof and there is not one egg in any of the nests. I had marked the eggs so I would know which one to take and now they are all gone. Someone has stolen them and I want you to find out who did it."

The little boy seemed to have told the entire story in one breath. When he was finished talking he had to take a deep breath and he sat down with both his hands on the arm rests, expecting a declaration from the old spy.

Coert had to smile about the request.

He never had any children but he was enjoying this little boy with all his talks about his little farm. He bent forward in his chair, acted as if he was conspiring a plan, and said in a whispering voice, "We need to set a trap for the thief so we can find out when he comes, then we can catch him and have him arrested." Cornelius liked the idea. This was real detective work, something different than riding on his bicycle seat behind his dad going through barricades.

"What we are going to do is, we will make an invisible wire from one end to the other and attach the end of it to an alarm device. Then, when the thief walks into the wire he will trigger the alarm and we'll catch him. Let's find a wire we can use for that. Do you have any fishing wire?"

"Yes," said Cornelius. "It is on my fishing rod, we can take some of it off."

They went to the backyard together and began to set the trap. "What are we using for the alarm, Mr. Coert?"

"Well, eh. Let's see if your mother has some lids from pans which we can hang up together and when the thief trips the wire, they will clatter and fall to the ground."

The two conspirers worked together to set the trap. Cornelius climbed on the roof and fastened the end of the wire to a pole about one meter off the ground. At the other side of the roof they had placed a pole with a groove in it; the wire ran through the groove down onto the backyard patio.

The pot lids were fastened and dangled two feet above the floor. The old man and the little boy wiped their hands on their trousers and laughed aloud.

"Tonight we may have to stay up late to make our arrest," Coert announced. Cornelius thought his was the best time of his life. Catching a thief was really fun.

Johanna called the two inside. "What are you two up to?" she asked. "Is anything wrong in the backyard?"

The young and the old both said "no" simultaneously. Johanna was secretly happy that the two such contrasting personalities could do things together they both enjoyed. She had heard Cornelius talk about the pigeon eggs which had become a real blessing for the family. "You say all the eggs were gone this morning, Corrie?" Johanna asked.

"Yes mom and someone is stealing them."

"But not for long," Coert budded in. "We have set a trap for the culprits and if they dare to come again they will be arrested."

"And who is going to do that?" Johanna asked with a smile.
"We are," the two answered in unison.

Chapter Forty Nine

ARRIVING IN PALESTINE

—— m ——

T he plane from Switzerland landed in Haifa, Palestine. It had
made its flight going through corridors used by neutral countries via the Pyrenees over Spain and then the Island of Gibraltar
going southeast, crossing the Mediterranean Sea into the country of
Palestine.

The passengers had all been nervous, having to go on an air-
plane for the first time in their life, but their fears were also about
the German Messerschmitt fighter planes which often came very
close.

They were all Jewish passengers and they all had one thing
in common: the Nazis had wanted to kill them and they had all
escaped. Some were from Poland, others were German Jews, and
they had come from all the occupied European countries. The other
thing they had in common was that they had all lost family members who had been lured to the concentration camps in Germany
and Poland.

"Lured" was the correct word because in each of those countries there had been a Jewish Council organized by the Nazis, and
the Jewish Councils had advised them to do what the Nazis told
them. Until it had become known that the concentration camps
were not really made to concentrate the Jews together, as the Nazis
had promised the Jewish Councils. They had believed that nothing

would harm them and that the temporary move would be to their own advantage. After the news got out that the camps were in fact death camps

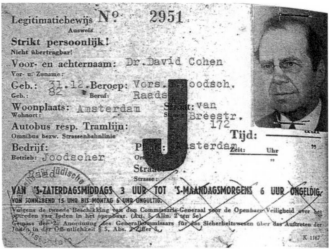

The leader of the Jewish council went to Auswitz too,

When he came back he was convicted and stripped from his Authority, and that millions of people had been gassed and incinerated in the camps, the Jews did obviously not go voluntarily any longer.

The Zionist movement had spread their secret agencies all over Europe and particularly in the neutral countries which were Sweden, Switzerland and Spain.

Together with the local Resistance of each country, the Zionist Councils were able to bring many Jews to the "promised land" where they were accepted as their own by the Kibbutzim communities which were spreading very fast across the country of Palestine.

The passengers on the plane did not know what to expect even though they had been prepared at the places of their origination. Films had been shown and plans had been read on how Palestine would become their new country of Israel, the promised land of centuries past.

Among the passengers exiting the plane was a young couple

who had been waiting in the city of Schaffhausen for several weeks
to obtain the proper paperwork allowing them to settle in Palestine.

Doctor Henk Ypma and his fiancée Hannah were very excited
to arrive in their new homeland. Henk had been promised a position as a General Practitioner in a Kibbutz near Haifa. They had
plans to get married as soon as they would be established and had a
place to live.

The fact that Henk was not Jewish had never been a problem
to Hannah. Henk was eager to become Jewish and learn everything
about the Jewish traditions. The couple was very much in love and
the pressure of the past was already wearing off.

The pictures of the death camps would never fade from Henk's
mind, nor did the fear that the Germans would follow him to
avenge the great escape he made happen.

Even in a secure country like Palestine was at the time, and
in the safe and well-guarded environment of a Kibbutz, the Nazis
could find him and either kidnap him or kill him. That was the
reason it took them so long to receive the proper papers to travel to
and stay in the promised land, the future state of Israel.

His name had been changed and was sounding so Jewish that
the Nazis would never find him because there was no paper trail
which linked him to the new name. He had simply vanished from
the earth.

Yet Henk was nervous about it and it would take him many
years to quit looking over his shoulders.

His new name was Ephraim Rosenzweig That name had been
his own choice. Henk had always loved roses and so did his parents. He was supposed to be the son of Aaron and Mary Rosenzweig, formerly living in Switzerland. Henk was the only Zweig,
which meant "shoot of the rose tree." A complete history of his
family had to be created in order to send the Nazis on a wild goose
chase and give him a new lease on life.

The Germans never found him and Henk became a successful
doctor of the Kibbutz until he was chosen in the new government
of Israel eight years later.

Chapter Fifty

THE VALUE OF FOOD

—⚊—

T he war was raging meaner every day. The Germans had
rationed food in such a way that no one should have to die of
hunger, yet many did. The malnutrition was taking its toll.

At the Van Rijn Residence, the official food ration was one loaf
of bread per week, one liter of milk, half a pound of butter every
two weeks, and five pounds of potatoes a week.

The rations, of course, did not include food for the number of
Jews who were hiding under the floor. At any given day there were
at least fifteen people who needed food under the floor. It was a
matter of ingenuity to scrounge up the needed food for all.

Luckily Cornelius' little farm helped a little. Kees had slaughtered two of the three ducks in the duck pen. Cornelius had been
begging him to go to the Brandwijk farm so he could find some
more duck eggs.

They had been eating all the cabbage he had grown and he had
a new crop coming soon.

One morning when Cornelius was playing outside in front of
the house, the Kapper from the corner came riding by on his bicycle. All the children were hungry and skinny. Whenever Cornelius
asked for something to eat, Johanna would tell him to just tighten
his belt and the hunger would go away for a while.

That particular morning became a little blessing for the Van

Rijn family. When the Kapper rode by on his bicycle, he threw a quarter of a loaf of bread into the group of playing children. Cornelius caught it and pushed it immediately under his sweater. The other boys wanted to take it from him but Cornelius ran quickly to his house.

His mother saw it all happen through the window and was right there to open the door for him. "Mom," he called out. "Mom, look what I got!" He took the piece of bread from under his sweater. "We have bread for tonight and I have some strawberries to go with it."

The treasure of a piece of extra bread made that evening meal a feast. Each had a slice of bread that they had never counted on.

The scarcity of food led people to make things edible which were normally used for other purposes. The farmers who grew sugar beets usually sold their products to a sugar factory instead of hungry citizens from the cities, who would often walk many miles to buy some sugar beets from the farmer.

They were heavy beets, some could weigh as much as ten pounds each. They were hauled in by baby carriages and self-made vehicles the Germans had no use for. At home the people would grate the beets and cook them in large pots on the fire if they had any firewood.

The resulting brew had two things which were useful – a heavy syrup would boil out of the beets which could be used to give them good quality carbs, and the pulp, which became a good base for pancakes. It tasted like cardboard and the pancakes were hard to chew. The more chewing had to be done, the more satisfaction came from eating the pancakes, particularly when they were drenched with the self-made syrup.

Other people would buy the skin of slaughtered pigs and boil them for food. A large amount of lard could be boiled out of the skin. The skin was cut into fine pieces which in turn were fried. The resulting "Kaantjes," as they called them, or "Cracklings," became a well-nourishing food. The only negative of the creative food chain was that it caused malnutrition.

The right and needed nutrients were not available. Many children had Hunger Oedema. Their little bellies would swell up as if they had been over-eating. The Nazis did not care. Their goal of starving the people was working. More and more people became members of the NSB, (The National Socialistic Movement.) This promised them larger rations so they could survive.

Many churches started the so-called "soup kitchens." Their supplies were donated by the few food factories which had been allowed to continue production for the benefit of the Germans.

For hours the citizens waited in line for a liter of soup. Often the waiting was so tiring that people fainted in the waiting line. More often than not there would be more people than the soup supply would allow, and people had to be turned away after having waited in line for several hours.

Johanna had volunteered with her church to help in the distribution. She helped for two hours but the misery had become too much. She had to go home and she would cry for days thereafter. It took strong people to deal with such human misery. Johanna had other worries – having a husband and child who were in continual danger when they went out to do their covert operations.

More than once they did not come home at the planned time. At those times Johanna would pray and pray and cry and cry. What if they had been arrested? What on earth would she do with all the guests down below?

A minister handing out soup to the hungry citizens.

Chapter Fifty One
RELEASED FROM CAMP WESTERBORK

—⁓—

Playing outside during war time was dangerous for any child. Nazi trucks and motorcycles could come racing around the corner. A chase could be in progress and shooting was rampant.

There were other dangers which could lurk in the streets. Nazi soldiers had picked up children and taken them to their local station for interrogation.

Cornelius had been told to stay close to the house and as soon as he would see soldiers coming he could run inside. Johanna knew that he would never tell about the hiding place, but one never knew about the cruel tactics that the Nazis and especially the Gestapo interrogators employed.

It was getting dusk in the city of The Hague; the playing boys were called inside by their parents gradually. Cornelius was still playing ball with two other kids when the ball was kicked into the bushes on the opposite side of the street. Cornelius ran after it and walked into the bushes when he heard a soft voice saying, "Cornelius." He looked up but saw nothing. It was getting darker by the minute.

Cornelius said with a whispering voice, "Who is calling me?""It is us, Mr. and Mrs. Sterenway, remember us? We were under your floor for two weeks about six months ago." He went deeper into the bushes and then he saw them. Yes, he did remember them.

They were nice people. His dad had brought them to the Ypen-burg farm and then he never heard of them again. "Cornelius, Mr. Sterenway and I want to talk to your daddy, could you please go tell him that we are here hidden in the bushes? You are such a good boy, we know you will help us. Go and tell your dad quickly."

Cornelius had to be careful. At any time he would be ap-proached by someone, even people he knew, he had to act as though he did not know them until he had told his dad. Besides, he had to act as if he was still searching for his ball or the other kids could tell on him and who knows? Their parents might be NSB-ers.

When he came out of the bushes with the ball he threw it to one of the other boys and went on playing for a few minutes. After a while he told the boys, "We better go inside because curfew will begin soon and we don't want to spend the night at the police of-fice, do we?"

He slowly walked to his house and Johanna, who was always watching her little son, quickly opened the door to let him in. "Mom, I need to speak to dad," he said very matter-of-factly. Dad looked up from a little nap he had taken and said, "What's the matter son?" Cornelius spoke very articulately. "Do you remember Mr. and Mrs. Sterenway?"

"Yes, what about them? They went away from here a long time ago. I would think they are either in Switzerland or Palestine already."

"No, Dad, they are here, across the street in the bushes. They asked me to come and tell you, they want to talk to you."

Kees got up and wondered what on earth had brought the couple back to The Hague. His mind began to race as he tried to recall what they looked like and how they had behaved when they were under his floor. They seemed to have been unproblematic, but one never knows. He also wondered how they got back here in broad daylight.

He decided to carefully investigate, first to make sure they were truly the Sterenways. Then he would go to Frans and talk the situation over with him. One could not be careful enough in these dangerous times.

He took his time and went outside casually walking in the opposite direction of the bushes in which the people were hiding. Then he turned around and walked by the bushes. He said softly and hoped they would be able to hear him. "Please wait until it is completely dark. There are too many NSB-ers here who could betray us. I will come back soon." He walked around the corner and quickly sped-up his walking toward the house of his friend and co-worker.

Frans had seen him coming through his secret pond and had the door open for him even before he could knock. "I have a problem," Kees began, getting straight to the point. "Across from my house are two Jewish people who were in my hiding place at one time about six months ago. I brought them to the Ypenburg farm and never heard of them again, which is normal. But now they are back here again and even though they used to be nice people, I cannot imagine how they got here and I don't want them in my house or yours until I know what is going on. I can't talk to them on the street, so what should I do?"

Frans was always the inventive person. Kees hoped he would come up with an acceptable solution. "We must not raise any suspicion that we distrust them either," Frans remarked. "I am thinking, I am thinking." He was rubbing his head again as usual when he was thinking real hard.

Finally after a long few minutes of silence he spoke, "I'll tell you what we can do. I have a friend in the police department who drives a small German truck. Another friend has a German uniform which he can wear. So let's stage an arrest. After the arrest we can drive the truck to a warehouse which is abandoned and then we can talk with them. It will scare them out of their wits but under the circumstances we cannot afford to take any risks.

If you can wait here I'll go and make the arrangements so we can get the show on the road. By now those poor people might begin to wonder why you are not coming to get them."

It took Frans only half an hour to get "the show on the road" like he said. He came back and told Kees to walk slowly to the bushes in which the people were hiding. "When the truck comes you act very surprised and just let it happen. Then you come back here and I will take you to the abandoned warehouse so you can talk to them."

The arrest and the entire covert operation took five minutes. Kees made eye contact with the Sterenways when they were loaded up on the truck. From the corner of his eye he could see several curtains move in the houses around him.

Nothing to report, thought the NSB-ers who saw the arrest happen. "No money in this one for us."

Twenty minutes later Kees was facing the two scared Jews in the abandoned warehouse. They had to be very quiet. The policeman had already left and the friend in German uniform remained just in case something strange would happen with the two captives.

Kees walked toward the two and opened his arms wide in an approach to embrace the two. They backed up when he came close and looked in horror at him. Kees thought he had better apologize, and said, "Mr. and Mrs. Sterenway, I am so surprised to see you back here. I am sorry for the shock we had to administer to you, please don't take it the wrong way. We are here to protect your people and we cannot take any risk of being detected. Please understand?"

The two shook their heads. "No, we don't understand, and what is happening with you Kees? Have you turned to the wrong side too?" They had tears in their eyes when they spoke and apparently they were convinced that Kees had changed sides and was now against them.

Kees took charge of the situation which was becoming more hostile as every minute went by. "Let's all relax and take a seat here on the floor. We just need to talk and clear the air." Reluctantly the Jewish couple sat down, still looking at Kees in horror. "In order to understand what is going on here, Mr. and Mrs. Sterenway, I must ask you to tell us first how and why you came back to The Hague. This is highly unusual and suspicious. We don't take risks in this business because we have to protect human lives. So please, tell us." Kees said, opening the conversation.

Mr. Sterenway took the floor and began to explain, "Whether you believe us or not, we have been released from the Westerbork camp with twenty-eight other 'volunteers.' They brought us back to several locations and cities. Some went to Amsterdam, some to Utrecht and some to Rotterdam and we were chosen to come to The Hague. They dropped us off around the corner from your house.

The deal is that they promised us freedom if all of us would go spying on the hiding places we had been at and tell the local Gestapo about them. They know, or at least up 'till a half hour ago, they knew where we were and where we would be going. They even gave us an address where we could stay overnight. If we don't report within the next few hours they will assume that we are not doing our job and they will come and find us."

Kees and Frans could not believe what they heard. Had the Nazis stooped that low, to persuade the Jews to betray their own by making false promises?

Mr. Sterenway went on, "We know our lives are worthless to them and we also know that there are Jews who would betray their own, but we are not like that, please believe me.

We came to warn you, we are the only ones who stayed with you and we will not betray your kind hospitality.

The others might do the same as we are doing, trying to hide and not tell, but on the other hand I know that there are several of the released ones who will do their dirty job. That is why we came to you. You might know a way to warn the other cities of this awful threat."

It was very quiet in the abandoned warehouse after Mr. Sterenway stopped talking. Each person had his own thoughts about the event.

Frans was wondering how the two could be so dumb as to accept the offer from the Nazis. They said themselves that their lives were worthless in the eyes of the Nazis.

Kees was thinking how he could hide the two and how soon could he get them safely out of the country, possibly to Switzerland and eventually to Palestine. Kees was very practical. How would he be able to hide them outside his home, because these people would get the entire Nazi army on their trail.

The man in the German uniform was thinking that if he would get caught in the presence of the two fugitives he would be shot in an instant.

The two Sterenways were thinking how else they could convince these people of their true experience and their dilemma by working with the Germans against their will. They were afraid that their idea of escaping their pending death sentences by betraying others was out of the question and unreal, and that the Germans had known that before-hand. The Nazis were just out to kill them if they would be caught.

The silence broke when Kees spoke. He first addressed the Resistance man in the German uniform. "Could you stay here in this warehouse and assist these people while I make certain arrangements for them?"

He answered, "Yes I could, but will there be someone who will bring us some food and drink?" Kees merely nodded and looked the man straight in the eyes.

He hoped the man could read what he meant in his eyes. Perhaps not, Kees thought, and he pulled the man by the arm toward the far corner of the building.

"What I mean," Kees whispered, "Can you guard these people on your own for two days here in this warehouse? This time the man's turn had come to nod his head without speaking a word.

The two walked back to the others where Frans was in a vivid conversation with the Sterenways. They heard him ask if they had names of the others who had been sent out to spy from Westerbork. The answer was, "Yes, but we only know a few names, just those of people we met and had to share a barrack with."

"Could you give me as many names as you can remember and write them here on this piece of paper?" He gave them a pencil and a small piece of paper he had in his pocket for weeks. It was all crumpled and dirty. "It will have to do," he added as he handed it over.

Chapter Fifty Two

RAZZIA AGAIN AND AGAIN

—⁓—

A t the Van Rijn residence there was a Razzia going on when Kees came home. He was accosted by half a dozen soldiers who demanded his Ausweiss. Kees was really getting mad at these Nazis for intruding on his privacy almost once a week. He demanded to speak with the commander of the troupe, who apparently had not come inside but was looking around at the neighboring houses.

When the soldiers sent for him, Kees made a big scene. "I work for you people," he said. "And almost every week you come back here. I am fed up with it. Tell me why you are doing this to me or I will go to Seyss Inquart himself and demand an explanation."No Dutchman had ever spoken to a German commander like that and the man addressed was taken by surprise. He began to apologize when one of the soldiers walked toward him and whispered something in his ear. The commander said to Kees, "Eine Minute," and went with the soldier to the front room where the table had been removed and the carpet pushed away.

The sawed-out square was clearly showing. No one had yet opened the hatch as they saw it. Three soldiers surrounded the hatch while one of them lifted it up. Three guns were at the ready pointing towards the hole. Kees looked at the scene and thought how many times they had done that and had been disappointed. As

Razzias

soon as the hatch was

removed the shooting began. All three guns went off and a cloud of dust came rising out of the concrete box which had been created by Frans one day.

The soldiers hoped to hear some screams or see some blood. Instead they saw nothing but dust coming out of the hole. Kees talked to the commander again. "See sir, this is about the hundredth time they have done this and all there is is a former safe-keeping for papers and valuables. As you can see there is nothing in it. Can you finally put an end to this charade?"

The commander seemed embarrassed by the situation and commanded everyone to leave. "Sir," he said to Kees. "I will personally file a report that you are good and should no longer be visited." That is a mild way of saying it, thought Kees. "At least I have given them a piece of my mind. Hopefully they will tell each other that at the Van Rijn Residence you will be embarrassed if you go do a

Hause Suchung.

There was much more important work to do for Kees. The interruption of the soldiers had made him anxious to get some people out of the country. He planned to go to the Ypenburg hangar in the early morning and organize an ambulance for the Sterenways.

Then he planned to go to the printers and ask for four new ID's two for the Sterenways and two for his cousins. They had been so restless and could explode as it seemed any day. He had to get them to Switzerland and the situation with the Sterenways justified their transport together.

Those were two people out of his house, which brought the total remaining to thirteen. He would also have to visit the Zionist office and explain the treasonous situation about the 28 Jews who had been released from Westerbork to do their traitorous jobs.

There was a lot of bike riding to do the next day because he also had to get the papers for a wounded military, hopefully an officer, from the doctors at the hospital. He had done it before and there was no reason why he could not do it this time. His only problem was that he had to go and work his slave labor job from four until twelve before he could make all his arrangements.

First he needed to talk to his cousins, but with the Nazis still in the street he should not risk to have them come upstairs. He decided to go downstairs and then take the two into the Groenendijk warehouse for a talk.

The guests down stairs were not surprised to see Kees come down the ladder. They had just finished coming back from their concrete bunker under the staircase and Kees would usually come down and explain what had transpired. Many inquisitive eyes were directed at him. Just one of them spoke in a whispering tone, "Razzia again?" Kees nodded and explained how he had made a scene over the shooting in the concrete box. He praised his friend Frans for coming up with the brilliant idea of it and commented that the idea had saved them and many others every time.

"But Ishmael and David, I need to talk to you both, would you please follow me upstairs?"

"No, we are not going into the house this time, too dangerous with all these Nazis in the street. Let's go the other way into the warehouse, there are no windows and it won't be opened until the morning."

The two Schmall brothers were anxious to hear what Kees was going to tell them. Were they finally going to be sent off to a safer place?

Kees began to tell them, "I have to tell you both that it is not easy to get you two out of the country. As much as I would like to help you, being family, I cannot show any preferential treatment to anyone. He saw the faces of the two tighten and a glimpse of disappointment began to appear. "However, you are blessed because today an incident happened which forces me to make a special arrangement for two other people who, if they would get caught, could betray a whole lot of Jews and their hiding places."

He explained what had happened with the appearance of the Sterenways and how they had been able to bring them to a temporarily safe place. "I think because of that situation I will be able to have you go along with them to Switzerland tomorrow evening. The two young men began to jump for joy and Kees had to put his finger to his lip to indicate to them to be quiet. He continued, "The Nazis are still in the street. Don't ruin it now or your trip will be going in a different direction." The brothers had a dozen questions and they could hardly wait for each other's turn to ask them. "How are we going," "what will we take," "will we get an Ausweiss," "how long is the trip?"

The questioning went on for half an hour when Kees decided to make an end to the meeting.

"Gentlemen, congratulations. Although I still have to make a lot of arrangements tomorrow, I need you to make sure you will be ready to move tomorrow evening. Please don't tell the others where and when you will be leaving. I have found that that leads to jealousy and sometimes rebellion. We cannot have that in these cramped surroundings, understood?"

They both nodded and then they all went back downstairs where a lot of curious eyes followed them coming back. Kees wished them all good night and promised to bring them food in the morning. "We have been able to bake some bread today and Cornelius had his egg farm back into production," he said. "So you may look forward to a small but tasty breakfast in the morning."

He went back up the ladder and into the living room where Johanna was reading her Bible. "It says here that the Jews will be persecuted in the last days. Do you think that is what we are experiencing? He looked at her and thought how strong she was to be able to deal with so much stress and problems. "No," he said. "I don't think these are the last days yet. Unfortunately it will be worse in those days than how it is now. God help the people who will live in those times.

If the Hoornbrug was an obstacle to pass through, it was only minor compared to the number of barricades which were installed on a September day in 1944. It was just before the longest winter of the century and at a time when many people needed their only form of transportation – the Nazis began to seize every bicycle they would encounter.

The entire city of The Hague seemed to be one big barricade. One could not leave his home or a barricade was right around the corner. That particular day as many as twenty one thousand bicycles had been seized.

The misery was complete because the minute a barricade was reached, the bicycle rider was coached into a line-up of other riders.

In groups of 50 and under armed escort, the riders had to bring their own bicycle to a warehouse which the Germans had seized and prepared for the great big two wheeler catch of the century.

Many Dutch citizens where wondering why there was the sudden change in policy and what the Nazis were going to do with their bicycles.

At the Binnenhof, Seys Inquart, the German Commissary of Hitler had made the decision, because his strategy of starving the Dutch was not even working.

He had received demands from Berlin, directly from the Ober Command to finalize and win this war against the Dutch. He had also received a report that there should be at least fifty thousand Jews still in Holland and that they needed to be captured and sent to the concentration camps immediately.

Special search specialists had been sent from Berlin to root-out

315

the hidden Jews. The lack of results in finding them had driven the generals to use un-real measures. They blamed the means of transportation for the Dutch – their Bicycles – on the successful hiding of Jews. They blamed the results, or lack thereof, of the starving of the Dutch on their use of bicycles.

The Nazis had seized any food they could find when bicyclists were stopped on the roads. The additional reason for seizing the bicycles was the shortage of transportation on the Eastern front. The generals had reasoned that if they could seize all the bicycles the Dutch owned they would be able to send a million more young soldiers to the Eastern front.

The seizing of all those bicycles lamed the city for a few days then the resourceful Dutch began to find other ways to do what they were used to doing on their bicycles.

There were no other forms of transportation than a few city trams and buses which had been running on irregular and sporadic routes. The tram conductors split up their tram cars and only ran single cars the next day. Volunteers came to run the additional tram cars which were much fuller than ever before. The only danger was that regularly a tram would be stopped and the passengers had to dismount in front of a German patrol and show their Ausweiss.

More Jews were caught, but more also went underground.

Chapter Fifty Three

ANYTHING WHICH CAN BURN

—ɱ—

T he few trees which had not yet been cut down began to change color. The always-beautiful fall had begun. Kees was on an errand, this time without Cornelius. He was on his way to the printer Jaap van Rooien, a person who worked all by himself.

The note had been delivered to the Deiman Straat by a twelve-year old girl and she had told him that he had to act immediately.

Kees knew that it would be safe to go to the printer because he was the only person who knew where Kees lived and the little girl was his daughter.

In the basement of an abandoned and partly bombed school, the printer had made his falsification headquarters.

There was a special way to get into the basement. First he had to climb over a wall. Behind the wall was a bombed part of the building. Kees had to climb on top of a pile of rubble in order to reach a door which was tumbled flat on the ground.

No one knew that the door was covering the staircase which led to the basement. The door had to be pulled up in order to get in and it would immediately fall back down over the entrance.

Down in the basement was a long hallway which smelled real bad because the sewer lines had been broken in the bomb blast. No one cared to clean up the mess. In a way, it was a good deterrent for possible intruders.

At the end of the basement hallway were two doors on either side of the hallway. The one was the print shop and the other the printer's bedroom.

Jaap van Rooien literally lived there and worked practically day and night. The need for food stamps was unlimited and the Resistance was always short.

When Kees entered the improvised print shop he found three people instead of the always lonesome Jaap de printer. The two men introduced themselves and Kees remembered the name – Johannes Post. He was the farmer from the east of the country who had become one of the most feared Resistance leaders.

The other person was Jan Toet, a former book-keeper. Kees stated that he was honored to meet the two men. He asked what brought them there and how could he be involved. They had a conversation which lasted the entire evening and when they finally broke up, the clock in the printer's office showed that it was past two in the morning.

Kees was thinking of Johanna and how worried she would be for him to stay out that late. Even though he had come with his bike, he left his bike with Jaap and stealthily took his time to get home safely.

Johanna saw him coming. For three hours she had sat in front of the curtains peeking through a narrow slit, waiting and worrying. She was not mad at him, how could she be? He was working so hard to save lives, to feed people and help them on their way to freedom.

Johanna wanted to know all about his meeting and who the special person he had to meet was. Kees began to tell the story he had heard that evening.

Johannes Post is a farmer from the Province of Drenthe in the east of the country. He had a well-run farm which he ran with his wife and five children. He was a hot-blooded, straight-forward farmer who could not stand the unjust occupation of the Nazis and the persecution of the Jews.

He left his family to help people. He traveled the entire country to save people and find hiding places, just like we do, and that is why he wanted to meet me. His slogan had always been, 'my life is in God's hands.' He is a very smart person. On a day not too long ago, before he became the leader of the Underground in the east of the country, he had a phone call from his pastor to see if he would come by and see someone who was visiting him.

He went and met Arnold, a young fellow from The Hague who had fled to the East because the Nazis were hot on his trail. This Arnold was probably as wild as Johannes and the two became partners against the Nazis.

They planned to terrorize the Germans and found a lot of like-minded people who joined their organization. They began by attacking local distribution centers and stole food stamps and ID cards. But he found out that that can never suffice for the growing multitudes of fugitives and the Jews.

He is the one who has organized the country-wide Boxer teams, groups of fighters who teach the Germans a lesson at unexpected locations.

They have put the fear into the Nazis in such a way that they dare not to operate in small platoons any more. Johannes called himself an experienced salesman. He deals in human lives and while traveling all over the country he brings the Jews from place to place and from farm to farm.

The people, who travel with him trust him because of his authority. His flaming eyes breathe power and respect. The country-wide Boxer Army has become as large as seven hundred men who plot attacks all over the country.

They call on each other to plan and perform the attacks. The Germans have become frantic to catch them. He is a rock-solid Resistance fighter. His wife sadly sees how the farm is deteriorating. Johannes is never at the farm and the children are too young to do all the hard farm work which needed to be done. She knows his ideals and his drive.

It is beyond family and country. It had become a passion to save the Jews, but also his co-workers. That is where the problem has arisen and that is why he was here in The Hague. He wants to free a hundred and fifty Resistance fighters who are awaiting their firing squad in the coming days.

More and more Resistance cells have been asking for his help to perform some kind of attack in order to free someone or to obtain something which could be a threat to their organization. Often they were NSB- ers who stood in the way of the Resistance and who repeatedly messed up the Resistance activities. Such NSB-ers are removed by Johannes and his Boxers, silently and effectively.

The people-saver had a problem which brought him here. He wants to free his friends from the Oranje Hotel, the prison in The Hague which is always the final stage before the firing squad. This attack has to be organized in a big way and it will become the final attack for Johannes Post.

For days in a row he has walked around the area of the prison in which his best friends are being tortured and prepared for the firing squad. Slowly he begins to realize that freeing them is all he wants to do, so he is visiting every Resistance fighter in The Hague to obtain help. He seems to have an elaborate plan in his head and nothing can possibly stop him from doing it.

Chapter Fifty Four

THE ZIONIST COUNCIL

—m—

I t was very early in the morning when the ambulance arrived at
the Groenendijk warehouse. As always the door was opened
and the ambulance drove inside. In minutes the doors were closed
and at that early time in the morning the NSB-ers were still asleep.
Besides, they had seen the ambulances come and go so many
times. After one of them had inquired as to why they came there,
there had been a very satisfactory answer: a technical problem only
Groenendijk was able to fix.

The people who were going to be brought to the Swiss border had been ready for an hour. They had received their new ID's
and they had prepared themselves for a ten hour drive, without
pit stops, to the south of Germany. The "wounded soldier" was
strapped in place. The way he had been disguised he looked like he
was ready to go to heaven. But nothing was more untrue than that.
His "destination" was a hospital in Munich and when they would
come close to Munich other papers would show that they had come
from the south of France. Once they passed Munich they would be
too far and they would not be able to explain why they had passed
Munich.

The preparation of the forged paperwork had been thorough. It
would be a shame if their plan would be ruined by one-time wrong
way of thinking. The ambulance was loaded up with Jews: the

Sterenways and Ishmael and David Schmall. Besides the wounded soldier there was the driver clad in German uniform who took the responsibility of driving the entire trip, seven hundred miles to be precise.

Once the ambulance reached the dirt road that ran close to the border, not far from the city of Basel, it would be met by a group of Zionist fighters who would walk them through the woods to free and neutral Switzerland.

The five passengers had been on a liquid fast since the day before and they had eaten as little food as they could. There would be no way to stop for any reason at all.

The Zionist Council in Basel had been sent a message by Telex in code of their arrival and who and when they could expect the new arrivals.

Mr. and Mrs. Sterenway had been very grateful to Kees. They had apologized for the nuisance they had created for Kees and Johanna.

Kees had been able to use the news which they had brought about the Judas role they had been forced into. Before they left and before the doors of the warehouse were opened, Kees and Johanna had prayed with them for a safe and easy trip. "The Lord knows," Kees said, "how much you will be needed in the promised Land, the future country of Israel."

Chapter Fifty Five

THE NSB-ER PRISON

—⟋ⲙ⟍—

I f the Nazis thought they were winning the war in Holland they had made a big mistake. They could be cruel and they became meaner by the day to suppress the Dutch. The citizens of Holland became more inventive to beat the oppressors.

When a German soldier was found killed by the Resistance in an attack on a public facility or a storage warehouse, the Resistance would immediately strip his uniform and use it for another attack.

`Hundreds of those German uniforms had been captured and were in use by the Resistance.

The man who had helped Kees in guarding the Sterenways in the abandoned ware house was one of those who used a German uniform. He spoke German fluently and acted the part. His name, Jan de Hartog, was changed into Hans Hertzog. His German made name-tag proved that. He worked together with a friend who drove the German three-ton truck.

They had worked with a printing artist and the three had created dozens of transfer papers for any occasion. They were prepared to go places, pick up and do errands, transport illegal printed materials to other cities or pick up captured Germans to remove them from a scene of an attack. The two specialized in surprising NSB-ers who were in the midst of a traitorous activity. Many NSB-ers disappeared for a while; sometimes they would show up

323

a hundred miles away from their home. Sometimes they would be kept captive for months depending on the severity of their crime.

There was a farm outside of the city of Tiel, nestled in-between orchards and close to the river The Rijn. The farm was specialized as being a NSB-er prison. The stable which once could house and feed sixty cows had been converted into a prison.

From the inside the small bow windows had been cemented shut. The half doors which had once been used to shovel out the cow dung had been replaced by brick from the inside too. There was only one door left to enter, it had been used as many as eighty times.

Until that point in time during the war it had never been used to exit.

The prisoners were fed just enough to stay alive with, sugar beet cookies and water. Each person was chained to a hook, ones the cows had been hooked to. It was a dismal place but it served a purpose and it saved probably thousands of Jewish lives.

The owner of the farm had a safety network around the perimeter of the farm and a second circle two hundred meters further. There was only one way to get to the farm and that was over a drawbridge which was always up.

Many times the Germans had come to search the farm but the sign at the draw-bridge had prevented them from going in. The sign read:

"Farm closed by the Dutch Health Department for severe Hogg Pest infestation. Warning Hogg Pest can be transferred to humans."

The Nazis who had made it as far as the draw-bridge had quickly turned back and they had told all their colleagues to shun that farm.

The farmer who owned the place worked outside in his beet field only after dark. During the daytime he spent time with his prisoners. Discussions had been high-spirited and gradually the farmer could sense that his speeches were falling on good ground.

He did not know how long he was going to have to keep these people. All he knew was that he could never set them free unless

the Resistance leadership told him so. In a way, the captured NSB-
ers were blessed because their lives were spared. If it ever came to
a liberation of Holland, they would be judged only for the things
they had done before their incarceration.

They had a lot in common these traitors of their own country
and countrymen. They had all expected to become leaders in a new
Nazi world. They had all expected to become leaders of the new
government and thought they had earned it by betraying their own.
This twisted way of thinking was what the Germans had taught
them, or rather what the Nazis had indoctrinated them with.

Some of them had become NSB-ers out of sheer greed and others because they had a very low self-esteem.

The two Germans in a three-ton truck arrived at the farm in
Tiel. They had two passengers in the back of the truck and they
were on their way to make a delivery. They ignored the warning
sign at the draw-bridge and when they stepped out of the cabin
they knew what to do. There was a large stone on the side of the
draw-bridge. A rope was tied to the stone. When they untied the
rope they could easily lower the draw-bridge and drive the truck
across the creek. The farmer knew they were coming. By means
of Morse code he had received the message that he was to expect
two more friends, the kind of friends he was used to at his estab-
lishment. The two German soldiers had not noticed that they had
been followed by a motorcycle all the way from The Hague. The
motorcycle had kept its distance just barely able to keep following
the truck.

The two "German soldiers" had no reason to suspect anyone
of following them. Unfortunately that was their downfall and their
death sentence.

When the draw-bridge had been raised again the truck drove
quickly toward the farm, unloaded their cargo and turned around.
On the way from The Hague they had stopped at another farm and
picked up four gunny sacks of potatoes.

That was what saved the prison but not the two this time. When
they came back, crossing the draw-bridge and raising it again, they
drove to the main road. A blockade had been erected in the short

time they had gone in and out of the farm. Several German trucks had blocked the road way. There was no escape this time.

A Gestapo officer demanded their papers which they duly produced. "Schwartz Haendler," the Gestapo officer proclaimed as he looked inside the truck and saw the sacks of potatoes. The two men froze. They had not counted on that angle of their trip. The commander barked "zum Kazerne mitt dem!"

Several soldiers grabbed the men and shoved them onto an enclosed prison truck. Another soldier took the three-ton truck and the entire blockade broke up.

They raced in high speed to their destination: the interrogation quarters of the Gestapo in the city of Tiel. The interrogators soon found out they had arrested Dutchmen and without a verdict or a judge. Without any further formalities the two young men, as brave as they had been during their time in the Resistance, were brought to the back yard.

Five minutes later three shots broke the silence of the city of Tiel. The peaceful town could not even be a witness of the execution. Standrecht had taken the lives of great, promising futures – if there had not been a war in Holland.

StandRecht, (Marshall Law) in the extreme, was used without delay.

Chapter Fifty Six

THE OLD SPY

—⚏—

T he pathetic old man who walked around in shabby clothes and a greasy hat scuffled around the barricades which closed off the city of The Hague. He was inconspicuous in his work and never talked to anyone. The special brigade which had closed off the city did not pay much notice to the shabby old man.

Coert van der Laan was the perfect spy in his own right, he thought he would never be arrested until he heard the call "Halt, Ausweiss!" from a soldier at the Hoornbrug.

This time they seemed to have suspected the old man of something. They frisked him and confiscated the entire contents of his pockets. He was told that he was under arrest and that he was going to be taken to the nearby Gestapo office for interrogation. His tiny little notebook was full of scribbles which made no sense to the Germans. He told the Gestapo interrogator that he was an insurance agent and that he was just taking a rest when they had arrested him.

They believed him and let him go. Coert had been scared to death. He was a spy, but he was scared because he had nothing and no one to fall back on. He was not a cool-blooded spy; he was just a brave citizen who felt he had to do what he did. He was often hungry and sometimes he slept under a bridge. He had commanded himself to do the work he did and with every evil he heard about done by the Nazis, he reminded himself how important his self-given command would be for eventual peace and freedom for the Hollanders.

In all his messages, he had given himself a code name. "I.B.," he called himself. The initials stood for the words "Isolation Breaker." The leadership of the allied forces in England did not know who I.B. was. His messages were used all the time and had become very valuable to them. No one in the Resistance knew him except Kees, who himself thought that Coert was personally known by the leadership in England.

One day Kees went with him on a trip to the south of Holland where they were to meet a Resistance worker who was in need of some new ID cards. Coert had asked Kees if he could follow him on a bicycle and meet the person in the city of Eindhoven.

It was one of the first times since Kees had met Coert that he heard him speak about espionage and the importance of getting his information to England.

When Coert told him how he transferred his information to England, the man was in awe about Coert's answer. "Why aren't you using the Swedish way, you live in Friesland?" "Well, you could get your messages to England much quicker and with a guarantee they will get there." The man went on to tell him about the Swedish way. He told him about a Resistance group with the code name "The Swan," which operated from the city of Dokkum in Friesland. The group worked with a number of fishermen who went fishing in the Oostzee and often docked their boats in the Swedish harbors. Sweden, which had remained neutral, had a Dutch Embassy which was sending all illegal information to England.

At the next opportunity Coert traveled to Dokkum and found the group The Swan. The old man had finally hooked up with the real Resistance and became known as "I.B." His information was so important that the Leadership in England even supplied him with all his needs. He received money to travel and to purchase food. But his job became more dangerous. One day he had sent a message to England which said, "Desperately in need of new tires for my bicycle." Two weeks later they were delivered at his house in Friesland.

Unfortunately, at the end of the summer of 1943 he became terminally ill. His messages stopped as quietly as they had begun.

Coert knew he was going to die. He took time to destroy all evidence of his spying career.

The Gestapo had found information he had sent and were desperately searching for a certain "I.B"

Coert had told his few friends that he expected the Gestapo to come. "They are welcome here," he had said smilingly. "All they will find is a sick old man, but make sure no one of the Resistance comes to my funeral. The Nazis might use it as bait to arrest anyone who knew me. So please don't come back here."

Only one time a Resistance worker came back to visit him.

In a secret radio message it had been announced, "Please tell I.B. that he has been honored with the Medal of Honor and has been given the Officer's Medal of The House of Orange."

Four weeks later Coert van der Laan went to be with the Lord. The Gestapo attacked his small and empty home just days later. All they found was the medal and six milk bottles painted with grey paint.

Chapter Fifty Seven

THE ATTACK ON THE JAIL

—⁓—

K ees had not agreed with Johannes Post at his visit at the printers' office in the ruined building. On the contrary, Kees had warned the stubborn farmer of the risks in getting such a large operation as an attack on the infamous jail. The Gestapo, the police and the Siecherheits Dienst, or S.D. were all involved in the security of the jail and you can bet that several NSB-ers are on the look out to betray anyone who contemplates anything against them.

"It is far too risky to get that many men involved, all men who are known by the Nazis, all of those who are on the most-wanted list, would jeopardize their secrecy and the work they are personally involved in."

They had parted as friends, Kees and Johannes, and they never saw each other again.

The local newspapers who were working for the Nazis had made the headlines several weeks later:

"Attack on Jail Ends in Blood Bath! Dozens of Rebels Killed!"

When Kees read the paper during his lunch break at the factory, his blood went cold in his veins. He knew it would fail and felt sorry he had not prayed with Johannes Post before he had left.

More than thirty men had been involved in the attack. Johannes had gathered them from all over the country. He had designed a map of the jail and had made several copies. One of the participants knew a reliable insider in the jail.

They made contact with this person.

The man was a Dutch S.S. member which should have rung a bell to Johannes. It was with great hesitation that Johannes had accepted his services. The man seemed to want to change his life and was willing to betray his German masters in exchange for rehabilitation after the war, a hiding place, and some money. He was willing to open the doors of the jail and let the attackers inside.

Blinded by the possibility of success, they prepared themselves for the attack. Unfortunately there were too many indications that the S.S. traitor could not be trusted. Several people warned Johannes of a pending disaster. Until the last minute, Johannes did not know that the head of security had visited the jail that afternoon.

The S.S. traitor had told him too many stories which sounded untrue. Was Johannes that much blinded by his intention to free his colleagues?

He could not force himself to stop the operation. He had gone ahead against his better judgment. The plan was that sixteen men would enter the jail when the door was opened. Meanwhile, Johannes took the responsibility to take the S.S. traitor and his mother and bring them to a safe-house.

He rang the doorbell of the living quarters of the nightwatch and forced himself and two others inside. The man who was not even surprised told them that he was a good Dutchman and asked them to beat him up and gag and tie him so that he could prove that he had resisted the intruders.

Then at that point in time, Johannes slipped away to keep his promise. He was now waiting for the games to begin. While his colleagues would free the freedom fighters that had been destined to die, Johannes would wait in the wings to finish his job and free the SS. traitor and his mother by picking them up at their home. His bicycle is waiting around the corner of the jail. He never thought how he was going to take the mother and son. Would they have to ride their own bicycle?

The work of the traitor had begun and while everyone in the

jail was asleep, the Nazis, armed to the teeth, were waiting for the signal. The signal of Judas, betraying his own.

The S.S. traitor had never left the jail. He was the one who had to give the directions, the commands to kill his fellow Dutchmen. The Nazis had machine guns in place. The Resistance fighters had only hand guns. The Nazis had the majority and the element of surprise.

The men of the Resistance were waiting for the pre-planned point in time. Their watches had been synchronized and so had the Nazis' watches. The S.S. traitor had known the exact time of the attack. When he was ready, he opened the door as planned and the Resistance men – all sixteen of them – stormed into the jail.

Then all hell broke loose. Machine guns began to rattle and shots were fired from every angle. The attack had become a total failure.

Of the sixteen men half of them found a way to escape. The other half were lying on the ground, wounded and dying.

They ended up in the very jail cells they had intended to open. Johannes did not know of the failed attack. He was on his way to save two more lives. When he arrived at the house of the S.S. traitor and rang the doorbell, he met his opponent, the S.D. blood hound who had staged the counter attack.

Johannes drew his gun and shot, but before he did he felt the penetration of a bullet in his hand. The revolver dropped on the street and Johannes was trampled by the Nazi boots. His ribs were broken and when he woke up he found himself in the place he had intended to empty – the jail, where all his friends were waiting to see him.

The next morning he got his chance to talk, but he did not say a word. The Nazis mutilated him but he never said a single word. The interrogation did not take more than five minutes. After two hours they took him and all the ones who had come with him for the attack to the dunes, without a conviction or a sentence.

The Nazis made the seventeen wounded men dig their own graves. The S.S. traitor was watching while the soldiers pushed the men down into their own dug pit and kicked them until they lay face down in the dirt. With shots to the neck, they finished their ugly mission. The proud farmer and his sixteen men gave their lives for their friends and their country. An army bulldozer covered the pit they had dug.

Chapter Fifty Eight

A RABBI'S QUESTIONS

—ɷ—

T here were still Rabbis in The Netherlands during the end of 1944. Those who had been sent to the concentration camps were no more. The Nazis did not show any favoritism to those who had the call of God on their lives.

The few Rabbis who were still in the country were in hiding. They were visiting other Jews in hiding to encourage them, to pray with them, and help wherever they could.

Rabbi Strauss was a clever Rabbi; he traveled as a sales person with an Ausweiss in the name of Han de Klerk. He had his hair bleached and wore wooded shoes to accentuate his Hollander-ship. Whenever he was stopped he spoke like a Dutch farmer and thus he had escaped every Razzia and barricade. His Ausweiss was never scrutinized or questioned.

On this late day in the fall, while the wind blew through his blond hair, no German had any intention to stop the Dutchman on his bicycle. He had a pass from the German Arbeits Einsatz that he was working for one of the food factories which formerly produced food for the Dutch but now only produced it for the German soldiers all over Europe. The pass was as fake as any, but it had always been accepted.

The doorbell of the Van Rijn residence rang. Johanna looked through the curtains to see who rang the door bell. She recognized the Rabbi and quickly went to open the front door. Across the street and above the Van Rijn Residence several curtains had moved. The always active NSB-ers had never had any success in reporting visitors to the Van Rijn residence. They immediately rang their Gestapo agent.

The NSB-ers had the privilege of having telephones in their homes for the sole purpose of reporting strangers around their homes.

Within minutes a Nazi truck stopped in front of the house and two soldiers banged on the door. The soldiers yelled "Aufmachen Schnell!" Kees knew the routine and was quietly laughing to himself. The soldiers did not wait at the door. Pushing Johanna aside they walked directly into the home. Then they saw him, the visitor, the person who did not live there, so he must be scrutinized.

The Rabbi stood up from his seat and introduced himself as if he was receiving a friend. "Han De Clerk," he said while stretching out his hand for a hand shake. The perplexed soldier took the outstretched hand and shook it before he knew what he was doing. The other soldier tried to be the harsh one and commanded the Rabbi to produce his Ausweiss.

"Of course, gentlemen," said the Rabbi. "Here it is, and please take a seat." This was unheard of and the soldiers seemed to act uncomfortably.

Within a few more minutes a second German vehicle came around the corner and two more soldiers entered the Van Rijn residence. This time it was a Gestapo sergeant with a soldier who demanded the Rabbi's Ausweiss. The embarrassment was complete. They all looked at Kees and Johanna and asked them who this stranger was and what he was doing at their home.

The answer was clear and simple. "This Gentleman is an insurance Salesman. We have asked him to come and quote us on health insurance, and you know about the new Third Reich insurance that your High Commander is recommending to all citizens?"

The soldiers had never heard of such a thing and commanded the Rabbi to produce documents supporting the statement. Han de Klerk took the hint and reached for his brief case. He showed them a folder which had a swastika on the outside and with big letters it said, "Third Reich Insurance Plan."

His bluff paid off. When they saw the folder they all turned around and without saying a word they closed the front door behind them.

A sigh of relief could be heard from all three people in the room, and Kees asked, "Do you have more papers to support what you just showed them?"

The Rabbi opened the folder and inside there was just one sheet of blank paper. "This is the application form," he said with a smile. "And it always worked."

After a moment of quiet Kees spoke, "What brings you to our humble home Rabbi? At this time we have only five people under our floor and you have given them a big scare by coming here so unexpectedly. By now they are still in their concrete bunker under the staircase. Johanna, don't you think we should give them the all-clear right now?"

"Oh yes, I forgot," she said. "This was such an unusual situation I did not even start the alarm by using the crack board. She got up and went to the hallway and came back a minute later.

"You have a very clever hide-out here Kees," the Rabbi began. "We have had numerous reports from people who have been in hiding here and who have been able to escape the camps with your help. In fact I have a letter here from your nephews who are now safely in Palestine. If it had not been for your help they would not have survived this Holocaust."

The Rabbi paused for a moment. It seemed he was searching for words to say. When he continued he had tears in his eyes and his voice was sounding like he was ready to cry. "What I would like to hear, Kees and Johanna, is how did you do it and how could you keep doing it in such a time as this, to speak in Biblical terms. In other words what gave you the strength to do it is what I would like to find out. We all know you are heroes, but what is it that made you the hero?"

Kees had to think about that for a long time. Here was a Jewish Rabbi asking where he received the strength to help God's chosen people. How could he tell him that he was following Jesus' command, the Jesus in whom they did not believe?

In silence he prayed, "Lord, how can I lift up your name and show them that you are the Christ, and that you give me the strength I need to do this work, how you sustain us and give us abundance where there is nothing?"

Kees was still thinking how to begin when the Rabbi spoke. "I know what you are going to say, Kees. Is it that difficult for you to tell me that Jesus is the one who did it?"

Kees and Johanna were shocked in surprise. What was this Rabbi going to say next, that they were wrong in doing what they had accomplished?

The man across from them smiled and jumped up from his chair he walked over to Johanna and gave her a big hug, without saying a word he did the same with Kees and then he said it. "I know that my Redeemer lives! Only He can accomplish what you have done."

The End of Part one.
Part two can be expected in the Spring of 2008

Biography of Dirk van Leenen

—ɯ—

He was born in 1940 just after the war had begun in The Netherlands.

He is married to Cynthia June van Leenen.

Together they have seven children and seventeen grandchildren.

They live in Arizona. Dirk has spent his life working with flowers. He has several degrees in Horticulture and floral design.

His interest in English Literature began when he was still living in Holland. At the University of Leiden he studied English and he worked a number of years in Holland as an English teacher.

For years he used to tell stories about his experiences during the Second World War in Holland. His children and grandchildren always urged him to write a book about those difficult times.

With Dirk's mother being Jewish, his parents were actively taking care of Jews.

It is out of their stories, anecdotes, and Dirk's memories that this book has been written.

Dirk has talked to many Holocaust survivors and gathered stories which have never before been told.

Glossary

Afsluitdijk	Dyke to close off the former Zuiderzee.
Ausweiss	German issued I.D.card.
Arbeitz Einsatz	A German way to justify slave the Dutch.
Binnenhof	Ancient Government buildings in the Hague.
Bitte	Please.
Briek	Horse drawn buggy.
Drogisterij	Pharmacy/drugstore.
Dr. Seiss Inquart	German appointed Governor over the Netherlands.
Gestapo	Nazi detectives and interrogators.
General Himmler	German General over Holland Occupation.
Groenendijk	Resistance worker who owned a box-tricycle rental place next door to the van Rijn house.
Hoornbrug	Bridge over a river entering The Hague.
Hollander	Dutch Citizen.
Het Oranje Hotel	Jail named after the Queen's family for housing
Krauts	Resistance fighters on their way to the firing Squad.
Heimweh	Home sickness.
Halt, Aufsteigen	Stop and dismount.
Joodse Raad	Jewish Council, installed by the Nazis.
Jordaan	Section of Amsterdam where mostly Jews lived.
Knok Ploeg	Fighting group of the Resistance.
Leidenaars	Inhabitants of the city of Leiden.
Moffen	Dutch slang for German soldiers,
Nazis	Members of the National Socialistic Party. all German military were called Nazis.
NSB-ers	Dutch citizens who became Nazis and Collaborators with the Germans.
Onderduikers	People who had to go in hiding.

Polders	Former lakes which had been emptied and changed into farm lands.
P.O.W.	Prisoners of War.
Razzia	Door to door search by large groups of soldiers.
Surro or surrogate	Artificial substitute for coffee.
Versperrung	Road block or Barricade.
Vernichtung	Annihilation.
Waffen SS	German storm troopers.

Known Concentration Camps, (death camps)

Auswitz
Birkenau
Bergen Belzen
Dauchau
Buchenwalt
New Gammen
Vucht
Westerbork
Sobidor
Oranien Stadt